The Minimum Wage

Recent Titles in the

CONTEMPORARY WORLD ISSUES
Series

Books in the **Contemporary World Issues** series address vital issues in today's society such as genetic engineering, pollution, and biodiversity. Written by professional writers, scholars, and nonacademic experts, these books are authoritative, clearly written, up to date, and objective. They provide a good starting point for research by high school and college students, scholars, and general readers as well as by legislators, businesspeople, activists, and others.

Each book, carefully organized and easy to use, contains an overview of the subject, a detailed chronology, biographical sketches, facts and data and/or documents and other primary source material, a forum of authoritative perspective essays, annotated lists of print and nonprint resources, and an index.

Readers of books in the Contemporary World Issues series will find the information they need in order to have a better understanding of the social, political, environmental, and economic issues facing the world today.

The Minimum Wage

A REFERENCE HANDBOOK

Oren M. Levin-Waldman

ABC-CLIO™

An Imprint of ABC-CLIO, LLC
Santa Barbara, California • Denver, Colorado

Library of Congress Cataloging-in-Publication Data

Names: Levin-Waldman, Oren M., author.
Title: The minimum wage : a reference handbook / Oren M. Levin-Waldman.
Description: Santa Barbara, California : ABC-CLIO, [2016] | Series:
    Contemporary world issues series | Includes bibliographical references and index.
Identifiers: LCCN 2015029353| ISBN 9781440833946
    (hardcopy : alk. paper) | ISBN 9781440833953 (ebook)
Subjects: LCSH: Minimum wage—United States. | Minimum
    wage—Law and legislation—United States—History. | Labor policy—United
    States—History.
Classification: LCC HD4918 .L4473 2016 | DDC 331.2/30973—dc23
LC record available at http://lccn.loc.gov/2015029353

ISBN: 978-1-4408-3394-6
EISBN: 978-1-4408-3395-3

20 19 18 17 16   1 2 3 4 5

This book is also available on the World Wide Web as an eBook.
Visit www.abc-clio.com for details.

ABC-CLIO
An Imprint of ABC-CLIO, LLC

ABC-CLIO, LLC
130 Cremona Drive, P.O. Box 1911
Santa Barbara, California 93116-1911

This book is printed on acid-free paper ∞

Manufactured in the United States of America

Portions of this book have been expanded from:

Levin-Waldman, Oren M. 2015. "Why the Minimum Wage Orthodoxy Reigns Supreme." *Challenge*. 58:1, 29–50.

Levin-Waldman, Oren M. 2011. "From a Narrowly Defined Minimum Wage to Broader Wage Policy." *Review of Social Economy* 69:1, 77–96.

Levin-Waldman, Oren M. 1998. *The Minimum Wage in Historical Perspective: Progressive Reformers and the Constitutional Jurisprudence of "Liberty of Contract."* Working Paper No. 256. The Jerome Levy Economics Institute. Online at: http://www.levyinstitute.org/pubs/wp256.pdf

Contents

Preface

In his State of the Union Address in January 2014 President Obama called for an increase in the federal minimum wage from its current $7.25 an hour to $10.10 an hour. Only a year before, President Obama had called for the federal minimum wage to be increased to $9 an hour. Congress never acted on the first call, and, as of this writing, the Republicans in the Senate blocked a vote on the current proposal. Calls for increases in the minimum wage are not new, and neither is opposition to it. But current calls come at a time when long-term unemployment still persists, and there has been an increase in income inequality with those at the top getting richer and those at the bottom getting poorer. Over the years, as the minimum wage has failed to keep pace with inflation and its value has continued to erode, the size of the middle class has only decreased. Beginning in September 2013, fast-food workers—the largest group of minimum wage workers—across the country went on a daylong strike for a $15 an hour minimum wage. They repeated this event a few months later. Then toward the end of 2013 and into the beginning of 2014, several states across the country raised their minimum wages above the federal level, largely because of the failure of the federal government to act. And yet, with this burst of state legislative activity, a new trend was born: local governments began adopting their own. San Francisco raised its minimum wage to $10.55 an hour, which was the highest minimum wage in the country until recently the state of Vermont adopted a $15 an hour minimum wage. At the same time, there appears to be broad support for raising the minimum wage in San Diego to $13.09 an hour over the next three years. Meanwhile, a measure was introduced in Switzerland to adopt a minimum wage of 22 Swiss Franc an hour, which is the equivalent of $22.88 an hour (in 2015 dollars), and which is also the highest minimum wage in all of Europe.

On one level, the momentum is clearly there to either adopt minimum wages or raise existing ones. But, as with any number of policy issues, the momentum has ebbed and flowed. The opposition to the minimum wage is no less now than it was when they were first adopted during the earlier part of the twentieth century. Ironically, we know little more about the effects of the minimum wage than we did in the past. And yet, as any number of policies in our policy toolbox have failed to assist the middle class, the ambiguity surrounding the minimum wage has perhaps translated into a greater willingness to at least experiment. At the same time, the protests for a $15 an hour minimum by fast-food workers are reminiscent of the calls by Progressive reformers at the beginning of the twentieth century for a minimum wage on the grounds that parasitic industries that were also sweatshops were paying beneath subsistence wages.

The minimum wage is a controversial topic in terms of both economic theory and political battle lines. The standard textbook theory is clear: raising the minimum wage will lead to job loss. This flows from the assumption that a minimum wage prevents workers from accepting wages below the minimum. But the lower the wage demands of workers, the more likely employers are to hire them. A minimum wage, then, creates a wage rigidity, thereby making workers less flexible in their demands. As a result, employers will hire fewer workers. Moreover, forcing employers to pay higher wages will only raise their prices or eat into their profits, which in turn will force them to lay workers off and/or substitute technology for workers.

Politically, battle lines have been drawn between free marke-
teers arguing that minimum wages only reduce employment,
efficiency, and personal freedom and those who argue that it
needs to be increased because those who work should earn a
wage that allows them to live in dignity and likewise support
their families in dignity.

Theoretically, the minimum wage is a statement about
how people behave in the market place, which similarly carries over to how they behave in the political arena as well. In
the real world, however, we often find that individual and firm
behavior do not always comport to theory. Additionally, what
might appear to be rational behavior for firms at the micro
level—minimizing costs, including labor costs—is not always
rational at the macro level—that is, if all employers minimize
their labor costs by paying as little as possible, then nobody
will have the wherewithal to purchase goods and services. The
English economist John Maynard Keynes popularized the idea
of the Paradox of Thrift, which suggested that consumers have
a propensity to save their money for a rainy day, which means
that they will consume less. But if everybody does that, then
there will be less consumption, thereby forcing an economic
contraction, because it is consumption that ultimately drives
the economy. The same lessons would appear to apply to the
minimum wage. And yet, as simple as that may seem, the minimum wage has been anything but simple. Ironically, this can
lead to the same unemployment that critics assert will happen
if the minimum wage is raised.

This book is not an argument for or against the minimum
wage. Rather, it is a reference book that seeks to present a
balanced overview of the issue so that individuals can make
informed decisions. All economics can do is say something
about how people behave or will behave in response to certain
stimuli. In that tradition, this volume seeks to do the same
thing. This volume will look at the history of the minimum
wage, the concept and its development here in the United
States and in other countries around the world. It will present

the various controversies surrounding the minimum wage in both the economics literature and the political sphere. Readers will be exposed to key figures and institutions on both sides of the issue, and by the end they should understand that it is the complexity surrounding it that has made simple solutions to the issue elusive.

The Minimum Wage

Introduction

A minimum wage is essentially a floor beneath which employers may not pay below. The current federal minimum wage of $7.25 an hour means that employers cannot hire workers for any amount below that wage. The reason why government would legislate such a wage is because workers, especially low-skilled workers, don't have any monopoly power in the market place (Galbraith 1998). Because they are plentiful and, for all intents and purposes, interchangeable, their oversupply in the market place, according to laws of supply and demand, effectively drives down their wage rates. Employers have also possessed sufficient market power that would enable them to pay these workers as little as possible, even if it is not sufficient to support themselves. Therefore, a minimum wage effectively gives these workers a measure of market power they otherwise lack in the absence of legislation.

A flywheel assembly line at the Ford Motor Company's Highland Park, Michigan, plant in 1913. The use of a moving line reduced a car's assembly time from 12 hours to 93 minutes. The world's first automatic conveyor belt not only revolutionized the Industrial Age, but inspired Henry Ford to institute an unprecedented $5 per day minimum wage and an eight-hour day at a time when auto industry workers were making $2.34 for a nine-hour shift. Faster assemblage meant quicker availability, giving impetus to America's car culture and an increasingly mobile society. Moreover, a $5 per day minimum enabled workers to move into the middle class and purchase goods like his cars. (Bettmann/Corbis)

Reasons for a Minimum Wage

There are perhaps four basic reasons for a minimum wage. The first reason is that because workers are earning below subsistence level wages, a minimum wage might enable that person to support himself or herself above the poverty line. Early arguments for a minimum wage during the late nineteenth and early twentieth centuries focused on the idea that workers should earn livable wages. These advocates specifically argued for minimum wages for women so that they could purchase necessary food and shelter. One such advocate was Emilie Hutchinson (1919), who argued that a minimum wage for women was necessary so that they could live in dignity. But they also saw it as a first step toward the attainment of what was then considered a living wage. During the 1870s, as the economy was undergoing its transformation toward a wage-labor economy, wage labor was often viewed as a mark of dependency and not a whole lot different from prostitution. By calling for a living wage, workers sought not only to give dignity to their work but also to achieve a measure of independence that could be distinguished from just another form of slavery.

Initially, labor leaders were opposed to a minimum wage for fear that it would undermine their efforts to organize workers and achieve better pay and working conditions through collective bargaining. The American working tradition was predicated on independent yeoman farmers—people who could be self-sufficient because they worked for themselves. Moreover, the idea of working for oneself was part of the American republican tradition that gave dignity to work. In the old order—the feudalistic world of Europe that Americans separated themselves from during the American Revolution—only the serfs worked. It wasn't considered dignified for aristocrats to work, but the republican tradition in America was predicated on the assumption that it was dignified for everybody to work, regardless of socioeconomic class.

The Industrial Revolution, which shifted masses of workers into low-paying factory jobs paying below subsistence, very much undermined these republican assumptions. Organizing men into unions was intended to give male workers dignity in their jobs (Glickman 1997). Women, however, were barred from joining labor unions, so reformers pushed for minimum wages for women. At times, the living wage for women was couched as a family wage. This was based on the prevailing assumption of the time that women's primary place was in the home (Lehrer 1987). Protective labor legislation played an important role in the process of defining the position of working women in an industrial economy. Social reformers viewed protective labor legislation as but one means of limiting the initial exploitation and orientation of women workers. At the same time, these laws also contributed to increasing productivity of labor by making employers use labor more "effectively." The language often used during this period in support for minimum wages for women was that of a "women's" wage, but it was intricately tied up with the concept of a living wage that men would earn. It was the idea that a living wage was that men should earn enough to support their wives and families, and that if employers were forced to pay women a higher wage, they would then opt to hire their husbands so that the women could stay home with their children (Kessler-Harris 1988). Therefore, it was often argued that the cost of women's low wages was not borne by women but by society as a whole. Many of those who argued for a minimum wage "often did so with a heartfelt preference for the idealized family wage and gendered welfare state" (Hart 1994, p, 16).

Other minimum wage advocates argued for a minimum wage on the grounds that it would lead to greater efficiency and productivity. English economist Sidney Webb (1912) argued that people who are paid better are able to work harder because they have greater energy, due in large measure to their ability to better sustain themselves. Moreover, the greater morale among employees deriving from higher wage rates also leads to greater loyalty to their employers. This was to be known as the "Webb effect" because a legal minimum wage would have the positive effect of increasing productivity. Webb also reasoned that employers would most appreciate the security a minimum wage would provide them against being undercut by dishonest or disloyal competition, and employees would be able to better maintain themselves, thus enabling them to be better workers. As a result of higher wages, productivity would increase naturally. Rather than eliminating competition for employment, it would transfer pressure from one element in the bargain (employers) to the other (employees). Moreover, the aggregate efficiency of the nation's industry would be promoted as the best available candidates are hired. A legal minimum wage, then, would positively increase the productivity of the nation's industry by ensuring that those who are left unemployed would be the least productive members of the workforce. Not only would employers be forced to look for the best workers so as to increase their overall productivity, but employees would also be forced to develop their skills so that they could be counted among the better class of workers.

In the United States, John Bates Clark (1913) was among the early economists to favor a legal minimum wage because, he argued, the absence of one essentially triggered a process whereby employers chose from the ranks of the most necessitous men and women. Trade unions would, of course, go a long way toward removing this evil, but in the absence of unions, the law might remove it. Adding to this H. LaRue Brown (1913) noted that nothing would make for greater inefficiency than hunger, worry, and discontent. Employees able to maintain themselves would surely be better workers, and minimum wages, then, had to be seen as part of a great social advance.

Even in the business community, there were supporters of the minimum wage on the grounds that it would lead to greater productivity. On the pages of the *American Economic Review,* the leading journal of the economics profession, Edward Filene (1923) argued that one way of increasing efficiency was for employers to pay wages that would command higher-quality employees. A higher wage would be more cost-effective because employers would not have to spend as much time providing direction and correcting the errors of those who were less well trained. Low wages simply resulted in employers having cheap standards, which only produced inefficient employees. These workers wouldn't be productive because they wouldn't earn enough to maintain themselves properly. Employers would not be able to get effective organization out of those who were unintelligent, and they could not be intelligent if they did not have enough to live on properly. A legal minimum wage would then help employers as well as employees, by enabling them to compete on an even playing field with other employers, and preventing employers from paying employees insufficiently to be consumers of their business. Moreover, employers would be more likely to take an interest in their employees by educating them to a level that would make them worth the wage. Ultimately, Filene reasoned that the state would assume the function of providing education and training to future workers. To this extent, the minimum wage would serve to enhance public efficiency.

Advocates of a minimum wage didn't simply appeal to the public's sense of fairness for defining the public interest; they also relied on the burgeoning field of statistics to show that the absence of a minimum wage was harmful. They tried to show that substandard wages paid primarily to young girls were simply inadequate. However, they didn't only estimate how much money a girl needed to earn in order to maintain herself in body but in morals too. Charles Persons (1919), for instance, reasoned that $7 per week represented the cost of maintaining subsistence for an individual, even though the general consensus among experts by 1915 was that the wage needed for subsistence in an urban area was roughly $8 per week. But as many as 75 percent of women were being paid below that level; indeed, 50 percent were earning less than $6 per week (Baer 1978). The issue, however, was more than merely economic; there was a moral dimension as well. Emilie Hutchinson (1919) made the point that the low (absolute) level of women's wages, which already were low relative to men's, was of particular concern because it affected a woman's ability to live a "moral lifestyle."

"It decides the girl's companionships, her amusements, her ability to gratify without danger her natural and reasonable tastes, her very capacity for resistance to temptation. Its physical effects open the way to moral dangers" (p. 50).

The idea that the absence of a minimum wage led to moral debasement was not merely a rhetorical appeal. Women who could not support themselves were more likely to earn subsistence through prostitution, an activity not altogether illegal at the time (Glickman 1997). Therefore, the ability to demonstrate that regulation would protect the moral fabric of the community could conceivably be justified as emergency legislation, given that the legal standard for allowing the state to interfere with one's liberty of contract was the protection of the community's "public health, welfare, and morals."

The third reason for a minimum wage, which would gain attention during the depths of the Great Depression in the 1930s, was that higher wages, especially at a point where wages were depressed, would afford workers greater purchasing power. This is generally referred to as the macroeconomic argument, which holds that insofar as a higher wage will offer low-wage workers more purchasing power, they in turn will be able to demand more goods and services. As they do this, business will produce more, and they in turn will hire more workers, which may have the inevitable result of naturally bidding up wages across the board.

It was this very type of macroeconomic argument that informed policy in the initial years of the minimum wage program. Higher wages, it was reasoned, would result in less labor strife because there would be less reason for workers to engage in labor actions against their employers. Higher wages, then, would have a stabilizing effect, because workers would have more money to spend and the economy as a whole would prosper. By creating a wage floor, there is a limit to how depressed wages become. By ensuring a minimum wage level, a minimum level of aggregate demand can also be assured. The minimum wage is then viewed as part and parcel of a movement to achieve a living wage so that the consumer base of the economy can not only be maintained but enlarged as well (Glickman 1997). But macroeconomic arguments also build on an institutional approach that assumes policy to be needed to ensure reasonably high wage rates. As wages are established by firms that possess market power, workers need institutions such as unions and statutory minimum wages to countervail the power of firms.

First Minimum Wages

The first country to pass a national minimum wage was New Zealand through its Industrial Conciliation and Arbitration Act of 1894. Two years later, Australia passed a form of minimum wage, although it wasn't a universal law that applied to all workers. Rather in 1896, Victoria, Australia, amended the Factories Act to create wage boards, which for years would become the model for European nations to enact national wage policies. This law in particular set basic wages in six industries that were considered to pay low. Although first enacted as a four-year experiment, the wages board was renewed in 1900 and then made permanent in 1904, which then encompassed more than 150 industries. Also by 1902 wage boards had spread to New South Wales and Western Australia.

The first minimum wage law in the United States, however, was not adopted until 1912 in Massachusetts, and it applied only to women and children. A year later, eight states followed suit. Although the Fair Labor Standards Act (FLSA) of 1938 would apply to men and women alike and fixed wages through legislative statute, the early laws applied only to women and were fixed either through wage boards or through commissions. The primary components of the first law, for instance, included a commission to administer the program and tripartite wage boards to make recommendations with regard to wage rates. Wage boards considered the subsistence needs of women, particularly in the sweated industries but also took into account the health of the industries to which these laws would apply.

In determining wage rates, these wage boards would typically weigh an employer's ability to pay higher wages against the needs of women for subsistence wages (Nordlund 1997). Recommendations were based on the principle of maintaining an adequate cost of living, with general consideration given to the financial health of those industries and occupations involved. Enforcement was to be through "public opinion" as opposed to legal sanction. In other words, employers would be encouraged to pay higher wages by moral suasion. The public thinking ill of them—viewing them as parasites—would suffice to compel them to pay their workers a true livable wage. At the same time, there had to be reciprocal benefits to the employers, which, of course, implied greater productivity.

Wage boards, however, became the basis for effective minimum wages in Great Britain, which passed the Trade Boards Act in 1909. This law was intended to wipe out "sweating." In sweating, manufacturers supplied materials to individuals who might work at home and small workshops, and then collected the finished goods. Workers were not paid wages per se but were paid by the pieces produced. The trade boards were actually intended to constitute the first steps toward either a universal minimum wage that would replace the wage boards or at least it was hoped that the trade board system would be expanded into most of the economy (Waltman 2008, pp. 42–49).

The first federal minimum wage in the United States was enacted in 1918 specifically for the District of Columbia, but it was to apply only to women under the model of protective legislation for women. The model of protective legislation for women followed the assumption that women needed special protection because of biological differences from men. Those differences meant that they were not entitled to the same liberty of contract as men were. Protective legislation for women rested on what were referred to as "essentialist" arguments, as they made reference to women's essentially different nature from men. But reformers drew on other arguments as well. They made the "pragmatic argument" that women were the lowest-paid workers and consequently they were in desperate circumstances. Because women weren't unionized, a legislated minimum would thus be an appropriate response. Moreover, a minimum wage, reformers argued, would be in the public interest on the grounds that the public would benefit from the next generation being healthy and brought up well. Women, as the mothers of the next generation, were viewed as a social asset, and children being brought up by women who were weak, sick, or immoral would in fact be contrary to the public interest. Therefore, it would be a matter of the public interest to maintain the social practices of the day that defined women as mothers, and to the extent that a minimum wage might serve to maintain this social convention, it too was to be deemed in the public interest (Figart, Mutari, and Power 2002).

The Supreme Court said as much when it upheld a maximum hours law for women in the 1908 case of *Muller v. Oregon*. Society had a compelling public interest in protecting a women's maternal function, and thus her "liberty of contract" could be infringed upon. Biological differences essentially required protective legislation. And the various arguments by reformers, whether essentialist or public interest, were essentially building on this underlying theme. Women, in short, needed to be paid a higher wage because they were in a vulnerable position (pp. 74–79). In this vein reformers were simply offering another variant of the efficiency argument. Still, the voluntarism upon which liberty of contract rested was considered a powerful argument during the time. Nobody was abandoning liberty of contract in favor of wage-setting institutions; only that some did not enjoy the same liberty of contract as others and, therefore, needed greater protection. In 1923, however, the Supreme Court in *Adkins v. Children's Hospital* (1923) reversed the *Mueller* decision and held that women were no longer entitled to special protection because the Nineteenth Amendment (giving them the right to vote) had eliminated the need for special protective legislation. Now that women too enjoyed the same liberty of contract as men, the District of

Columbia's minimum wage was held to be an unconstitutional abridgement of individual liberty of contract (Levin-Waldman 2001, Chapter 3).

The precursor to the Fair Labor Standards Act, which would be passed in 1938, was actually the National Industrial Recovery Act (NIRA) and later the National Recovery Act (NRA), which contained codes that established minimum wages on an industry-by-industry basis. The NIRA, passed in early 1933, was designed to maintain price and market stability by adopting industry codes that would safeguard against unfair competition. The codes contained provisions on wages, hours, working conditions, union membership, and collective bargaining. Essentially Congress delegated authority to the executive branch, for a federal administrator to supervise the making of codes, which often was a collaborative venture with representatives from industry. And in many cases, the codes were written by trade associations. Section 3(a) of the act specifically authorized the president to approve codes of "fair competition" after making certain prescribed findings (Kirkendall 1974). Section 7 dealt with issues of collective bargaining, maximum hours, and minimum wages. With this section it was established that as a matter of fair competition that (1) employees were to have the right to organize and bargain collectively with representatives of their choosing; (2) they were not to be coerced into joining a company union; and (3) their employers were to comply with maximum hours and minimum wages as they were approved and prescribed by the president (NIRA 1933). Once the president approved a code, it would have the force of law. Although maximum hours and minimum wages were to be prescribed, they were not uniform but would vary from industry to industry. The underlying purpose behind the NIRA was to prohibit those practices regarded as unfair by industry because they might have the effect of destroying the price structure without justification. The codes were also intended to prohibit the unfair practice of exploiting workers by cutting their wages and increasing their hours of labor.

It didn't take long, however, for this measure to be challenged in the courts. In *Schechter Poultry Corp. v. United States* (1934), the law was challenged on the grounds that the codes (1) violated the separation of powers because Congress delegated its legislative authority to the president; (2) the codes weren't in regulation of interstate commerce but intrastate commerce; and (3) the wage and hours provisions in Section 3 violated the Constitution's Fifth Amendment's due process clause. In the case of the code that applied to the poultry industry, the "Code of Fair Competition for the Live Poultry Industry of the Metropolitan Area in and about the City of New York," approved by executive order, the code established maximum hours of 40 hours a week and a minimum wage of 50 cents an hour. Among the arguments made by the plaintiff, the A.L.A. Schechter Poultry Company, was that the minimum wage wasn't restricted to women and children, as were minimum wage provisions of the past. Specifically, the NIRA threw overboard "old-fashioned" limitations and represented a sharp departure from the health and welfare standard that had been used in the past.

Speaking for the Court, Chief Justice Charles Evans Hughes made it clear that the code-making authority constituted an unconstitutional delegation of legislative power, and for this reason alone the NIRA could not stand. From the point of view of wages and hours, those working in the poultry plants had no direct relationship to interstate commerce. And it was on this point that the Court appeared to raise the specter of a slippery slope. If the federal government could determine wages and hours of employees within a state because its commerce might cross state boundary lines, what was to stop it from determining wages when there were no interstate commerce issues involved?

Meanwhile, there were states willing to take the lead and pass their own minimum wages, even though it wasn't clear the courts would maintain them. In New York State in 1933, the state legislature added Article 19 to the state's labor law, which authorized the state's labor commissioner to fix the wages of women. The act extended to all occupations in which women and children were gainfully employed, but did not include domestic help. The state of New York tried to claim that its law was different from the D.C. law struck down in the *Adkins* decision. In the case of *Morehead Warden v. Tipaldo* (1936), the Supreme Court took up the constitutionality of New York's minimum wage. New York attempted to argue that a state minimum wage was a piece of emergency legislation for women and children (the emergency being the Great Depression) that had depressed wages. The Court, however, did not consider minimum wages in this instance to be a matter of emergency legislation. That is, the Court did not view the circumstances to be constitutive of an emergency, where in the absence of this legislation, some severe economic consequences would result. Since the statute related only to wages of adult women and minors, as opposed to hours regulation that would affect employees' safety, it could not be considered an emergency law. Also, men were just as susceptible to exploitation as women and the effect of this legislation would be to restrain women in their competition with men. Thus the Court affirmed the precedent in the *Adkins* case, and struck down the New York state minimum wage legislation.

A year later, however, the Supreme Court reversed itself in *West Coast Hotel Co. v. Parrish*. This case involved a minimum wage statute in Washington State that had been on the books since 1913. Here the state of Washington argued that minimum wages were necessary to preclude the possibility of wage disputes that would result in a disruption of normal business activity, hence presenting an inconvenience to all concerned. What was particularly interesting about this case was that the decision came within a month of a plan by President Roosevelt to pack the Court. Frustrated with the Court's invalidation of early New Deal measures, Roosevelt introduced a bill to add a new justice to the Court for everyone who failed to retire upon attaining the age of 70 up to a maximum of 15 justices.

Although the plan failed, the justices did understand that such a plan might not fail in the future and began to reassess some of their earlier positions. Now the Court asserted that liberty only implies the absence of arbitrary restraint—not immunity from "reasonable" regulation. Therefore, there was nothing in the minimum wage law that necessarily extended beyond the state's broad protective power. In fact, the Court made it clear, as it echoed Justice Oliver Wendell Holmes's dissent in *Adkins,* that "this statute does not compel anybody to pay anything. It simply forbids employment at rates below those fixed as the minimum requirement of health and right living (*West Coast Hotel* 1936, pp. 396–397). This case was decided against the reality of the Great Depression where the problem was specifically deflated prices and wages. As policy makers understood it, economic stability required measures intended to inflate both prices and wages (Nordlund 1997). Congress in 1935 passed the National Labor Relations Act, which was intended to bring about wage stability by encouraging collective bargaining as a way of avoiding strife, but also by equalizing the power imbalance between labor and management. The Court in this case was also clear that workers' unequal position in bargaining power and their helplessness as they are being denied a living wage not only threatens these workers' health, but it also imposes a social cost on the community. Still, what is important in this case is that the path was now cleared, constitutionally, for Congress to pass the nation's first minimum wage law in its own right that would not be folded into a larger national recovery bill.

The Road to the Fair Labor Standards Act (FLSA)

The nation's first federal minimum wage law was enacted in 1938 in the Fair Labor Standards Act, but the road to this milestone was a difficult one. Considerable opposition came from Southern states, where wage rates were lower than in the North, and where antipathy to a federal law was a holdover to the carpetbagging days following the Civil War (Wright 1986). There were several reasons for why a federal minimum wage was needed and that the matter could not be left to the states. Aside from the argument that a national economy required a national standard, a major reason for a minimum wage was that it would spur economic development, particularly in the South, which, compared to the industrial North, was considered backward. The South was especially considered to be ripe for economic development.

Southerners, however, opposed the minimum wage for several reasons. First and foremost, a national minimum wage was viewed as an intrusion on the Southern way of life, which was traditionally agrarian, and also based on a system of patronage. Second, as the South was new to industrial development, it was not ready to achieve national parity with the North. Third, it did not take into account the lower standards of living and natural reasons for a lower standard of living. Fourth, it did not take into account freight differentials that actually put the South at a disadvantage. And fifth, it wouldn't increase purchasing power; instead, it would increase unemployment through the closing of firms that would not be able to pay their employees (Nordlund 1997, pp. 39–40).

Those in the North may have viewed the minimum wage as a basis for improving efficiency, but those in the South didn't quite see the need to incur whatever costs would attend those efforts. It wasn't just a question of rehabilitating a region, but liberal politicians in the South especially wanted to uplift the region's poorest people. In seeking to expand the activities of the national government, they sought to remove control of federal programs from local elites and concentrate that power in the hands of federal officials like themselves. From their perspective, the national government could become a major force in the South and ultimately overthrow the region's traditional political and economic arrangements. They were partly driven by a report titled *Report on Economic Conditions of the*

South (1938), which underscored how much the South lagged behind the rest of the nation.

The bill that would become the nation's first minimum wage was introduced as the Connery–Black bill after its sponsors, Representative William Connery of Massachusetts and Senator Hugo Black of Alabama. The bill was reported out of the Senate Education and Labor committee and passed on its first vote in the Senate in July 1937. In the House, however, the bill was blocked by the Rules Committee, and there it sat until a compromise could be reached, which would effectively increase the number of exemptions. In other words, the minimum wage that would be finally passed in 1938 was actually quite limited in terms of its coverage.

The first minimum wage went into effect in October 1938 at a rate of 25 cents an hour. The original act provided that the statutory minimum would be raised to 30 cents an hour one year later. At the same time, it established a procedure for raising the minimum wage by stages to a level of 40 cents an hour within seven years, thereby obviating the need for legislative action for some time to come. Among the administrator's responsibilities would be the appointment of an industry committee for each industry engaged in either commerce or goods production. Committees were to be composed of representatives from among employers, employees, and the general public, and they were to be responsible for making recommendations to the administrator for the highest possible minimum wage rate within an industry that would not adversely affect employment. At the same time, these recommendations were supposed to take into account the respective industry's economic and competitive conditions. The act also provided for maximum hours and child labor. Instead of the Labor Board envisaged by the initial Connery–Black bill, the FLSA, as it was passed, simply established a framework for recommendations that would presumably be acted on by Congress at a later date.

The objective was to establish a minimum set of standards that would ensure that producers in one region of the country would not have unfair competitive advantage over producers in another because they were either paying substandard wages or working their employees excessively long hours. There were, however, a number of exemptions from the law. For the most part, the only workers covered by the law were those engaged in goods production and interstate commerce. Excluded from coverage were those engaged in local retail sales, intrastate commerce, transportation, and agriculture. Executive, administrative, and professional workers were also excluded, as it was assumed that (1) their wages were considerably more than the minimum and (2) the nature of their work was such that a time clock could not be imposed. Still, many of those whom we today associate with the lower, if not the lowest, end of the wage scale were simply not covered by the provisions of the FLSA. And those for whom the law did apply, they were more likely to be members of a trade union, in which case their wages would be higher than the statutory minimum anyway.

Within six months of its passage, Elmer Andrews, the wage and hours administrator, was proclaiming it a success insofar as it successfully became a permanent part of the law of the land. At the same time, he was careful to note that its popularity perhaps derived from the modesty of the statute itself that better enabled business to adjust. Because of its limited scope, compliance was the rule, not the exception (Andrews 1939). Studies, however, suggest that many, particularly in the South, simply evaded the law. There may well have been employment consequences that were simply ignored. Later studies, however, suggest that the law perhaps wasn't quite as free of adverse effects. The hosiery and lumber industries, for instance, had among the highest levels of employment of any Southern industries covered by the act. Both these industries also paid low wages prior to the FLSA's implementation. Labor costs also comprised a high proportion of the total costs in both industries. The law clearly increased labor costs in those industries, and trend increases in employment began to reverse following implementation in 1938. According to a sample from the Bureau of Labor Statistics, Southern employment decreased 5.5 percent from 13,868 to 12,689. Meanwhile, employment in the North increased by 4.9 percent from 4,437 to 4,657 over the same period. Employment effects probably would have been greater had it not been for the fact that many Southern firms continued to pay less than the minimum rate. Many individual firms simply chose to evade the law. In fact, a majority of firms avoided paying the minimum wage either by withdrawing from interstate commerce, which made them exempt, or by illegally paying below the minimum (Seltzer 1997). Nevertheless, the law did create a major precedent for federal involvement in wage regulation, but the more important accomplishments were yet to come in the subsequent amendments.

Expansion of Minimum Wage in the United States

The initial law mandated that the minimum wage would increase from $.25 an hour in 1938 to $.40 an hour by 1945. Otherwise, each subsequent increase in the minimum wage was to require an act of Congress. The next congressional action was not to come until 1949, and was introduced in President Truman's State of the Union address. The goal was to bring the lowest paid workers up to a level that corresponded to the price and wage structure that evolved immediately after World War II (Nordlund 1997). This was to be done through amendments to the FLSA. Whatever was necessary as late as 1945 was no longer adequate in 1949. There were also several problems with the initial legislation that these amendments sought to address. First, there was no definition of working time for which an employer was obliged to account to his employees in minimum wage and overtime pay. Second, there wasn't any formula or guidelines for calculating the "regular rate" on which an employee's weekly overtime pay would be based. Third, the initial law omitted any specific definition of many of the key terms used in coverage and exemption provisions. And finally, the law failed to include a direct prohibition on employment of "oppressive child labor" in those establishments subject to child-labor provisions.

Still, the 1949 amendments raised the minimum wage to 75 cents an hour. Additionally, the administrator was to appoint a special industry committee to recommend either a minimum wage rate or a set of rates to be paid to those employees engaged in commerce or goods production for commerce in Puerto Rico and the Virgin Islands. The 1949 amendments also began the process of expanding coverage. Whereas all employees in retail sales were excluded from coverage, the FLSA was now amended to exclude only those employees in retail establishments in which more than 50 percent of its annual sales volumes were in the states where they were located. Then again in 1955, President Eisenhower in his State of the Union Address urged Congress to modify the FLSA again on the grounds that the economic growth during the preceding five years would support an expansion of the minimum wage. Although opposition was as strong as it ever was, and for many of the same reasons during the 1930s, the minimum wage was raised to $1 an hour. But the 1955 amendments also mandated a comprehensive evaluation program related to the FLSA, and it also established procedures to expedite a wage order program in the Virgin Islands and Puerto Rico (Nordlund 1997, p. 88).

In 1961 the minimum wage was raised again to $1.25 an hour and coverage was expanded for an additional 7.6 million workers. In addition to increasing the minimum wage to $1.25 an hour, the 1961 amendments expanded the definition of *covered industries*. Retail and service establishments with gross sales in excess of $1 million and who sold across state lines in excess of $250,000 were now covered. Transportation workers in either urban or intraurban systems in which gross sales exceeded $1 million were to be covered by the minimum wage too. And so too were those who worked for gas stations, if gross sales exceeded $250,000. Despite these expansions, most retail and service workers—those whom today might be termed "low-skilled"—were still excluded from coverage (*Statutes at Large* 1961). The 1961 amendments did strengthen the back wage recovery process and required a variety of studies to determine the consequences of maintaining several exemptions to the law. But it would be the amendments of 1966 that would mark the biggest expansion of the program since its initial passage in 1938.

The 1966 amendments would extend coverage to an estimated 9.1 million workers, of whom more than half were estimated to be earning less. According to a majority report in Congress, the graduated increases were intended to rectify substandard living conditions "without substantially curtailing employment or earning power." Moreover, the increases that were expected to increase the national wage bill by $800 million could be absorbed because the graduated increases were roughly equal to the productivity gains of prior years (*Congressional Quarterly Almanac* 1966, p. 825). The 1966 amendments would raise the minimum wage to $1.60 an hour over the next couple of years, where it would remain until increased again in 1974 to $2 an hour, $2.10 an hour in 1975, and $2.30 an hour in 1976.

Over the course of these amendments, the American economy had been growing, but by the 1970s the growth had slowed down. A turning point in the expansion of the minimum wage in the United States came in 1977. The major impetus for increasing the minimum wage had been high inflation that had significantly devalued the wage from its 1974 level. Supporters were calling for an immediate 30 percent increase from the existing rate of $2.30 to $3. They also called for an automatic mechanism to be grounded into law that would keep the minimum wage at 60 percent of the average hourly manufacturing sector wage. The Carter administration, however, was only willing to propose an immediate increase to $2.50 an hour, with future minimum levels to be adjusted annually so that they would always remain equal to 50 percent of average manufacturing wages (Eccles 1977, p. 640). As with other bills, a compromise was reached that would increase the minimum wage through four steps to $3.10 an hour by 1981, but it would not be indexed to inflation. The amendments of 1977 called for the minimum wage to increase to $3.35 an hour by 1981, and the minimum wage would not be raised again until 1989, thereby resulting in its serious stagnation.

Contraction of Minimum Wage in the United States

During the 1980s the political climate changed and became more conservative and market-oriented. As part of the 1977 amendments evaluation program, a Minimum Wage Study Commission (MWSC) was set up to review the minimum wage and assess its costs relative to its benefits. The MWSC report came out in 1981 and concluded that a 10 percent increase in the minimum wage would reduce teenage employment by about 1 percent. Other estimates have placed the disemployment effect even higher. At the same time, the effects were judged to be proportionately smaller among adults 20 to 24 years old, and that adults on balance appeared to be better off under a wage floor. It was also during this time that the nature of the political debate over the minimum wage began to change. With the election of Ronald Reagan to the presidency came a whole new outlook on the economy. For economists like Milton Friedman, the White House finally had an occupant who viewed government as the problem, rather than the solution to the nation's economic and social problems. Summing up the goals of economic policy, George Stigler argued that "the supreme goal of the Western World is the development of the individual: the creation for the individual of a maximum area of personal freedom, and with this a corresponding area of personal responsibility" (Stigler 1986, p. 93). As noble as policies intended to provide a safety net or reduce income inequalities might be (which would also include the minimum wage), they were fundamentally at odds with the tenets of freedom.

Table 1.1 Percentage of Workers Earning at or Below Prevailing Federal Minimum Wage

Year	Both Sexes	Men	Women
1979	13.4	7.7	20.2
1980	15.1	9.7	21.6
1981	15.1	9.6	21.3
1982	12.8	8.6	17.3
1983	12.2	8.4	16.4
1984	11.0	7.5	14.8
1985	9.9	6.9	13.2
1986	8.8	6.9	11.9
1987	7.9	5.4	10.5
1988	6.5	4.4	8.6
1989	5.1	3.5	6.7
1990	5.1	3.4	6.9*
1991	8.4	6.0	10.9*
1992	7.7	5.9	9.7
1993	6.7	5.1	8.4
1994	6.2	4.7	7.8
1995	5.3	3.9	6.8
1996	5.4	3.9	6.8
1997	6.7	5.1	8.3*
1998	6.2	4.7	7.7*
1999	4.6	3.4	5.9
2000	3.6	2.5	4.8
2001	3.0	2.0	3.9
2002	3.0	2.2	3.7
2003	2.9	2.0	3.8
2004	2.7	1.8	3.6
2005	2.5	1.7	3.3
2006	2.2	1.5	2.9
2007	2.3	1.4	3.1*
2008	3.0	1.9	3.9*
2009	4.9	3.9	5.9*
2010	6.0	4.5	7.3
2011	5.2	3.9	6.4
2012	4.7	3.4	6.0
2013	4.3	3.3	5.4

* Reflects changes in the minimum wage that took effect during those years.

Source: Drawn from Table 10, U.S. Department of Labor, Bureau of Labor Statistics, "Characteristics of Minimum Wage Workers, 2013" Report 1048, BLS Reports (March 2014): www.bls.gov.

Beginning in the 1980s several things actually happened. The number of minimum wage workers declined, poverty increased, and the value of the wage dropped considerably. Table 1.1 shows the declining percentage of those earning minimum wage.

Between 1979 and 2013 the number earning the minimum wage dropped by 67.9 percent for all minimum wage earners, 57.1 percent for men, and 73.3 percent for women. Despite these decreases, a greater percentage of minimum wage workers have been women. It is interesting to note that in most years that the minimum wage increased, the number of minimum wage workers also increased, which would suggest that higher minimum wages serve to attract more workers into the labor market. But it should also be noted that these percentages only tell us about who is earning the statutory minimum wage. What might be more important is who is earning around the minimum wage, which would encompass a much larger segment of the labor market. As this is but one of the controversies surrounding the definition of the minimum wage population, more will be said about it in the next chapter. Still, the most important drop was in the value of the minimum wage, which fell below 40 percent. The minimum wage, which hovered around the poverty line through 1979, began to decline sharply afterward. By 1989, it was only at 70.5 percent of the poverty line, and even following some increases during the 1990s, the minimum wage never reached above 80 percent of the poverty line until the last few minimum wage increases during the 2000s. It is also important to note that earlier on in the history of the minimum wage program, or at least since 1950, the minimum wage represented more than 50 percent of average hourly wages. But during the 1980s its value fell precipitously so that by 2012 it represented less than 30 percent of average hourly wages. This can be seen in Table 1.2.

This all coincided with the emerging consensus following release of the MWSC's report. Opponents of the minimum wage now found data that they could use to their advantage. Because

Table 1.2 Comparison between Minimum and Average Annual

Year	Minimum	Annual Average Wage	Minimum Wage as a Percentage of Annual Average Wage[a]	Minimum Wage as a Percentage of Poverty Line
1938[b]	$.25	NA	NA	NA
1939[b]	.30	NA	NA	NA
1940	.35	NA	NA	NA
1941	.35	NA	NA	NA
1942	.35	NA	NA	NA
1943	.35	NA	NA	NA
1944	.35	NA	NA	NA
1945	.40	NA	NA	NA
1946	.40	NA	NA	NA
1947	.40	$1.13	35.4	NA
1948	.40	NA	NA	NA
1949	.40	NA	NA	NA
1950[b]	.75	1.33	56.4	NA
1951	.75	NA	NA	NA
1952	.75	NA	NA	NA
1953	.75	NA	NA	NA
1954	.75	NA	NA	NA
1955	.75	NA	NA	NA
1956[b]	1.00	1.80	55.6	NA
1957	1.00	NA	NA	NA
1958	1.00	NA	NA	NA
1959	1.00	NA	NA	89.5
1960	1.00	NA	NA	88.2
1961[b]	1.15	2.14	53.7	100.4
1962	1.15	NA	NA	99.2
1963[b]	1.25	2.28	54.8	100.6
1964	1.25	2.36	53.0	105.1
1965	1.25	2.46	50.8	103.1
1966	1.25	2.56	48.8	100.5
1967[b]	1.40	2.68	52.2	109.4
1968[b]	1.60	2.85	56.1	105.0
1969	1.60	3.04	52.6	113.8
1970	1.60	3.23	49.6	107.4
1971	1.60	3.45	46.4	103.1
1972	1.60	3.70	43.2	99.7

(continued)

Table 1.2 (*continued*)

Year	Minimum	Annual Average Wage	Minimum Wage as a Percentage of Annual Average Wage[a]	Minimum Wage as a Percentage of Poverty Line
1973	1.60	3.94	40.6	93.8
1974[b]	2.00	4.24	47.2	105.7
1975[b]	2.10	4.53	46.4	101.7
1976[b]	2.30	4.86	47.3	105.4
1977	2.30	5.25	43.8	99.1
1978[b]	2.65	5.69	46.6	106.0
1979[b]	2.90	6.16	47.1	104.3
1980[b]	3.10	6.66	46.5	98.2
1981[b]	3.35	7.25	46.2	96.1
1982	3.35	7.68	43.6	90.6
1983	3.35	8.02	41.8	87.8
1984	3.35	8.32	40.3	84.2
1985	3.35	8.57	39.1	81.3
1986	3.35	8.76	38.2	79.8
1987	3.35	8.98	37.3	76.9
1988	3.35	9.28	36.1	73.9
1989	3.35	9.66	34.7	70.5
1990[b]	3.80	10.01	38.0	75.9
1991[b]	4.25	10.32	41.2	81.4
1992	4.25	10.70	39.7	79.0
1993	4.25	10.96	38.8	76.7
1994	4.25	11.26	37.7	74.8
1995	4.25	11.60	36.6	72.7
1996[b]	4.70	11.81	39.8	78.9
1997[b]	5.15	12.17	42.3	83.7
1998	5.15			82.4
1999	5.15			80.6
2000	5.15	18.76	27.5	78.0
2001	5.15	19.27	26.7	75.8
2002	5.15	19.70	26.1	74.7
2003	5.15	20.33	25.3	73.0
2004	5.15	21.24	24.3	71.1
2005	5.15	21.89	23.5	68.8
2006	5.15	22.86	22.5	66.6
2007	5.85	23.95	24.4	73.6
2008	6.55	24.56	26.7	79.4

Table 1.2 (*continued*)

Year	Minimum	Annual Average Wage	Minimum Wage as a Percentage of Annual Average Wage[a]	Minimum Wage as a Percentage of Poverty Line
2009	7.25	24.77	29.3	88.2
2010	7.25	25.38	28.6	86.8
2011	7.25	26.06	27.8	84.2
2012	7.25	26.47	27.4	82.5
2013				

[a] These percentages are author's calculations based on the poverty rate for a family of three. The percentage for a single minimum wage earner would, of course, be higher and that for a family of four would always be lower.
[b] Except for 1945, 1947, and 1996, the years selected are the years in which increases in the minimum wage took effect.

Source: U.S. Department of Labor, Employment Standards Administration; Bureau of Labor Statistics, "History of the Federal Minimum Wage Rates under the Fair Labor Standards Act—1938 through 1991," *Current Employment Statistics*, Labstat Series Report, Series EEU00500006. U.S. Department of Commerce, Bureau of the Census, Historical Poverty Tables, Table 1, "Weighted Average Poverty Thresholds for Families of Specified Sized: 1959–1996," http:/www.census.gov/hhes/poverty/histpov/hstpov1.html; U.S. Bureau of Census, Current Population Survey, Annual Social and Economic Supplements, http://www.census.gov/hhes/www/poverty/histpov/; also OECD StatExtracts, http://stats.oecd.org/Index.aspx?DataSetCode=AV_AN_WAGE

the report noted that most minimum wage earners weren't primary wage earners, the image of the minimum wage as a luxury of teenagers was only reinforced. Meanwhile, economists championing the youth disemployment effect also found their voice, especially given the administration's support for it. A two-tiered wage system quickly became the political strategy for attacking the minimum wage. By allowing for a subminimum wage, it was reasoned that employers would opt for teenagers over their parents, which in time would only lead to the elimination of the program.

If the minimum wage was primarily benefiting teenagers and not benefiting those working to support a family, what was the logic of the minimum wage at all? It was simply irrelevant. At the same time, it was relevant because it did not bear on the poverty rate. First those who argued against increases in the minimum wage suggested that only teenagers would derive benefit from increases, with the implication that in a policy calculus in which one of the variables is poverty, this group simply wasn't important. Or at least they weren't important enough that countless numbers of businesses should incur rising labor costs. Now the same group that wasn't considered important before was becoming the reason for why the minimum wage should not be increased. Raising the minimum wage now would hurt teenagers because they wouldn't be able to find employment.

By 1989 the minimum wage had dropped to less than 40 percent of average annual hourly earnings. But this episode actually began in 1987 when Senator Edward Kennedy of Massachusetts and Representative Augustus Hawkins of California introduced legislation to increase the minimum wage to $4.65 an hour by 1990. President Reagan had indicated that he might soften his opposition to the minimum wage hike if a provision for a youth subminimum wage was also included (Card and Krueger 1995, p. 318). Arguments against the minimum centered on the more traditional academic arguments that the minimum wage had a disemployment effect on the teenage labor market. Because the administration was ideologically opposed to any type of government interference in the economy, it became all too easy to latch onto a group of studies that would buttress its position. Meanwhile, the case for the minimum wage became increasingly mired in poverty arguments: the minimum wage had to be increased because it would provide assistance to the working poor.

By the time the new Bush administration took office in 1989, it was willing to lend its support to an increase because growth in the economy would allow for it, but it wanted a short-term subminimum, which would be referred to as a "training wage." And yet, it was not prepared to fully support the Democratic proposal, H.R. 2, which would have raised the minimum wage from $3.35 to $4.55 in three stages and included a two-month training wage only for those who never held a job before. Rather, when both houses passed H.R. 2, President Bush, in an effort to demonstrate that he could not be pushed around, vetoed it. Nevertheless, a compromise bill was introduced, which in the end was signed into law, and raised the minimum wage from $3.35 to $4.25 in two stages and included a training wage equal to 85 percent of the minimum for those aged 16 to 19.

The early part of the 1990s certainly held the prospect of being radically different from the preceding decade. With the election of Bill Clinton as president in 1992, after 12 years of Republican reign in the White House, the prevailing political mood was one of change. Clinton had campaigned on a platform of improving the economy and putting people first. The administration did not immediately address the minimum wage, but Labor Secretary Robert Reich was clear that raising the wage was central to assisting those at the lower end of the wage scale. Meanwhile, during the first term of the administration, the earned income tax credit (EITC), a refundable credit that would benefit the working poor, was successfully expanded. For those earning the minimum wage, which was then $4.25, the credit would effectively raise one's wage to $6. Still, the credit was not considered to be enough; the administration was also working on welfare reform, with the intent of moving people off the welfare rolls and into the labor market within two years. Therefore, in order for work to be considered a viable option for the typical welfare mother, even assuming the EITC, the minimum wage would need to be raised. By 1994, however, the political climate had changed dramatically. Both houses of Congress had changed hands in the midterm elections and were now controlled by Republicans, who saw no reason to raise the minimum wage. The sentiment among many in the Republican Party was that workers not worth $4.25 an hour should be paid less (Reich 1997, p. 232). The public, however, did not share this viewpoint. Although the public firmly believed that welfare recipients should work, it also believed that those who worked should be paid a living wage. Now the issue was one of simple fairness. Corporate executives were getting richer. Many in the middle class were experiencing the pains of downsizing.

In 1996, Congress passed draconian cuts in welfare, which only dramatized the inequity of maintaining the minimum wage where it was, for how could the nation now demand that people go to work at wages below subsistence? In the end Congress voted to amend the FLSA again in 1996, but only because the legislation included tax relief and other benefits to small business. The 1996 amendments to FLSA called for a 90-cent-an-hour increase to be phased in in two steps. The first phase-in was to take place during the fall of 1996, with the second phase-in taking place a year later. As a result, the minimum wage was increased to $5.15 an hour in 1997.

During the 2000s the value of the minimum wage declined again. The political composition of Congress made it unlikely that the minimum wage would be increased during the early part of the George W. Bush administration. It was during the midterm elections of 2006, when the Democrats took control of the House of Representatives, that there was a new political momentum to raise the minimum wage from $5.15 an hour to its current rate of $7.25. As part of its effort to pass a swath of legislation during the first 100 days of the new Congress, a minimum wage increase was passed in January 2007 and would be increased in increments, first to $5.85 in 2007, then $6.55 in 2008, and finally to $7.25 in 2009. But the value of the minimum wage was still declining. In 2013, during his State of the Union Address, President Obama called for a minimum wage increase to $9 an hour, but the Republican-controlled House of Representatives refused to take action on the measure. Then again in 2014 in his State of the Union Address, President Obama called for an increase in the minimum wage to $10.10 an hour. Again, the Republican-controlled House of Representatives refused to take action and Republicans—even in the Democrat-controlled Senate—were able to block a vote on the minimum wage. Meanwhile, in an effort to set the tone, and perhaps circumvent Congress through Executive Orders, President Obama issued an executive order that would require all companies doing business with the federal government to pay their workers a minimum of $10.10 an hour or risk losing their federal contracts. But this measure was more symbolic than real, and its reach was still limited to those with federal contracts. It would not affect employers without federal contracts. To expand coverage to everybody else would still require an act of Congress.

Minimum Wages in Europe

The minimum wage in the United States is by statute. In European countries where there are minimum wages, they often function differently. In some countries there are statutes, and in others there are wage boards that set different rates for different industries. In France, labor market institutions have been in stark contrast to the United States. France has been characterized by high minimum wages and strong employment protective legislation. Wage rates in France tend to be set in a more centralized fashion. In the aftermath of World War II, the first national legal minimum hourly wage was introduced—the Minimum Interbranch Guaranteed Wage (SMIG), which was also indexed to inflation. Conceived of as a "fair wage," it was thought that it would balance the relationship between wage earner and employer in the face of disequilibria that would tend to favor employers. This was later transformed in 1970 into the SMIC—the interprofessional, indexed-linked growth minimum wage—and was automatically indexed to both inflation and particularly to real growth (Caroli and Gautie 2008). Although France has been characterized by higher rates of unemployment, it also had much reduced incidence of low-wage work. Low-wage work in France is not necessarily the same as poverty. In the United States, however, it tends to be associated with poverty. The minimum wage in France has played a key role in compressing the distribution of wages at the bottom. One of the key explanations for the small number of low-wage workers in France is the existence of the minimum wage. Another consequence of the high minimum wage has been a deficit in the number of low-skilled, potentially labor-intensive activities (Caroli, Gautie, and Askenazy 2008).

Denmark also presents an interesting contrast, as it tends to be characterized by what is referred to as the "Danish model," which is composed of agreements between employers and trade unions. These agreements are much more important as a regulatory mechanism than legislation and government interventions. One of the features of the Danish labor market is that the wage distribution in Denmark is much more compressed than in the United States. This means that there isn't quite the same gap between the top and the bottom. Denmark has a thoroughly organized labor market, and labor market issues have historically been settled in centralized negotiations between employers and employee representatives without government interference. As a consequence of the Danish model, Denmark does not have a minimum wage law as do other countries. Employers, however, did respond to union pressure at general wage bargaining in 1977 and agreed on minimum tariffs concerning all employees and members of the Danish Employees' Federation. For the trade unions, the introduction of a minimum tariff was seen as a victorious step in the ongoing struggle to raise the wages of low-wage workers, concentrated among women and low-skilled men. The new wage policy was called the "solidarity wage policy." And yet, despite unionism as the primary form of wage policy in Denmark, Danish workers still aren't as well protected as they are in the rest of Europe. In some cases, they are as unprotected as they are in the United States (Westergaard-Nielson 2008).

The Netherlands, on the other hand, actually parallels the British model of wage councils. The debate over low pay and employment dates back to the aftermath of World War II. For a majority of workers under the 1950 Worker Council Act, workers were entitled to representation in joint work councils in the firm, initially chaired by employees. Prior to 1980, low pay was an integral part of general wage formation. After the war until the early 1960s, all outcomes of collective wage negotiation had to be officially approved by government-appointed officials. In 1964, social partners—a variety of different actors in business, labor, and government—agreed between them on an economy-wide minimum wage. Consequently, low pay, which was identified as the minimum wage, came to be treated separately from wages in general following 1964. And yet, the evolution of both wages and social insurance changed dramatically during and after the deep recession and the second oil crisis of 1980, thus beginning a period of prolonged wage restraint and welfare reform. From the 1980s on, negotiated real wage growth was moderated (Salverda, van Klauveren, and van der Meer 2008).

Sweden too, influenced by the Rehn–Meidner model, has long had what might be described as an active labor policy. In the aftermath of World War I, a strong emphasis was placed on work, and cash advances and support were discouraged. Unemployed workers were expected to either obtain a job on the open labor market through employment agencies or accept a poorly paid public works job. A continuing theme of labor market policy was that the labor market should come to work better. Labor market policy was a key issue of the Labor Movement's committee *Program for the Post-War Period,* published shortly before the end of World War II. Although the three main components of active labor policy were full employment, a fair income distribution and higher standard of living, and higher efficiency and greater democracy in the economy, the later component of "solidaristic wage policy" is ultimately what became the most important from the vantage point of wage policy (Wadensjo 2001). On one level, solidaristic wage policy implied equal pay for equal work regardless of the profitability of the companies, but on another the aim was to establish fair wage differentials rather than general wage equalization.

As much as wage differences between earners were to be expected, it was also believed that those differences should reflect objective differences in the working environment, responsibility, experience, and education, not short-run profits or labor conditions. For Rehn and Meidner, solidaristic wage policy would encourage economic growth, mainly through structural change and alleviating inflationary wage–wage races. As Lennart Erixson (2001) explains: "By solidaristic wage policy, a pull mechanism is replaced by a push mechanism, or better, a rationing mechanism, in labour markets. Labor mobility is maintained by the threatened unemployment in unprofitable sectors but also by greater number of vacancies in profitable sectors" (p. 19).

In Britain where there is no official equivalent of the U.S. poverty threshold, there is what is now called the living wage, which essentially functions as a minimum wage. Nevertheless, the aim of the living wage is similar to that of the United States: to increase the wages of poorly paid workers. Living wages, then, are seen as part of a wider concern in the labor movement with tackling poverty (Grover 2005). Between 1979 and 1997, under a Conservative government, the United Kingdom experienced rising levels of income disparities and poverty, and also a growing percentage of low-paid workers. By 2005, an estimated 22.1 percent of workers in the United Kingdom were categorized as "low pay." Low pay in the United Kingdom was also associated with female employment, part-time work, and low-skilled occupations. And compared to continental Europe, the United Kingdom never had a highly regulated labor market. A rapid increase in earnings inequality and a sharp increase in the number of households during the 1980s and early 1990s led to a substantial increase in household poverty (Mason, Mayhew, and Osborne 2008). Historically, trade unions provided significant protection for many workers at the low end of the labor market. Union membership peaked at 53 percent in 1979, but that peak was followed by a sustained decline, precipitated initially by the severe recession at the end of the

1970s through the beginning of the 1980s. Union density now stands at 29 percent. In 1989 when density was 53 percent, about 78 percent of the workforce was covered by collective agreements. Now with 29 percent density, only 36 percent of the workforce is covered by collective agreements. In the vast majority of firms, there is no negotiation or consultation regarding pay and working conditions, including unionized workplaces. In contrast to other Western European countries, there never was a single, all-encompassing system of industrial relations in the United Kingdom. Under the Thatcher government new laws were introduced, which not only reduced the scope of unions to act but also essentially created an environment whereby employers were able to withdraw recognition of trade unions. Until 1999, the United Kingdom didn't have a national minimum wage, but there were other forms of low-wage protection—through a broad system of wage councils (Mason, Mayhew, Osborne, and Stevens 2008).

In 1999, the British Parliament finally passed the National Minimum Wage (NMW), which effectively supplanted the Trade Boards Act of 1909 that would attempt to establish minimum wages on an industry/occupational basis. Now there would be a uniform minimum wage covering the entire country. A key feature of this act was the establishment of the Low Pay Commission (LPC), which would be an independent body that would report on the state of the low-wage labor market and make periodic recommendations for wage increases. The LPC effectively removed the issue of the minimum wage from the political will of Parliament. By creating the commission, the Parliament would be forced to publicly respond to the LPC, which also ensured that the minimum wage could not be kept off the political agenda at times the Parliament might be dominated by those who weren't as friendly to the minimum wage. Not only did the NMW raise wages, but it did so with no negative effects (Waltman 2008). It certainly raised the wages of the less well-off, although their income gains were modest, but the result was that more people in Britain had more discretionary income as a result. And because of wage compression engendered by the NMW, there was a slight reduction in income inequality. At the same time, studies of the NMW have repeatedly failed to turn up evidence of disemployment effects. On the contrary, employment levels actually rose following the introduction of the minimum wage. Moreover, objective observers even attributed recent increases in unemployment to increased supply factors rather than increases in the minimum wage.

In Australia, the concept of a living wage is actually an integral element in a national system of wage determination. At the center of Australia's unique wage-setting institutions are quasi-judicial tribunals that were established around the turn of the century to manage and resolve industrial disputes. The idea of a living wage was a founding concept in the Australian industrial arbitration system. The Australian Council of Trade Unions (ACTU) launched its living wage campaign in 1996 as a claim before the Australian Industrial Relations Commission to vary awards. With the living wage campaign, the ACTU was attempting to mount a counteroffensive against the newly elected government that was committed to breaking union power and deregulating the labor market. The living wage has, in short, been about preventing the collapse of hourly wage rates in an economy plagued by chronic unemployment and underemployment (Buchanan, Watson, and Meagher 2004).

And in New Zealand, the living wage has been about achieving fair labor standards. In New Zealand's labor market, wage determination occurred principally through centralized bargaining systems until the mid-1980s. "Fair wages" were initially defined with reference to prevailing wage rates, but over time they became conflated with appropriate living standards. For nearly a century, the Industrial Conciliation and Arbitration Act of 1894 had established a basic framework for industrial relations. As part of a 1925 statement of the Arbitration Council, the living wage was considered to be a minimum rate earned by a man that would be sufficient to maintain himself, his wife, and two dependent children. Until 1984, the labor market had been governed by the full-income concept—a social wage—that included all nonwage benefits paid by employers, as well as contributions from government revenue to wage earners or the entire population. But between 1984 and 1990, the Labour Party, which was always closely linked to the trade union movement, began a process of dismantling market regulations. In 1991, the national government enacted the Employment Contracts Act (ECA), which didn't even mention trade unions; rather, they were subsumed under bargaining agents, thereby weakening their ability to recruit and represent workers. Given this climate, the living wage in New Zealand, as is the case in Britain, has been about improving the national minimum wage, which always fluctuated widely in its ratio to average wages (Hyman 2004).

Germany, by contrast, has been one of seven among the 28 European Union countries not to have a national minimum wage. Rather, it has relied on trade unions and business groups to fix wage rates. In this regard, it has followed the more corporatist model found in countries like Sweden. In corporatist arrangements, wages are usually set as part of agreements reached by big business, organized labor, and government. Germany, however, is moving in the direction of a national minimum wage. In April 2014, German chancellor Angela Merkel approved the country's first minimum wage of 8.50 euros, the equivalent of $11.75 an hour, to begin in 2015. The German parliament is set to take up the issue during the summer of 2014. Still, the wage will not cover minors, interns, trainees, or the long-term unemployed during their first six months at work. Also, those employers using temporary and seasonal workers will have six months to phase in the new law.

The Current Context

The minimum wage is currently still at $7.25 an hour and calls for its increase come amid two trends. The first is that the minimum wage has declined in value and represents a much lower proportion of the federal poverty line than it once did. And the second is that income inequality, especially wage inequality, has been increasing in the United States, particularly since the 1980s. President Obama's call for a $10.10 minimum wage has specifically been against the backdrop of rising inequality. A minimum wage, in and of itself, would not eliminate inequality, but it would certainly reduce the gap between the top and the bottom. But the call for an increase in the minimum wage also comes within the context of more states, and even localities, enacting new minimum wages. Vermont has the highest minimum wage law in the country at $15 an hour, and San Francisco and San Diego have raised their citywide minimum wages. In New York, many localities are seeking permission from the state legislature to enact their own minimum wage according to the respective living standards of the community. More localities are beginning to see more local governments take the lead on the minimum wage. In New York State, several localities have petitioned the state legislature for permission to enact minimum wages that would be appropriate for their respective communities. New York City's mayor, Bill de Blasio, similarly intends to seek Albany's permission to create a citywide minimum wage for New York City.

Currently, 29 states have minimum wages that are higher than the federal minimum. Vermont recently passed legislation to raise its minimum wage to $10.50 an hour by 2018. Washington State has a minimum wage of $9.32 an hour, but Seattle has the highest minimum wage of $15. San Francisco has had its own minimum wage for several years now. As of January 1, San Francisco has one of the highest minimum wages at $10.55 an hour. Moreover, there is broad support in favor of raising it to $15 an hour, and labor activists are poised to put it on the ballot for voters to decide the issue. In San Diego, Mayor Todd Gloria proposed a ballot initiative that would raise the minimum wage to $13.09 over three years, with the argument that the entire local economy will benefit. That states and localities are taking the lead on this issue only highlights the reality of the federal minimum wage failing to keep pace with inflation.

Rising inequality has become a permanent phenomenon in the world's industrial countries. Between 1947 and 1973, the incomes of families in the bottom fifth of the income distribution in the United States grew more rapidly than the income of families in any of the other countries. Meanwhile, the incomes of families in the top fifth of the distribution grew more slowly than the incomes of families in other quintiles. After 1973, however, that changed. Low-income families in the United States experienced a steady decline in real income from the late 1970s through the middle of the 1990s. And it was only because of economic growth that accelerated during the course of the 1990s that the decline in their incomes came to an end. Those countries with the greatest increases in income inequality also had the most decentralized labor markets, whereas those countries with centralized wage-setting institutions tended to have less income inequality (Pontusson 2005).

Peter Gottschalk (1997) suggests that income inequality increases when the growth of income is greater among those at the top than among those at the bottom, even though bottom incomes have improved in absolute terms. While mean wages grew rapidly during the 1950s and 1960s, the dispersion around the growing mean changed very little. But as mean wages grew slowly during the 1970s through the 1990s, inequality rapidly increased. So long as those at the bottom of the income distribution gained along with everyone else from secular growth in the mean, it was a foregone conclusion that poverty rates would be kept down. Indeed, income growth of those at the top was greater than the growth of those at the bottom. Between 1976 and 2008, the percentage increase in income among the 10th percentile was 316.7 percent compared to 360.4 percent among the 50th percentile and 431 percent among the 90 percentile. Among the bottom quintile, average incomes increased by 326.7 percent compared to 480.2 percent among the top quintile.

Between 1989 and 1999, the average family's income increased by 3.9 percent. Meanwhile, the income of those families in the top 5 percent increased by 11.6 percent. More unequal than income, however, has been wealth. In the United States in 1998, for example, the top 1 percent received 14 percent of all income, but enjoyed 38.5 percent of all net worth and 47.2 percent of all net financial assets. The top 10 percent received about 40 percent of all income, but held about 83 percent of all financial assets. During the mid-1990s, the United States had the highest poverty rate among the 16 developed countries, while it also continued to have the highest per capita income in the world (Hodgson 2004, pp. 91–94). In the aggregate, the amount of money in American households rose from $2.9 trillion in the mid-1970s to $4.8 trillion in the mid-1990s. And while average household income rose from $39,415 to $47,123 in constant dollars, the average incomes of the top 5 percent rose from $126,131 to $201,684. Although incomes of those in the middle fifth ranged from $27,760 to $44,000 with an average income of $35,486, this middle fifth had only 15.1 percent of the total. The median pay for a full-time worker in the United States was $25,480, with 51.9 million men earning more at a median of $28,964 and 39 million women earning less at a median of $21,736 (Hacker 1998, pp. 10–16).

Income inequality has been on the rise in recent decades. Those at the top of the distribution have seen their incomes increase, while those at the bottom have seen their incomes decrease in real terms. This has effectively narrowed the middle class, whose wages have stagnated in aggregate terms since the 1970s (Phillips 1990; Newman 1993; Hungerford 1993; Wolff 1994; Danziger and Gottschalk 1995). Income inequality and poverty are both greater in the United States than in other industrialized nations (Smeeding, O'Higgins, and Rainwater 1990; Smeeding and Sullivan 1998). While inequality in the United States has been increasing for decades now, the sharpest increase appears to have occurred during the early 1980s, and then again during the 1990s (Bernstein and Mishel 1997). But it was also during this period that the United States saw a decline in unionism and a deterioration in the minimum wage. Those declines weren't nearly as great in other countries where income inequality has tended to be less, which is to say that inequality has been less in those countries with stronger minimum wages. Between 1963 and 1989, for instance, the wages of the least skilled, those in the bottom 10th percentile, fell by 5 percent, while the wages for the most skilled, those in the 90th percentile, increased by 40 percent (Juhn, Murphy, and Pierce 1993). The net result of this divergence was an enormous increase in wage inequality.

The standard model holds rising income inequality to be a function of structural economic transformation. Technological change has tended to be biased toward those with higher levels of education and skills. As the economy has evolved from industrial-based manufacturing to postindustrial service, there has been a growing mismatch between good paying jobs and the skills available to workers. According to this school of thought, the labor market is divided into a primary market where high premiums are placed on skilled workers, and a secondary market where unskilled workers are trapped in the lowest-wage service sector of the economy. The growth in wage inequality between the primary and secondary labor markets has been caused by increasing skills differentials between the two (Katz and Krueger 1992; Katz and Murphy 1992).

Institutionalists, on the other hand, and a tradition from which the concept of active wage policy is derived, hold rising income inequality to be a function of deliberate policy choices biased toward the interests of business. Those choices included an assault on the institutions that long served to bolster the wages of those at the bottom of the distribution, as well as the working class: mainly the minimum wage and unions (Howell and Huebler 2001; Card and DiNardo 2002). During the late 1970s, the United States began experiencing a sharp ideological shift toward a preference for competitive market outcomes and solutions, and this ideological shift did have direct effects on bargaining in the workplace (Moody 1988). Those countries with the greatest increases in income inequality also had the most decentralized labor markets, whereas those countries with centralized wage-setting institutions tended to have less income inequality. The institutionalist school will argue that in the absence of institutions to prop up the wages of those at the bottom of the distribution, income inequality is bound to increase.

Understood in greater context, then, the current debate over the minimum wage is within the context of rising inequality, and rising inequality is understood to be in part due to public policy decisions that have resulted in the decline of important labor market institutions, including the minimum wage (Volscho 2005). It isn't just that there has been a widening of the gap between the top and the bottom, but that the very top has effectively pulled away from the rest of the country. Journalist Hendrick Smith (2012) argues that policies favorable to business have resulted in America's superrich accumulating trillions in new wealth while the poor have gotten poorer, and the middle class has all but disappeared. The result is essentially two Americas. At the same time the minimum wage was under political assault, there was a power shift in favor of pro-business policies. Had this shift not occurred, Smith believes that the typical American family would be earning an average of $12,000 more per year. Instead, the period beginning in the 1980s became one of great wage stagnation.

Economist Joseph Stiglitz (2012) also argues that rising income inequality is the product of policy choices made. As much as market forces shape the degree of inequality, those same forces are shaped by government policies. Inequality often means that those with vast resources are able to use their resources to influence public policy in ways that favor them, and often at the expense of those lacking in resources. Those at the top typically use their power to shape the rules of the game in their favor, and to extract from the public as much as they can for themselves. If individuals believe the economic and political system is unfair, the glue no longer works and societies do not function well. In short, Stiglitz would appear to be talking about maintaining institutions that ensure the economy functions both efficiently and fairly. Stiglitz would appear to be calling attention to the fact that the American political system is more responsive to those with money, and the more unequal the distribution becomes, it is only a foregone conclusion that policies pursued by elected officials will favor those at the higher end of the distribution (Bachrach and Botwinick 1992; Bartels 2008).

Another variant of this theme is the argument by Gordon Lafer (2002) that economic policy over the last couple of decades has been predicated on the assumption that more policy efforts, because of the dominance of the skills mismatch thesis, need to be focused on efforts to retrain workers rather than actually creating jobs. The skills mismatch thesis has become a convenient explanation for falling wages and rising inequality. By the logic of the skills mismatch theory, those lacking in skills are not in a position to command wages higher than the minimum wage. Moreover, they are not worth more than the minimum. At the same time, the skills mismatch theory cannot explain completely the reasons for low wages at the bottom and the stagnant wages in the middle. Rather, the decline in unionism appears to have played a greater role in determining wages of most workers than less education.

Among the reasons for high middle-class wages, at least until the 1980s, was that more workers were members of unions. Union wages were generally 28.4 percent higher than those of unorganized workers. In traditional human capital theory, competitive markets guarantee that wages will be exactly equal to the workers' marginal productivity. But the union premium underscores this central flaw, which has only been obscured by mismatch theories. The union premium makes it clear that institutions are key in setting wage rates and determining worth. This would also imply that some employers—nonunionized employers—are enjoying substantially greater profits. And yet focusing policy on job training allows us to obscure the reality that institutions that deliberately propped up wages have been targeted because they cut into profits. But as union membership declined, so too did the value of the minimum wage. It is no accident that the longest period in which there were no minimum wage increases—1981 through 1989—was also one of significant declines in union membership. The minimum wage tended to be increased more frequently when there was a constituency behind it, and that constituency was organized labor. With the decline of unions, the minimum wage no longer had a constituency and was less likely to be increased (Levin-Waldman 2001).

Also arguing the deliberate policy hypothesis, Jacob Hacker and Paul Pierson (2010) argue that the shift in income from the bottom to the top has been a long-term trend that began around 1980, and not one that was obviously related to either the business cycle or the shifting partisan occupancy of the White House. The top reaped massive gains while the economy stopped working for middle- and working-class Americans. More than an increasing gap between the top and the bottom, the very top has been pulling away from the rest of the country. Meanwhile, government has been doing much less to reduce inequality through taxes on the top and benefits for those at the bottom, in large measure because those at the top have been in a position to dictate policy. The rules of the game make a huge difference in people's lives. Government policy not only failed to push back against the rising tide at the top of finance, corporate pay, and winner-take-all domains, but it also consistently promoted it. The absence of a government response to rising inequality can be regarded as a form of policy when it takes the form of "drift"—the deliberate failure to adapt policies to the shifting realities of a dynamic economy. One example of this is that intense opponents of the minimum wage have worked tirelessly and effectively to prevent it from being increased to prior levels or to be pegged to inflation. But drift is the opposite of how laws are actually made. They are a passive-aggressive form of politics and policymaking. Political scientist Larry Bartels (2008) notes that in the 2006 vote on the minimum wage, members of the Senate tended to be less responsive to lower-income constituents than to higher-income constituents. To the extent that rising income inequality means that those at the top are able to dictate the rules of the game in their favor, it only means that the likelihood of support for minimum wage increases for those at the bottom is less.

Thomas Piketty (2014) in his celebrated book on the growth of income inequality also defines it as the very top pulling away from the rest. He argues that the history of the distribution of wealth has always been deeply political and cannot be reduced to so-called neutral economic mechanisms. Rather, the history of inequality has been shaped by the way that economic, social, and political actors view what is just and what is not, and also the relative power of those actors and the collective choices that result. And yet, much of this has been obscured by what Piketty refers to as the economic discipline's "childish passion for mathematics" (p. 32). This obsession has only served to create the appearance of being scientific, without having to answer the far more complex questions posed by the real world in which we live. It is because this preoccupation has also created the appearance of neutrality that it could more easily embrace the skills-biased toward technical change hypothesis without stopping to consider the larger political and social context in which those forces were operating.

In comparing France to the United States, Piketty observes that the minimum wage in France did play a role in reducing wage inequality in the post–World War II years while wage inequality in the United States rose as the minimum wage was in decline. In France a national minimum wage was created in 1950, but was seldom increased thereafter and only fell farther behind the average wage. But in 1970, the minimum wage was officially indexed to the mean wage. Moreover, governments from 1968 to 1983 felt obligated to increase the minimum wage significantly almost every year in a seething social and political climate. Between 1968 and 1983, the purchasing power of the minimum wage also increased by more than 130 percent, while the mean wage increased by only 50 percent. The result was a significant compression of wage inequality. In the United States, however, subclass of "supermanagers" emerged. Inequality had reached its lowest ebb between 1950 and 1980, whereby the top decile of the income distribution claimed 30–35 percent of the nation's income. After 1980, however, income inequality exploded with top decile share of the national income rising to between 45 and 50 percent in the 2000s. The causes of rising income inequality in the United States are largely due to the unprecedented increase in wage inequality, and especially the extremely high compensation of managers at the top of the distribution. Although the skills mismatch argument is acknowledged to be the accepted theory for this rise, it does not offer a satisfactory explanation of the rise of the supermanager or of wage inequality in the United States after 1980. Within this context, the decline in the minimum wage, or at least its failure to keep up with inflation, is seen as a contributing factor to

Table 1.3   General Trends in Wage Inequality (Percentage)

	90/10	90/50	50/10	Ratio of Top Quintile to Bottom Quintile
1982	20.0	2.2	8.9	15.6
1992	12.3	2.3	5.4	12.4
2002	8.5	2.4	3.5	13.1
2003	9.0	2.5	3.6	13.3
2004	8.5	2.4	3.6	13.0
2005	8.8	2.5	3.6	13.6
2006	8.9	2.4	3.7	12.9
2007*	8.5	2.4	3.5	12.3
2008*	8.7	2.4	3.6	12.2
2009*	8.8	2.4	3.5	11.3
2010	8.4	2.4	3.5	11.5
2011	8.3	2.4	3.4	11.3
2012	8.6	2.5	3.5	11.9
2013	8.3	2.5	3.3	12.5

* Years in which there were increases in the federal minimum wage.

rising income inequality. Of course, nobody believes that raising the minimum wage would by itself eliminate inequality.
But it would reduce the gap between the top and the bottom
because the percentage increase among those at the bottom has
to be greater than the percentage increase among those at the
bottom (Gottschalk 1997).

Table 1.3 shows several different measures of wage inequality
for full-time workers working for wages. Overall wage inequality appears to have declined between 1982 and 2013, but at
least by the measure of the ratio between the top quintile and
the bottom quintile it did increase between 1992 and 2002. By
the other measures it decreased. Despite variations in the rates
of inequality, there was a decline in wage inequality between
2006 and 2009. One of the reasons for the decrease despite
the literature to the contrary is that the Current Population
Survey, which is also census data, topcodes the income and
wage variable. Therefore, it is not capturing super wages over
$1 million, which might otherwise skew the ratio upward.
Then, beginning in 2010 inequality, according to the quintile ratio measure, ticks up again. What is important about
this period is that in 2007, the first phase of a three-phase
increase in the minimum wage took effect, with the last
phase occurring in 2009. Between 2009 and 2013, inequality increased because the mean income of the top quintile
increased by 10.9 percent, while it decreased by 0.4 percent
among the bottom quintile. But between 2006 and 2009,
the mean income of the bottom quintile increased by 28 percent, while it only increased by 11.9 percent among the top
quintile.

Analysis

The minimum wage in the United States was born out of a changing economic structure, mainly the Industrial Revolution, that
resulted in masses of workers being forced into essentially low-
paying jobs. Although it expanded considerably to cover more
workers, and increasingly more industrial nations around the

world have adopted minimum wages, it has also been a deeply divisive political issue, fraught with ideology. Politics have essentially stalled further growth of the program. Whereas calls for a minimum wage were against the backdrop of rising inequality in a new industrial economy paying barely subsistence wages, today calls for increases are also against rising inequality and stagnant middle-class wages whereby the top has simply pulled away from everybody else. What is important to bear in mind is that the minimum wage is but one policy in a larger policy toolbox aimed at bolstering working people's income and ultimately achieving prosperity. In short, the minimum wage speaks to a fundamental reality, which, as the next chapter will show, isn't always that obvious—that institutions matter.

References

Adkins v. Children's Hospital. 1922. 261 U.S. (October).

Andrews, Elmer F. 1939. "Making the Wage-Hour Law Work." *American Labor Legislation Review.* 29, 2 (June): 53–61.

Bachrach, Peter and Aryeh Botwinick. 1992. *Power and Empowerment: A Radical Theory of Participatory Democracy.* Philadelphia, PA: Temple University Press.

Baer, Judith A. 1978. *The Chains of Protection: The Judicial Response to Women's Labor Legislation.* Westport, CT: Greenwood Press.

Bartels, Larry M. 2008. *Unequal Democracy: The Political Economy of the New Gilded Age.* Princeton, NJ: Princeton University Press.

Brown, H. LaRue. 1913. "Massachusetts and the Minimum Wage." *Annals of the American Academy of Political and Social Science.* 48: 13–21.

Buchanan, John, Ian Watson, and Gabrielle Meagher. 2004. "The Living Wage in Australia: History, Recent Developments, and Current Challenges." In Deborah M.

Figart, ed. *Living Wage Movements: Global Perspectives*. London; New York: Routledge.

Card, David and Alan B. Krueger. 1995. *Myth and Measurement: The New Economics of the Minimum Wage*. Princeton, NJ: Princeton University Press.

Card, David and John DiNardo. 2002. "Skill Based Technological Change and Rising Wage Inequality: Some Problems and Puzzles." *Working Paper No 8769*. National Bureau of Economic Research (February).

Caroli, Eve and Jerome Gautie. 2008. "Low-Wage Work: The Political Debate and Research Agenda in France." In Eve Caroli and Jerome Gauti, ed., *Low-Wage Work in France*. New York: Russell Sage Foundation.

Caroli, Eve, Jerome Gautie, and Phillipe Askenazy. 2008. "Low-Wage Work and Labor Market Institutions in France." In Eve Caroli and Jerome Gautie, eds. *Low-Wage Work in France*. New York: Russell Sage Foundation.

Clark, John Bates. 1913. "The Minimum Wage." *The Atlantic Monthly*. 112, 3 (September): 289–297.

Congressional Quarterly Almanac. 1966. 22.

Danziger, Sheldon and Peter Gottschalk. 1995. *America Unequal*. Cambridge, MA: Harvard University Press.

DiNardo, John and Thomas Lemieux. 1997. "Diverging Male Wage Inequality in the United States and Canada, 1981–1988: Do Institutions Explain the Difference?" *Industrial and Labor Relations Review*. 50, 4 (July): 629–650.

Eccles, Mary Eisner. 1977. "Labor 'Disappointed' in Carter's Performance." *Congressional Quarterly Weekly* (April 9).

Erixson, Lennart. 2001. "A Swedish Economic Policy— The Rehn-Meidner Model's Theory, Applicability and Validity." In Henry Milner and Eskil Wadenjos, eds. *Gosta Rehn, The Swedish Model and Labour Market Policies: International and National Perspectives*. Aldershot, UK; Burlington, VT: Ashgate Publishing Co.

"Fair Labor Standards Amendments of 1961." 1961. *Statutes at Large of the United States.* 75. Public Law 87-50 (May 5).

Figart, Deborah M., Ellen Mutari, and Marilyn Power. 2002. *Living Wages, Equal Wages: Gender and Labor Market Policies in the United States.* London; New York: Routledge.

Filene, Edward A. 1923. "The Minimum Wage and Efficiency." *American Economic Review.* 13 (September): 411–415.

Galbraith, James K. 1998. *Created Unequal: The Crisis in American Pay.* New York: Basic Books.

Glickman, Lawrence B. 1997. *A Living Wage: American Workers and the Making of Consumer Society.* Ithaca, NY; London: Cornell University Press.

Gottschalk, Petter. 1997. "Inequality, Income Growth, and Mobility: The Basic Facts." *Journal of Economic Perspectives.* 11, 2 (Spring): 21–40.

Grover, Chris. 2005. "Living Wages and the 'Making Work Pay' Strategy." *Critical Social Policy.* 25, 1: 5–27.

Hacker, Andrew. 1998. *Money: Who Has How Much and Why.* New York: Touchstone/Simon & Schuster.

Hacker, Jacob S. and Paul Pierson. 2010. *Winner-Take-All Politics: How Washington Made the Rich Richer—And Turned Its Back on the Middle Class.* New York: Simon & Schuster.

Hart, Vivien. 1994. *Bound by Our Constitution: Women, Workers, and the Minimum Wage.* Princeton, NJ: Princeton University Press.

Hodgson, Godfrey. 2004. *More Equal Than Others: America from Nixon to the New Century.* Princeton, NJ: Princeton University Press.

Howell, David and Friedrich Huebler. 2001. "Trends in Earnings Inequality and Unemployment across the OECD: Labor Market Institutions and Simple Supply and Demand Stories." *Working Paper No. 23*. Center for Economic Policy Analysis, New School University (May).

Hungerford, Thomas L. 1993. U.S. Income Mobility in the Seventies and Eighties." *Review of Income and Wealth*. 39, 4: 403–417.

Hutchinson, Emilie. J. 1919. "Women's Wages: A Study of the Wages of Industrial Women and Measures Suggested to Increase Them." *Studies in History, Economics and Public Law*. New York: Columbia University. 89(1): 1–179.

Hyman, Prue. 2004. "The Fight for Living Standards in New Zealand." In Deborah M. Figart, ed. *Living Wage Movements: Global Perspectives*. London and New York: Routledge.

Juhn, Chinhui, Kevin Murphy, and Brooks Pierce. 1993. "Wage Inequality and the Rise in Returns to Skills." *Journal of Political Economy*. 101; 3: 410–442.

Katz, Lawrence and Kevin M. Murphy. 1992. "Changes in Relative Wages, 1963–1987: Supply and Demand Factors." *Quarterly Journal of Economics*. 107: 35–79.

Kessler-Harris. Alice. 1988. *A Woman's Wage: Historical Meanings and Social Consequences*. Lexington, KY: The University Press of Kentucky.

Kirkendall, Richard. 1974. *The United States 1929–1945: Years of Crisis and Change*. New York: McGraw-Hill Book Co.

Lafer, Gordon. 2002. *The Job Training Charade*. Ithaca, NY; London: Cornell University Press.

Lehrer, Susan. 1987. *Origins of Protective Labor Legislation for Women, 1905–1925*. Albany: State University of New York Press.

Levin-Waldman, Oren M. 2001. *The Case of the Minimum Wage: Competing Policy Models*. Albany: State University of New York Press.

Mason, Geoff, Ken Mayhew, and Matthew Osborne. 2008. "Low-Paid Workers in the United Kingdom: An Overview." In Candice Lloyd, Geoff Mason, and Ken Mayhew, eds. *Low-Wage Work in the United Kingdom*. New York: Russell Sage Foundation.

Mason, Geoff, Ken Mayhew, Matthew Osborne, and Philip Stevens. 2008. "Low Pay, Labor Market Institutions, and Job Quality in the United Kingdom." In Candice Lloyd, Geoff Mason, and Ken Mayhew, eds. *Low-Wage Work in the United Kingdom*. New York: Russell Sage Foundation.

Moody, Kim. 1988. *An Injury to All: The Decline of American Unionism*. London & New York: Verso.

Morehead, Warden v. New York Ex Rel. Tipaldo. 1935. 298 U.S. (October).

Muller v. Oregon. 1907. 28 *Supreme Court Reporter* (October).

National Emergency Council. 1938. *Report on Economic Conditions of the South*. Washington.

National Industrial Recovery Act (NIRA), *Statutes at Large* 73rd Congress, Session 1 Chs. 89, 90 (June 16, 1933).

Newman, Katherine S. 1993. *Declining Fortunes: The Withering of the American Dream*. New York: Basic Books.

Nordlund, Willis J. 1997. *The Quest for a Living Wage: The History of the Federal Minimum Wage Program*. Westport, CT: Greenwood Press.

Persons, Charles E. 1919. "Estimates of a Living Wage for Female Workers." *American Statistical Association*. 125 (March): 567–577.

Phillips, Kevin. 1990. *The Politics of Rich and Poor: Wealth and the American Electorate in the Reagan Aftermath*. New York: HarperPerennial.

Piketty, Thomas. 2014. *Capital in the Twenty-First Century*. Cambridge, MA; London: Belknap Press of Harvard University Press.

Pontusson, Jonas. 2005. *Inequality and Prosperity: Social Europe v. Liberal America*. Ithaca, NY: Cornell University Press.

Reich, Robert B. 1997. *Locked in the Cabinet*. New York: Alfred E. Knopf.

Salverda, Wiemer, Maarten van Klauveren, and Marc van der Meer. 2008. "The Debate in the Netherlands on Low Pay." In Weimer Salverda, Maarten van Klaveren, and Marc van der Meer, eds. *Low-Wage Work in The Netherlands*. New York: Russell Sage Foundation.

Schechter Corp. v. United States. 1934. 295 U.S. (October).

Seltzer, Andrew J. 1997. "The Effects of the Fair Labor Standards Act of 1938 on Southern Seamless Hosiery and Lumber Industries." *The Journal of Economic History*. 57, 2 (June): 396–415.

Smeeding, Timothy M. and Dennis H. Sullivan. 1998. "Generations and the Distribution of Economic Well-Being: A Cross-National View." *AEA Papers and Proceedings*. 88, 2 (May): 254–258.

Smeeding, Timothy M., Michael O'Higgins, and Lee Rainwater, eds. 1990. *Poverty, Inequality and Income Distribution in Comparative Perspective: The Luxembourg Income Study (LIS)*. Washington: The Urban Institute Press.

Smith, Hendrick. 2012. *Who Stole the American Dream?* New York: Random House.

Stigler, George J. 1986. "The Goals of Economic Policy." In Kurt R. Leube and Thomas Moore, eds. *The Essence of Stigler*. Stanford, CA: Hoover Institution Press.

Stiglitz, Joseph E. 2012. *The Price of Inequality*. New York: W.W. Norton.

Volscho, Thomas W. Jr. 2005. "Minimum Wages and Income Inequality in the American States, 1960–2000." *Research in Social Stratification and Mobility*. 23: 347–373.

Wadenjso, Eskil. 2001. "The Labour Market—Rehn or Rubbestad." In Henry Milner and Eskil Wadenjos, eds. *Gosta Rehn, The Swedish Model and Labour Market Policies: International and National Perspectives.* Aldershot, UK; Burlington, VT: Ashgate Publishing Co.

Waltman, Jerold L. 2008. *Minimum Wage Policy in Great Britain and the United States.* New York: Algora Publishing.

Webb, Sidney. 1912. "The Economic Theory of a Legal Minimum Wage." *The Journal of Political Economy.* 20, 10 (December): 973–998.

West Coast Hotel Co. v. Parrish et al. 1936 300 U.S. (October).

Westergaard-Nielson, Niels. 2008. "Low-Wage Work in Denmark." In Niels Westergaard-Nielson, ed. *Low-Wage Work in Denmark.* New York: Russell Sage Foundation.

Wolff, Edward N. 1994. "Trends in Household Wealth in the United States, 1962–83 and 1983–89." *Review of Income and Wealth.* 40, 2: 143–174.

Wright, Gavin. 1986. *Old South, New South: Revolutions in the Southern Economy since the Civil War.* New York: Basic Books.

2   Problems, Controversies, and Solutions

Introduction

The minimum wage has long been a controversial issue, largely because there may be unintended consequences. The standard model holds that raising the minimum wage will either result in lower employment or lead to higher productivity. Because it may lead to less employment, its costs are often assumed to outweigh the benefits. But what about other models? How do they affect our understanding of the consequences of minimum wage?

Those who support the minimum wage claim that it helps the working poor. But this too is a controversy because there is a question as to whether minimum wage earners are really poor. Many of the earlier studies noted that most minimum wage earners were primarily teenagers or secondary earners rather than primary earners. And yet, these principal controversies revolve around both the problem of measurement and definition. The first problem is just precisely what the size of the minimum wage population is, and this very much hinges on definition. If we are looking at only those who earn the "statutory" minimum wage, then we are talking about only 2 percent of the labor force. Given that, critics might have a point that the costs may outweigh the benefits. But if we are talking about

Historian, educator, socialist, and author Sidney Webb was one of the most influential social reformers in Great Britain during the late 19th and early 20th centuries. Webb was the first to articulate an efficiency wage justification for the minimum wage. (Hulton Archive/Getty Images)

who earns around the minimum wage, then we are defining the minimum wage in terms of the "effective" minimum wage, whereby the statutory minimum is merely a reference point for the general low-wage labor market. If this is the case, we are now talking about close to 20 percent of the labor market, in which case a sizable portion of the labor market will derive benefit from minimum wage increases.

Additionally, there is the problem from a policy standpoint of whether we should be focused on the micro-effects—how they affect the firm—as opposed to the larger macro-effects—how they affect the economy as a whole. Consider the following dilemma: an increase in the minimum wage will lead employers to reduce their workforces, thereby leading to higher unemployment. Therefore, workers should be paid less so that more will be employed. But if all employers follow suit and pay their workers poorly, then the purchasing power of workers will be reduced, thereby resulting in reduced aggregate demand for goods and services. The same thing happens when prices continue to rise but wages fail to rise along with them. As aggregate demand for goods and services fall, then the economy contracts, in which case more workers will lose their jobs. The macroeconomic argument for the minimum wage holds that raising the minimum wage will benefit the economy because workers' increased purchasing power will enable them to demand more goods and services, and this is what drives the economy.

Still, there is another controversy, which is just what the source of low wages is. Institutional economists hold that it in the absence of institutions like labor unions and the minimum wage to bolster wages, wages will be low—as little as employers can pay. There is an asymmetrical power relationship between employers and their workers. Market purists, however, maintain that the source of low wages in an increasingly global economy is a mismatch between the skills possessed by workers and those demanded by employers. Rather than raising wages, more efforts should be placed on training and education. As we will see in this chapter, there are no easy solutions to any of these controversies, except that economic studies should simply be used by policymakers to make decisions. This too speaks to a controversy in recent years: the politicization of economics, of which the minimum wage has been a casualty.

Competing Minimum Wage Models

The major controversy in the minimum wage debate concerns which model is used to understand the issue. The claim that the minimum wage leads to lower employment is based on the *competitive market model,* sometimes referred to as the *standard model.* But data in recent years showing that the minimum wage actually leads to higher employment, specifically in the fast-food industry, is based on what is known as the *monopsony model.* A third model, known as the *efficiency wage model,* holds that increasing the minimum wage will lead to greater efficiency because productivity will rise. And yet, a fourth model, known as the *macroeconomic model,* holds that society prospers from a higher minimum wage in the long term because it enhances the purchasing power of workers, who are able to demand more goods and services. The existence of these different models suggests that there is no right approach to take to the issue. But it also illustrates how different groups with different interests in the outcome of the debate can employ the model which best serves their respective interests.

Standard Model

The standard model holds the costs to society of raising wages to be greater than any benefits. Predicated on the assumption of perfectly competitive markets, market-clearing wages are achieved when the demand for labor is exactly equal to the supply of labor. In such a market, there is no such thing as unemployment because wages either rise or fall until the demand for labor is exactly equal to the supply of labor. At the wage at which demand equals supply, all those willing and able to work at that wage will be employed. If more people are willing to work, the wage will fall further, thereby inducing firms to hire more workers, with the result being that the supply of labor once again equals the demand. Conversely, when firms are unable to hire as many workers as they would like, the wage rises to induce additional people to enter the workforce until supply and demand are once again equal.

A wage floor, such as a mandated minimum wage, prevents the cost of labor from dropping below that minimum. When the minimum wage is higher than the equilibrium wage, fewer workers will be hired than are willing to work, with the result being unemployment. In a competitive market, each worker receives the value of his or her marginal revenue product, which is the amount of increase in the output that results from an increase in, say, a unit of labor. If adding an additional worker results in a rise in total revenues, the firm's output will rise as a result. Firms typically use the marginal revenue product of labor as a criterion for determining how many more workers to hire because they are able to calculate how much more output can be expected based on how many units are added. Therefore, a minimum wage, if it is effective, will do one of two things: it will either result in the layoff of those workers whose value is less than the minimum, or it will result in an increase in productivity among low-efficiency workers (Stigler 1946; Ehrenberg 1997).

Consequently, the minimum wage ends up hurting low-wage workers—precisely those whom it was intended to help. As the cost of labor is increased (due to a mandated minimum wage that is higher than the market-clearing wage), firms are willing to hire fewer workers and employment drops. Only if the demand for goods and services on the part of consumers is increased can it be expected that there will be an increased demand for labor that will effectively bid up wages. A minimum wage, then, benefits some—those who will be paid more money—at a cost to others—those who will either lose their jobs and/or not be able to find other jobs because employers do not believe their value to be worth the new minimum wage.

A policy that artificially raises wages to help some at the expense of others is simply inefficient, because an economy forced to lay workers off as a function of artificially inflated wages isn't utilizing its full labor capacity. Even if there is some outward appearance of benefit to be derived from an increase in the wage floor, there will invariably be a cost to be borne whether in the form of job loss, lost opportunity for jobs, lost benefits, or increased output per man hour—the demand for higher productivity.

One problem already with the model is that it is just that: a model that is a theoretical construct with characteristics that simply may not exist in the real world. In the real world, the minimum wage is likely to affect different people differently (Brown, Gilroy, and Kohen 1982). More to the point, the model of perfect competition assumes the minimum wage to be irrelevant because the source of low wages is not a function of distorted market power, but the failings of individuals. They simply are not worth more than the low wages they have been receiving. Therefore, it is up to them to improve themselves, and a minimum wage cannot solve this problem. Rather, all that it can do is artificially inflate wages, thereby absolving low-wage workers of their responsibility for themselves. As the locus of the model is on the individual, it tends to negate structural variables that may affect individual behavior. The competitive market model also assumes full employment. There is no such thing as unemployment because workers can always lower their wage demands until employers are willing to demand their labor services. A minimum wage prevents workers from lowering their wage demands below a certain point. Unemployment, then, is caused by wage rigidity.

The model simply assumes a good and efficient outcome to arise from individuals freely making choices and pursuing their interests. This emphasis on free choice and efficiency, however, may also mask the particular vision of society contained in the standard model's normative conception of the economy. In this vision, workers can always determine whether they will be employed by virtue of their willingness to be flexible when it comes to their wage demands. Figart, Mutari, and Power (2002) call this conception *the wage as price*—what one in an exchange relationship is going to pay for one's labor services. But there may be other ways of conceiving of wages: mainly wages as living—the notion that the purpose of wages is to provide an adequate level of support for workers—and wages as social practice, which emphasize the socially and historically specific process of wage setting. Worker flexibility may be efficient for the overall market place, but that does not mean that it is efficient for the needs of individual workers.

Still, the model fails to address the consequences of a world where wages could be allowed to drop to a level whereby demand would be equal to supply. It is also blind to power, and that low wages may be the result of a power imbalance between workers and employers. To a large extent, the standard model holds there to be no difference between labor and other goods and services. Both firms and individual workers in competitive markets are considered to be "wage takers," and are therefore assumed to have no bargaining power. As we noted in Chapter 1, the origins of the minimum wage lay in institutional economics, which, during the Progressive Era, categorically rejected this analysis. On the contrary, workers faced a marked inequality of bargaining power and consequently suffered from the exploitive and otherwise unjust wages that were offered them (Kaufman 2005). Early institutional labor economists emphasized that the labor market imperfectly gave employers superior bargaining power relative to individual employees. Because of the inequality in bargaining power, there really was nothing to prevent the economic coercion of workers. Among the early Progressive thinkers, Robert Hale reformulated the problem of coercion to demonstrate that the sphere of private "voluntary" market relations was indistinguishable from public power exercised in a direct fashion. Capitalists especially, through their state-conferred property rights, enjoyed coercive power through their ability to compel exchanges on terms that they would consent to. By virtue of their ability to threaten to withhold their capital or the products of their capital from those who required them, they would be able to compel. The one who did not own property (i.e., the typical low-wage worker whose only option was to bargain with the property owner for a job in order to attain subsistence) was essentially being coerced. If background circumstances were such that individual choices were effectively circumscribed, then there was no question that coercion was ubiquitous and that workers, especially those that did not own property, really did not enjoy the same freedom as those with property, that is, employers. As far as Hale was concerned, absolute freedom wasn't really possible, and that all one could really hope for at best was relative freedom (Fried 1998).

The competitive market model also assumes that both individuals and firms are purchasing and selling on the basis of preferences. In other words, they are *wants* traders. Workers, however, often have no choice but to sell their labor services, which only makes them *needs* traders. But if the worker *needs* to sell his or her labor services, the assumptions of the model fall apart. A wants trader has the option of withdrawing from the market if the proposed exchange fails to meet his/her profit-maximizing criteria. The wants trader is, by definition, then, less dependent on the market due to his or her ability to withdraw at any time. The needs trader, however, does not enjoy the same luxury and may be forced to accept an exchange that is less than ideal, and which in some cases may be considered exploitive because it meets a basic need such as eating (Prasch 1995). The reality is that in most bargaining situations whereby the power balance is asymmetrical, workers are needs traders while employers are wants traders. Employers become needs traders only when the workers possess skills that employers absolutely have to have, which in turn can drive up wages. As most minimum wage earners are essentially needs traders without real bargaining power, they are in reality forced to accept whatever conditions are offered at the lowest wage rates because they don't really have the ability to hold out for something better.

Consequently, they don't enjoy the same freedom as those with greater bargaining power.

By not taking into account the power imbalance between employers and workers, policy decisions made solely on the basis of a theoretical model may be simply flawed. The greatest flaw, however, is the assumption that workers, through the wages that they demand, determine whether or not they will be employed. It isn't the wage demands that workers make that determine whether they are employed; rather, it is the aggregate demand for goods and services (Minsky 1986, pp. 123–124). The English economist John Maynard Keynes (1964) explained that it was a fundamental assumption of classical theory that labor could always reduce its real wage by accepting a reduction in money wages. Workers could always ensure their continued employment by adjusting their wages downward to the point where employers would demand their labor. But there was no available means by which labor collectively could "bring the wage-goods equivalent of the general level of money wages into conformity with the marginal disutility of the current volume of employment." As far as Keynes was concerned, a reduction in money wages would have no lasting tendency to increase employment other than by virtue of its consequences with regard to either the propensity to consume for the entire community or the schedule of marginal efficiency of capital. A reduction in money wages would reduce prices somewhat, and would involve a redistribution of real income from wage earners to other factors. And this transfer from wage earners to other factors would in most likelihood diminish the propensity to consume, which in turn would only result in lower demand for goods and services, thereby resulting in an even greater contraction of productive industry (pp. 14, 262). The point is that flexible wages would not assure full employment if effective demand was deficient (Weintraub 1978–1979).

The fundamental defect of wage deflation was that it would lead to reduced production and employment. Keynesian economics is predicated on the assumption that unemployment is the result of a deficiency in aggregate demand. Therefore, a general reduction in wages and prices is not likely to lead to a readjustment; it will only make things worse. Even if it is assumed that the demand for labor is inversely related to the real wage, an exogenous decline in the level of money wages cannot increase employment even if the price of wage-goods declines proportionately. Moreover, if wage-deflated wages lead to a redistribution of income from wage earners to non-wage earners, it will also result in less spending. An episode of deflation could also result in a decrease of net financial wealth (Brown 1992). But there is also a limit to how much prices can be reduced following wage reductions. Employers still have fixed costs, and if they cannot reduce their prices to meet the new lower wages, the result will be a drop-off in demand because of reduced purchasing power. In a survey of business executives during the 1930s and 1940s, Richard Lester (1946), a later institutional economist, observed that business executives tended to think that costs and profits were contingent on the rate of output, and not the other way around. As far as these executives were concerned, employment levels were not determined by wages rates, but by the rate of output. This would, of course, suggest that no matter how low workers are willing to reduce their wage demands, if there is no demand for their firms' goods and services, they simply will not be employed.

Monopsony Model

The second model is known as the monopsony model. In simple terms, a labor monopsony exists when there is only one purchaser of labor services. In a labor monopsony, either one firm or one industry possesses sufficient monopoly power that it can effectively establish wage rates. This model assumes there to be something called market power and because of that power firms are in a position to pay low wages (Card and Krueger 1995). Because they are the only firms willing to employ minimum wage workers, these workers have no other choice but to accept those low wages they are offered. They don't have the option of offering their services anywhere else. Unlike the competitive market model, where minimum wage increases lead to lower employment, minimum wage increases in the monopsony market may actually result in employment gains. At a minimum, there will be no employment losses. This is because the market-clearing wage is often below that of a perfectly competitive market. Because an increase in the minimum wage is still likely to be less than the market-clearing wage of a perfectly competitive market, the minimum wage in the monopsony is likely to result in greater employment and efficiency because it will still be less than the equilibrium wage in a perfectly competitive market (Houseman 1998).

The monopsony model, then, implies supply-side effects—that by increasing the minimum wage, the effect will be to pull people into the labor market, who for whatever reason may have shunned it prior to the increase. An increase in the minimum wage, then, should serve to empower low-skilled workers. This model, which has by and large been ignored, suggests that there are potential benefits from increases in the minimum wage that may counter most of the negative consequences. Essentially, individual behavior will be affected because higher wages will offer greater incentives to work. The higher the minimum wage, the more likely it is to attract individuals into the labor market.

While the monopsony model does recognize a power dynamic, it also calls into question those assumptions of equal bargaining power between employers and employees in the market place that lay at the heart of the competitive market model. Given the unequal relationships between those who work and those who hire workers, institutional structures (such as wage floors and unions) are necessary for a more level playing field. In the absence of all workers being unionized, the minimum wage offers a modicum of monopoly power to workers, especially in low-wage and low-skilled labor markets, that counterbalances the monopoly power of employers.

Efficiency-Wage Model

The third model is the efficiency-wage model; it often finds expression in two basic forms, neither of which is mutually exclusive. The first expression necessarily flows from the assumptions contained in the standard model. In a competitive market, workers will produce more efficiently, and will take steps to avoid shirking if employers pay them higher wages. Because employees receive higher wages, they have a stronger incentive to hold onto their jobs because the costs associated with job loss are also now higher. Employers too derive benefit because the costs of higher wages are offset by the savings in monitoring costs (Shapiro and Stiglitz 1984; Weiss 1990). Therefore, raising the minimum wage might have the effect of offering positive inducement to work. Moreover, employees will work harder and thus be more productive.

The second expression, often referred to as the "Webb" effect after Sidney Webb, argues that a wage floor can lead to greater efficiency because workers become more productive. Although an increase in the minimum wage may well result in a wage exceeding the marginal product of the worker, the employer now has incentive to find ways to increase productivity either by getting his workers to produce more or by substituting technology for labor. The worker, too, has incentive to improve his or her skills so the value of his/her labor will justify the new wage (Webb 1912). Subsumed under this model is the notion that a minimum wage would also make workers more productive because it would better enable them to maintain themselves physically, which in turn would sustain them spiritually.

This model does not receive much attention today, but it was very influential during the early part of the twentieth century, and it figured prominently in the array of state reform efforts that ultimately culminated in the Fair Labor Standards Act of 1938. And yet, despite the lack of attention, it nonetheless assumes the supply and demand function contained in the competitive model, but essentially turns those assumptions flowing from it on their head. That is, those who are forced to pay higher wages would simply be forced to find ways to improve their productivity (Gordon 1995). More importantly, it calls attention to the fact that society, through a wage policy, is essentially expressing a value preference. It also reflects the more institutionalist school in economics. Rather than assume that the economy operates by natural law, the economy is as much a function of institutions and power relations (Palley 1998).

On one level it represents a preference for minimum wages above some poverty threshold. But on another, it suggests a preference for a higher wage economy on the assumption that a higher wage floor will offer managers incentive to provide the type of on-the-job training that would make their workers more productive. Michael Piore and Charles Sabel (1984) have couched this choice as the difference between the low- and high-roads. The low road assumes a mass production industrial economy in which most functions can be performed by cheap and low-skilled workers. If labor is not cheap at home, work can easily be outsourced to those locations where labor costs are substantially lower. The high road, by contrast, entails developing an innovative information-based economy with a flexible and high-skilled labor force able to command higher wages. The skills, and ultimately productivity of the labor force, are developed through education and training programs. Although a higher wage alone will not stand as the sole path toward a high-wage economy, it might provide a necessary stick for employers to invest in the necessary education and training for their workers to make them "worth" the new wages. Such arguments were quite persuasive during the early part of the century when many in industrial mass production were earning anything but a "living wage." The problem is that productivity is difficult to measure, and, with the advent of greater empiricism to the evaluation of the minimum wage during the 1970s and 1980s, it has become easier to focus on a particular segment of the labor market.

The efficiency model also holds that there could be other costs savings from higher wages. Workers who are paid more are less likely to leave their employers for other jobs. This reduces turnover, and employers are then able to save on recruitment and training costs. Turnover in low-wage jobs tends to be higher precisely because the wages are low. Employers often contend that because the turnover is so high it does not pay to invest in their workers. But following the logic of the Webb effect, a higher minimum wage would force employers to invest in their workers to make them more productive.

Another side of the efficiency wage assumes costs savings to employers from higher wages. These employers now experience lower turnover and therefore save on recruitment and training costs as a result (Howes 2002; Fairris 2003; Reich, Hall, and Jacobs, 2003). Edward Leamer (1999), for instance, argues that most economists have been trained with a simple partial equilibrium model that associates minimum wages with unemployment. The problem with this is that the labor contract is assumed to be one-dimensional, in that it covers wages but overlooks working conditions. It also does not take into account varying degrees of effort on the part of workers. Instead, a competitive labor market offers a set of wage effort contracts with higher daily wages that can offset the disutility of higher work effort. In other words, an efficiency wage is essentially a wage for greater effort. A minimum wage, then, does not necessarily cause unemployment; instead, it forces effort in the low-wage and low-effort contracts up enough to support the higher wage. This isn't to say that there aren't benefits to capital that could not hurt labor. An increase in the minimum wage in the low-wage market may cause a reduction of wages and an increase in effort in the high-wage, high-effort market not directly affected by the minimum wage. As a result of greater effort in both the high-wage and low-wage sectors, output levels rise in both. Gross domestic product is increased and income inequality is reduced, which may make the representative worker worse off. But by forcing effort levels to more closely conform, the minimum wage creates comparative advantage in the labor-intensive sector, which is the opposite of what might be expected. In exchange for the higher wage, employers are getting greater effort. The goal is not to equalize but to ultimately push up wages through productivity gains. If capital is then interpreted as human capital, and if workers themselves invest in their own education, the message of the model is that those who choose education are also choosing higher effort. In other words, if the labor contract is multi-dimensional, a minimum wage law that sets a floor for one aspect of the contract will most likely be met with adjustments to other aspects of the contract. And if effort is variable, then a minimum wage could generate enough extra work effort to compensate for the increased wage level, thus ensuring that everybody is happy.

Similarly, Drazen (1986) argues that a minimum wage can be Pareto-optimal, if we consider a labor market in which the quality of labor is sensitive to the wage increases. To say it is Pareto-optimal is to say that it will make a group better off without making another group worse off. In his simple model, he assumes that entry into the labor market depends on maximizing income. There are two markets: a primary one with higher wages and a secondary one with lower wages. Individuals enter the primary labor market if their expected income is higher than the forgone (and lower) income in the alternative or secondary market. It is also assumed that a worker's productivity in the primary market is an increasing function of his forgone income. These two assumptions together imply a positive relation between an individual's acceptance wage and his or her productivity. Therefore, there is a role for minimum wage legislation because firms would prefer to pay higher wages if they knew that labor quality would improve to reflect the higher wage level. And they would also prefer to pay above market-clearing wages if they knew that other firms were behaving the same way. By fixing wages above the market-clearing level, government can achieve a preferred equilibrium, which private competitive behavior cannot. In other words, left to their own devices, employers will not pay higher wages to achieve greater efficiency, because in the uncertainty that others will do the same, they are forced to lower their wages in order to remain competitive. Employers, in other words, need a little push.

The macroeconomic model suggests that insofar as a higher wage will offer low-wage workers more purchasing power, they in turn will be able to demand more goods and services. As they do this, business will produce more, and they in turn will hire more workers, which may have the inevitable result of naturally bidding up wages across the board. In this view, the model calls into question some of the assumptions contained in the competitive model. The quantity of labor is not determined by the price of labor but by the aggregate demand for goods and services. Therefore, an increase in the minimum wage, though it may lead to some short-term adverse consequences, will lead to long-term benefits to the economy as a whole.

It was this very type of macroeconomic argument that informed policy in the initial years of the minimum wage program. Higher wages, it was reasoned, would result in less labor strife because there would be less reason for workers to engage in labor actions against their employers. Higher wages, then, would have a stabilizing effect. Because workers would have more money to spend, the economy as a whole would prosper. By creating a wage floor, there is a limit to how depressed wages become. By ensuring a minimum wage level, a minimum level of aggregate demand can also be assured. The minimum wage is then viewed as part and parcel of a movement to achieve a living wage so that the consumer base of the economy can not only be maintained but also enlarged (Glickman 1997).

Unemployment Consequences

Data on the effects of the minimum wage are also controversial because the data have been ambiguous at best. The principal focus of much of the empirical literature has been on the youth labor market. In 1981, the U.S. Minimum Wage Study Commission (MWSC) issued a report on the minimum wage. Although there was something in the report for different sides of the issue to take away, opponents of the minimum wage were able to focus exclusively on what the report had to say about the impact of the minimum wage on the teen labor market. The commission staff estimated that a 10 percent increase in the minimum wage would reduce teenage employment by about 1 percent. Other estimates have placed the disemployment effect even higher (MWSC 1981, pp. 35–38). It has since been the prevailing wisdom that the minimum wage takes its greatest toll on the youth labor market, that a binding floor reduces employment for younger and less skilled workers. Following this report, a consensus emerged among mainstream economists that a 10 percent increase in the minimum wage will result in a 1–3 percent reduction in teenage employment (Kosters and Welch 1972; Welch 1974, 1978; Meyer and Wise 1983; Kosters 1996). At the same time, effects were judged to be proportionately smaller among adults aged 20–24 (Neumark and Wascher 1992), and that adults on balance appear to be better off under a wage floor. Although the MWSC too noted the smaller effects among adults, they have not been the focus of much of the research. Herein lies a problem, for there have not been many studies estimating just how many people might be attracted to the labor force were the minimum wage to be increased. That is, the issue is demand-side-oriented, not supply-side-oriented. In attempting to estimate how many fewer workers will be hired following a minimum wage increase, that is, their labor services being demanded, it misses how many more workers might be attracted into the labor market in search of higher wages, that is, their labor services being supplied. This is not a trivial point because lower employment predicted by the standard model is in part due to the supply-side effects arising from a higher wage.

Ironically, however, the MWSC report implies supply-side effects. By distinguishing between reduced employment and higher unemployment, the commission effectively acknowledged that a higher wage would effectively attract people into the labor market. Because workers actively looking for work constitute the formal definition of unemployment, the official unemployment rate would increase due to an expanded market of job seekers. Most studies that suggest lower employment usually mean that fewer workers will be hired as a result of higher wages and that in some cases there will be an increase in unemployment due to a potential layoff of existing minimum wage workers. But to formally acknowledge that unemployment will rise because more workers may look for jobs at higher wage rates is to acknowledge that there are supply-side effects. And yet, this very technicality raises another problem when discussing potential unemployment due to the minimum wage. Lower employment and higher unemployment may not mean the same thing. Employment could be lower because of a disemployment effect—that employers responded by laying off workers. But employment could be lower because employers are less likely to hire in the future. That is, there may not be as much low-wage job creation. Or employment could be lower because a higher minimum wage attracts into the labor market those who previously shunned work. With more people in the labor market now chasing the same number of jobs, employment is effectively lower than it was before. In other words, lower employment and unemployment are not necessarily the same.

Still, another variation of the model holds that it simply contributes to wage rigidity that affects not only short-term unemployment but long-term as well. Mark Partridge and Janice Partridge (1999) argue that the minimum wage is positively related to long-term unemployment rates. Because, according to the standard model, a minimum wage prevents workers from lowering their wage demands, employers will demand less labor. If low-skilled workers with a low value of marginal product cannot take a job below the minimum wage, the probability of them being offered a job at all will only diminish and the duration of their unemployment will increase. And yet, this speaks more to the problem of not creating more jobs in the future.

Researchers in recent years have actually addressed the data issue by collecting new data with results that not surprisingly have called into question the efficacy of the conventional wisdom flowing from the more standard model. The principal challenge to the standard model has been from studies of the fast-food industry conducted by Card and Krueger (1995, 1998) and others (Katz and Krueger 1992). Specifically in studies of the fast-food industry in New Jersey with Pennsylvania serving as a control group, Card and Krueger found the minimum wage to have no disemployment effect at all. On the contrary, employment in New Jersey restaurants was actually found to have increased. There was also no substitution effect, and even though the minimum wage increase did lead to price increases for meals, there was no evidence that prices rose faster in New Jersey stores that were most affected by the wage increase. Moreover, the minimum wage increase did not negatively affect the number of store openings. In a follow-up study several years later, Card and Krueger (1998) only confirmed their earlier results.

These studies, however, have been controversial, and as such have raised a whole host of other research questions. Much of the criticism centers around the issue of measurement and the quality of available data. The basic problem is that just because no adverse effects were observed, it doesn't necessarily follow that there wouldn't be were the minimum wage raised beyond a certain point (Kennan 1995). These increases may not have had the consequences predicted by the standard model because the minimum wage was still so far below a market-clearing wage (Freeman and Freeman 1991).

Perhaps more than anything else, these studies demonstrate that a major limitation of the standard model is that it only predicts unemployment in competitive labor markets. By their own admission (Card and Krueger 1995), the fast-food industry is a monopsony to the extent that it is the principal employer of minimum wage workers, and therefore, it is not representative of most industries. Kevin Lang and Shulamit Kahn (1998) even go so far as to suggest that higher minimum wages, contrary to the effects claimed by those who argue the youth disemployment effects, actually shift employment toward youth and students, especially in the fast-food industry.

The controversies, however, do not end with these studies because employment may have increased because employers engage in rescheduling. While wage increases will lower employment in the standard model, minimum wages in an alternative model can actually increase employment because the wage floor actually increases the relative costs of hours, in which case the employer has greater incentive to increase the mix of jobs relative to hours. In other words, the number of hours a worker works is determined by the hourly wage rate. Therefore, the minimum wage can increase employment (Palley 1998). Employment can increase because the number of hours per worker may actually decline while the number of workers working actually increases. As the hourly cost of workers increases, employers have greater incentive to reduce the workweek and hire more workers. This is simply another form of substitution. Thomas Michl (2000) found that wage increases led employers to hire more workers while simultaneously reducing the workweek. Looking at Card and Krueger's data, he found that hours in New Jersey restaurants declined by around 6 percent or by about an hour and fifteen minutes per week. But in later work, economists Sylvia Allegretto, Arindrajit Dube, and Michael Reich (2011) observed that higher minimum wages may have led the workers themselves to reduce their hours. In other words, it was not clear whether reduced hours were the result of employers forcing employees to work less or workers opting to work less because now they were making more per hour.

Still, there have been other studies that only support the Card and Krueger studies of no disemployment effects. In a survey of small business, Levin-Waldman (2000a) found that not only had a minimum wage increase in September 1997 to $5.15 an hour, not affected most small businesses, but that at least 79 percent still would not be affected were the minimum wage to have been increased again to $6 an hour. And in a follow-up study, it was observed that more than 86 percent of small business would not be affected by an increase to $6 and that still 64 percent of small businesses wouldn't be affected by a further increase to $7.25 an hour (Levin-Waldman (2000b).

Adding to this, Dube and Reich along with Suresh Naidu (2007) looked at the effects of a minimum wage law that was enacted by a public ballot measure for the city of San Francisco in 2003. While the federal minimum wage was still $5.15 an hour, San Francisco's was now $8.50, which was still 26 percent higher than California's minimum wage of $6.70. Looking at primarily the restaurant industry because it was considered to be the primary employer of fast-food workers, they found that the benefits to the increases did outweigh the costs. The city wage floor did significantly raise the wages of those at affected restaurants and compressed the wage distribution among restaurant workers, and increased the average wages of fast-food workers twice as much as those at sit-down restaurants. And yet, there was no increase in business closure or employment loss detected. To the extent that such findings undermine the standard model, they also add to the ambiguity surrounding the effects of the minimum wage. Moreover, they reinforce some of the evidence that suggests that we may know very little about the minimum wage or its actual effects. Still, that new studies show that the standard model may not be accurate doesn't mean that the earlier studies that held there to be disemployment effects were wrong. Clearly, the findings from those studies are what researchers observed. The problem may have been the prism through which they were viewing the data.

In a subsequent study, Dube and Reich along with Sylvia Allegretto (2011), on the basis of data from 1990 to 2009, found no real evidence to support disemployment effects associated with minimum wage increases, although there may still have been an effect on hours. Firms did not necessarily decrease their demand for workers, but they may have decreased their demand for the number of hours worked by teenagers. Or teenagers themselves opted to work less following minimum wage increases, thereby supplying fewer hours of their labor services. All in all, their findings added to those of the previous study that minimum wage increases, again in the range that have been implemented in the United States, do not reduce employment among teens.

Much of the data currently support the notion that raising the minimum wage would help low-income families. Although the minimum wage would have an impact on both men and women, data suggest that more women earn the minimum wage than men, thereby making the issue a potential women's issue. For female-headed households, then, a minimum wage increase can be expected to provide a real benefit.

Problem of Data

Much of the controversy over the effects of the minimum wage has to do with the quality of data that are actually available. Most of the data are individual-level census data from the Current Population Survey (CPS). It is not firm-level data. Researchers are often looking at rates of employment on the basis of individual responses to specific employment questions at various times—before and after minimum wage increases occurred. At best, we can establish a correlation between an increase and a change in employment. This does not prove, however, that a change in employment was specifically due to a minimum wage increase. In other words, the data cannot establish a causal relationship. Moreover, because it is individual-level data, it does not tell us anything about firm behavior. We don't really have any data that tell us how firms respond to minimum wage increases. Dube, Lester, and Reich (2010) argue that a major problem with the data is that economists have been taking two different methodological approaches. Traditional national-level studies use all cross-state variation in the minimum wage over time to estimate the effects. Meanwhile, case studies typically compare adjoining local areas with different minimum wages around the time of the policy change. In an attempt to control this, they specifically compared all contiguous county-pairs of restaurants in the United States that are located on opposite sides of a state border. For cross-state contiguous counties, they found strong earnings effects and no employment effects. When looking at local comparisons while also controlling for heterogeneity in employment growth, they found no detectable employment losses from the types of minimum wage increases that have been taking place over the years in the United States.

Michael Reich (2010) argues that much of the CPS data suggesting large negative effects due to minimum wage increases only show these large negative effects to be among teenagers. Although one typically looks at trends prior to minimum wage increases and then trends following minimum wage increases, one might still find a negative trend following an increase. And yet, it is still incorrect to attribute a post–minimum wage trend to minimum wage policy. The negative post–minimum trend could be due to other factors, especially when there is often a good six-month lag time between the enactment of an increase and the implementation of that increase. Placed in larger context, between 1955 and 1996, the minimum wage was increased 16 times, and these increases were also more likely to occur in times of relatively strong employment growth. But these increases have also been occurring in the context of more and more states raising their minimum wages above the federal level, beginning in the late 1980s. Moreover, these states with higher minimum wages are not limited to areas above-average living costs, or those that necessarily tend to be more liberal. But instead of taking the standard position that one possible reason for this may be that the minimum wage is still much lower than market-clearing wages, he suggests that it may be that higher wage floors can significantly reduce employers' recruitment and retention costs. Low-wage employers typically experience above-average turnover and job vacancy rates. Therefore, it is likely that job vacancy rates would fall if a higher wage served to make those jobs more attractive. While it may still reduce the desired level of employment, it might leave the actual level of unemployment unchanged, which is to say that minimum wages do not kill jobs; they kill job vacancies. Put another way, minimum wage increases do not necessarily lead to disemployment because workers were fired; rather, they decrease the number of jobs created in the future for low-wage workers.

Even attempts to get around the inherent weaknesses of time-series data have their limitations. Janet Currie and Bruce Fallick (1996), for instance, using individual-level data from the National Longitudinal Survey of Youth (NLSY) examined disemployment effects of minimum wage increases in 1979 and 1980. They also examined the effects of the minimum wage on individual year-to-year changes. Their approach was specifically to measure the effects by identifying a group of workers that would most likely be directly affected by the minimum wage and then compare their employment to the employment of a group of workers who were least likely to be affected. Affected workers were found to be 3 percent less likely to be employed a year later. At the same time, no evidence was found that minimum wage increases affected the wages of those workers who remained employed a year later. Still, they were not able to establish that it was the increase in the minimum wage that was a direct cause of their not being employed a year later as opposed to other factors. In the end, all that can be made are inferences, and to the extent that it provides the basis for inference, it serves to support the theoretical construct contained in the traditional textbook. On the contrary, all that can be made is a plausible inference based on statistical tests bound to show a high likelihood. And yet, based on changes in employment patterns following, say, a minimum wage increase, a further inference is made about the behavior of firms, which only reinforces the reigning orthodoxy.

Measuring the Minimum Wage Population

Debate over the minimum wage has often revolved around youth disemployment effects versus anti-poverty benefits. Those who oppose the minimum wage tend to focus on the teen labor market, with the claim that most minimum wage workers are teenagers. And those supporting increases often focus on the benefits that will accrue to the working poor. To a certain extent, both sides really speak past one another. One of the things missed, as we saw in Chapter 1 regarding the historical evolution of the minimum wage, is that the minimum wage was intended to be a labor-management issue. But the focus of the current debate may also have much to do with how we are defining the population. The principal focus on the teen labor market, at least in the past, may have been because most minimum wage earners tended to be younger. Earners of the minimum wage are for the most part teenagers or contributing members of a household budget (Burkhauser and Finegan 1989; Brown 1996). Therefore, it was argued, that because they weren't primary earners, the costs to society, in terms of higher unemployment, were simply not worth the costs.

The MWSC estimated that 68 percent of minimum wage earners were in families headed by married couples. Of these, 1.5 million were the only earners in their families, thereby making up 14 percent of low-wage workers. Fifty-four percent of all minimum wage workers were in families with two or more earners. Still, the commission made it clear that minimum wage earners were not the primary earners in families with more than one earner (MWSC 1981, p. 13). Because only a small fraction of the labor market actually earns the statutory minimum wage, the potential benefits are presumed to be so small that they could not possibly offset the more likely larger costs.

On these grounds, it is often concluded that raising the minimum wage would not greatly help the poor. On the contrary, raising the minimum wage is more likely to hurt the poor because at a higher wage, employers are more likely to hire more skilled labor as a substitute for unskilled labor. Because low-skilled individuals are heavily overrepresented among the ranks of the poor, minimum wage increases will effectively result in employers discriminating against recipients (Finegold 1998). These studies, however, might well miss the point. Even if most minimum wage earners are not the primary earners in their households, it does not follow that the income of those earners isn't necessary to the sustenance of the family unit.

A commonplace criticism of the minimum wage is that because only a small fraction of the labor market earns the minimum wage, the issue is really insignificant. Most of the debate and the research that has been done focus on a limited subsegment (roughly 2 percent) of the labor market: those specifically earning the statutory minimum wage. And yet, the minimum wage really speaks to a broader segment of the labor market: low-wage workers who make up what could be referred to as the "effective" minimum wage population. But this can be understood only if we take a broader view of the minimum wage population. Levin-Waldman (2011) has argued that if we look at the issue from the vantage point of wage contours, the minimum wage takes on a whole new dimension.

The classic model of the wage contour was developed by John Dunlop (1957) to explain how a firm's internal wage structure might be as much affected by external forces as internal ones. Wage contours were to be defined as a group of workers with similar characteristics working in similar industries and earning similar wages. And for each group there would be a group of rates surrounding a key rate, and these group rates would be affected by changes in the key rate. Within an industry, the key rate would essentially be defined as any rate serving as the reference point for that industry. Since key rates were specific to industries, they could also vary from industry to industry. But it also implies that there is nothing necessarily natural about wage rates. On the contrary, wage rates are determined more by institutions than the natural market place.

Data from the Integrated Public Micro-use Data Series (IPUMS) for 1940–2000 have shown that the effects of a minimum wage increase would generally be greater than commonly supposed because the population earning around the minimum wage was actually substantially larger than usually supposed (Levin-Waldman 2002; 2005a). Therefore, the effective minimum wage population would have to be defined as those earning around the minimum wage, that is, wage contours. Wage institutions like unions and minimum wage laws did make a difference, particularly in explaining wage differentials between different regions of the country. This would also imply that wage institutions like unions and the minimum wage also serve as key rates of change in particular wage contours, and that the focus on only those earning the statutory minimum is simply too narrow to make a determination regarding the utility of the minimum wage as a policy tool for both assisting low-wage workers and potentially narrowing the wage gap between the bottom and the top.

William Spriggs and Bruce Klein (1994) also observed that the minimum wage's greatest import is its function as a reference point for wages around it. They found that despite changes in the statutory minimum wage, firms merely maintained their internal wage structures. Increases may have resulted in employment consequences in some cases, but the effects were not found to be significant. Rather, firms simply viewed the minimum wage as a reference point for what starting wages should be. Building on this construct, David Gordon (1996) later argued that a decline in the real value of the minimum wage also affected those earning in between the point where the statutory minimum wage used to be and the point where it is at the end of the dip. An increase in the minimum wage, then, might lead to an upward pressure on wages because employers would feel compelled to pay higher wages even to those not directly affected (pp. 214–215). The real importance of the minimum wage lies in its impact on wages from the statutory minimum to some point above. Moreover, one could not even begin to measure more accurately the size of the minimum wage population unless the minimum wage was looked at in real terms rather than statutory terms. This, of course, would imply that as the statutory minimum wage increases, so too does the starting wage, thereby shifting upward the general wage structure. Using a wage contour construct similar to Spriggs and Klein, Deborah Figart and June Lapidus (1995) estimated that an increase in the minimum wage from $4.35 in the mid-1990s to $4.75 would result in an increase of women's average wages from $9.79 to $10, although the effects for those earning less than the previous average would be larger.

Only recently, however, has this issue been looked at from a more empirical standpoint, particularly in the work of David Neumark, Mark Schweitzer, and William Wascher (2004). Despite their general conclusions that the minimum wage had negative effects for those throughout the wage distribution, they did acknowledge that the minimum wage appeared to have so-called wage contour effects, particularly for those earning immediately above the minimum wage. Still, they concluded the effects of increases throughout the distribution to be negative because low-wage workers were bound to be hurt through a reduction in hours. And the fact remains: workers' wages fall into wage ranges or contours, and that a shift in one is going to result in a shift in others. Looking at state minimum wages from 1960 to 2000, Thomas Volscho (2005) estimated that each $0.81 increase in the minimum wage would result in a 35.5 percent reduction in the Gini coefficient ceteris paribus (all other things being the same or unchanged). Moreover, state wages on average had the effect of reducing the degree of income concentration in the top quintile, thereby lending support to the "ripple effect," or what we might otherwise refer to as wage contours.

Using data from the CPS to measure the effects of minimum wage increases in New York, New Jersey, and Connecticut between 2003 and 2006 with Pennsylvania as a control, Levin-Waldman (2009a) also found that when the minimum wage was increased, the median wages in the first three contours of the distribution also increased. For instance, following New York's minimum wage increase in 2006 from $6 to $6.75, the median wage of those in the first contour—an interval ranging from the statutory minimum to 25 percent above—rose from $7.05 to $7.21. But it also rose from $8.57 an hour to $9.61 in the second, and from $10.33 an hour to $12.01 in the third. Similar effects were observed in New Jersey and Connecticut. In the rest of the United States and also Pennsylvania, where the minimum wage still remained at $5.15, the median wage continued to be $5.77, $7.21, and $9.21 an hour in the first three contours respectively. The effect of the minimum wage contours was for the median wages of those earning up to 91 percent above the statutory minimum to rise. This would suggest that to the extent that there are wage contour effects, they should be viewed positively, not negatively. It would also imply that the minimum wage really has larger macroeconomic welfare benefits. None of this, of course, denies the inflationary impact that concerns Neumark et al. (2004). Rather, the benefits arising from wage contour effects do introduce a new metric into the discussion. It suggests that inflation—if for the purposes of bolstering the wage distribution—does have a social value.

Levin-Waldman (2011) extended the interstate analysis, which relied on three contours, to a national one relying on 10 contours and spanning a 46-year period from 1962 to 2008. Using data from the IPUMS CPS for 1962–2008, he then constructed 10 contours, which range from the statutory minimum wage of a given year to 25 percent above the statutory minimum. Successive contours pick up where the preceding contour left off and ranges to 25 percent above. The sum total is that those earning in the first 10 contours above the statutory minimum, which comprises roughly 70 percent of the labor force, are earning up to 500–700 percent above the minimum wage in any given year. When attempting to measure how many people are earning the statutory minimum wage, the data produce no measure at all, as if nobody at all earns the statutory minimum wage. And yet, when a contour is constructed around the statutory minimum—the first contour—the data produce a significant measure.

Between 1962 and 2008, median wages in each contour increased in years when there was an increase in the federal minimum wage. In years when there was no increase, median wages remained unchanged for the most part. These trends alone would imply wage contour effects and that the reach of a minimum wage increase extend far beyond the limited submarket that actually earns the statutory minimum wage. Arguably there may be other factors to explain increases in median wages, especially in the upper contours, but those other factors don't appear to be present in years when there was no increase in the minimum wages? The lack of increases in median wages during those years when there was no minimum wage increase, and the long periods when there was no minimum wage increase, suggest that wage stagnation may well be attributable to the absence of wage policy, or at least its latent nature. Moreover, consistent with the literature on the impact of centralized wage setting on wage and income inequality, the data here similarly reveal an impact through the effects of wage contours. And yet, to the extent that there may be middle-class welfare benefits associated with the minimum wage, we aren't talking about a narrow segment of the labor market as critics claim, but of at least two-thirds. In other words, contrary to the conventional wisdom that the minimum wage benefits only a small segment of the labor market, or that its intended beneficiaries are poor, the minimum wage is really about the middle class. That idea may be controversial in and of itself, because it runs contrary to the conventional wisdom that those earning above the minimum don't really benefit from increases and therefore it is of no use to them.

The notion of an effective minimum wage population was given support by a Congressional Budget Office report in early 2014, which itself was controversial. This report suggested that a minimum wage increase to $10.10 an hour as proposed in President Obama's State of the Union address would lead to a total reduction in employment of 500,000 jobs by 2016 once fully implemented. Despite this, the economy was still going to be better off. Citing the conventional economic analysis, employment would be reduced because an increase would force employers to pass some of the increased costs onto consumers, which in turn would lead consumers to purchase fewer goods and services. As they would then produce fewer goods and services, they would hire fewer workers. Therefore, employment might be reduced through the "scale" effect. Or a minimum wage increase would raise the costs of low-wage workers relative to other inputs, which would lead some employers to respond by reducing their use of low-wage workers toward other inputs. In this case, employment would be reduced by the substitution effect. At the same time, the report suggested that the conventional analysis might not apply in certain circumstances. As an example, a firm hiring new workers finds that it has to increase the wages of existing workers doing the same work. An increase in the minimum wage thus means employers have to pay existing workers more. Consequently, it lowers the additional cost of hiring a new worker, thereby leading to increased employment. Still, the report was unclear about what it meant to talk about a reduction in total employment.

A disemployment effect occurs when employers respond to increases in the minimum wage by laying off existing workers. The report, however, never used the term *disemployment effect*; rather, it talked about a reduction in total employment, which is significant. This could occur in three different ways. The first is for employers to lay off workers. The second is for low-wage employers not to hire in the future, in which case total employment is reduced. And the third, which the report does not really get into, is that a higher wage will attract back into the labor market those who may have shunned work because the prior minimum wage was considered to be too low. Now there are more people in the labor force, which means that employment on the whole is lower. Even though the CBO report does not come out and say it, it is nonetheless alluding to a very important distinction, which is the difference between rising unemployment because of disemployment and lower total employment because fewer low-wage jobs will be created in the future. The CBO report seemed to be implying the latter.

Nevertheless, the CBO went on to say that at least 16.5 million Americans would see their incomes increase and that on the whole a minimum wage increase would be good for the economy, and that it would potentially lead to some economic growth. This would be because some of the people earning slightly above the new minimum wage of $10.10 an hour would also receive pay increases. Moreover, a few higher-wage workers would owe their jobs to the increased demand for goods and services that would result from a minimum wage increase. Here the CBO was offering the standard macroargument for increasing the minimum wage: more people earning higher wages have greater purchasing power, which enables them to demand more goods and services. In time, this might lead to job creation. But the CBO suggested that there would be even larger macro benefits from its impact on the federal budget deficit. On one level, federal spending and taxes would be affected by increases in real income for some people and the reduction in real income for others. One group of workers with higher income would then pay more in taxes and receive less in various types of federal benefits than they otherwise would have. Another group of workers who become jobless because of increases or because higher prices reduce consumption would see a reduction in real income, meaning that they would pay less collectively in taxes and receive more in federal benefits.

Here the CBO concluded that the net effect of raising the minimum wage would most likely be a small decrease in budget deficits for several years to come, but a small increase thereafter.

Without going into contours, the CBO was suggesting that there are clearly ripple effects for those wages around the minimum wage. The suggestion of 16 million benefiting would be consistent with at least the first two to three contours of the distribution. The explanation would appear to be simple enough. Those earning just above the old minimum wage would have to get pay raises as well as those earning the minimum because those earning the new minimum are now approaching the wages of the next interval. The more people who received higher wages, the more demand for goods and services, which in turn would drive the economy. But there was something else about the CBO report, which is who earns the statutory minimum wage may not be as important as who earns *around* the minimum wage. The distinction between those earning the statutory minimum wage and those earning around it is a critical one because it is suggestive of why the minimum wage elicits the strong political opposition it often does. If only a small fraction of the labor market earns it as critics claim, then it should really be a nonissue politically. But if the minimum wage is really a reference point for the low-wage labor market, and the minimum wage could have implications for the overall wage distribution, then the issue is quite significant whereby many interests have a stake in the outcome.

Politicization of Data

The standard model's predicted unemployment consequences have conveniently found a home in conservative political circles. During the 1980s the nature of the political debate over the minimum wage began to change. With the election of Ronald Reagan to the presidency came a whole new outlook on the economy. For pure market theorists and defenders of the standard model like Milton Friedman, the White House finally had an occupant who viewed government as the problem, rather than the solution to the nation's economic and social problems. Summing up the goals of economic policy, George Stigler (1986), from the same Chicago school of thought as Friedman, argued, "The supreme goal of the Western World is the development of the individual: the creation for the individual of a maximum area of personal freedom, and with this a corresponding area of personal responsibility" (p. 93). As noble as policies intended to provide a safety net or reduce income inequalities might be (which would also include the minimum wage), they were fundamentally at odds with the tenets of freedom. Consequently, the older institutionalist arguments emphasizing the role of government, to the extent they had been listened to at all during the 1970s, had lost their voice.

The Reagan administration made no secret of its views that too much interference in the economy was the principal reason the economy had been in a recession during the 1970s. Moreover, inflation was by and large a product of workers demanding too much from their employers without returning sufficient productivity, which meant that labor unions were part of the problem because they prevented wage flexibility. Wage floors that also contributed to wage rigidity were also part of the problem. Politicization of the standard model, however, was not difficult to do. The standard model has always had an anti-labor bias. Economist Thomas Paley (1998) suggests that the political dominance of business and the intellectual dominance of laissez-faire have meant that economic policy over the last few decades would consistently favor business at the expense of labor. Competitive market theory is generally anti-labor because labor market institutions like unions and the minimum wage that raise wages contribute only to unemployment. But it is also anti-labor because labor is treated as a commodity. Workers are simply inputs in the production process and, as such, have no personalities of their own. Consequently, the standard model's view of the minimum wage nicely serves the interests of those who believe that all government interferences—whether in the form of regulation, public programs, and other interventions—greatly undermine free market ideology and free choice.

A good example of this is Milton Friedman's (2002) argument that political freedom means the absence of coercion. By separating economic activity from political authority, the market has eliminated the source of coercive power. Government's role is merely to do what the marketplace cannot: maintain, arbitrate, and enforce the rules of the game. When government intervenes, it limits freedom. The excuse over the last few decades for governmental intervention has been what Friedman calls "full employment" and "economic growth." But government intervention does not increase employment; it results in greater unemployment, thereby justifying even more intervention, which in turn will only limit further individual freedom. For Friedman, the greatest achievement of capitalism isn't the accumulation of property and wealth, but the opportunities it affords individuals to develop and improve themselves. If, as Friedman believes, the minimum wage, has the opposite effect of what was intended, poor people and/or otherwise low-skilled workers who are displaced from their jobs as a result will no longer be able to improve themselves. And in the name of helping people who will be hurt the most, all that government will have achieved is precedent for further intervention and infringement of personal freedom and autonomy (Budd 2004). Moreover, the assault on autonomy is deemed to be more egregious because it was in essence inefficient.

The key point here is that the minimum wage in the standard model by itself merely results in inefficiency. When the standard model is politicized, as it was during the Reagan years with the help of economists like Friedman, the minimum wage results in an abridgement of individual freedom, and it is freedom and liberty which is what the country is all about. To make a political appeal against the minimum wage on the grounds that it is inefficient most likely will not resonate with too many people. But to couch government intervention as an assault on personal freedom, as the Reagan administration did, ended up having great political appeal. And yet, when one side politicizes the argument, so too does the other. Freedom to contract, after all, necessarily assumes the individuality of each worker. The standard model, however, just reduced each worker to no more than interchangeable commodities lacking in personality. The other side of the freedom argument is that low wages deprive workers of the freedom—their ability to make choices. It deprives them of what economist and philosopher Amartya Sen (1999) calls their capabilities. By capabilities he means their capacity to reason for themselves, make rational choices, and act on their choices. Therefore, there are those on the political left who would argue that contrary to being an assault on personal freedom, the minimum wage is at root a political class struggle over capitalist wage relations because not everyone enjoys the same bargaining power (Kamolnick 1993). Now the issue isn't a matter of freedom, efficiency, but one of justice. A just society, in other words, does not exist when the market place in the name of efficiency results in great disparities in income with those at the bottom not being able to meet their basic subsistence needs. Rather, low-wage workers are in effect being exploited.

Source of Low Wages

When the minimum wage was first adopted during the early part of the twentieth century, it was considered to be a corrective to the low wages resulting from an economic transformation that saw the replacement of skilled work with mass production staffed by unskilled workers barely receiving subsistence wages. But it was also viewed as a measure to address the rising income inequality that also resulted from the industrial revolution. Today, we are still addressing issues of economic transformation. In the post–World War II years, the country, and indeed much of the industrial world, underwent economic change whereby the base of the economy changed from manufacturing to services. Manufacturing jobs (many of which were also unionized) that paid middle-class incomes have disappeared and what has replaced them have been service-sector jobs in what has come to be characterized as a dual economy. At the top are high-paying jobs requiring great levels of skills and at the bottom are low-paying jobs, where workers have very little by way of education or marketable skills that could command higher wages. With the loss of the manufacturing base, the middle class has all but dropped out. This, in part, accounts for the rise in income inequality, particularly since the early 1980s. More importantly, however, it signifies the disappearance of the middle class.

Still the debate over the minimum wage raises a fundamental problem for economic theory: just what are the sources of low wages? The standard model, it will be recalled, posits that individuals earning low wages, especially around the minimum, are not worth more than the wages that they are receiving. This corresponds to the assumption that setting wages is a natural process. The idea that a wage floor would be necessary to ensure that individuals earn a subsistence wage only turns these assumptions on their head. First of all, it underscores the fact that there really is nothing natural about wage-setting mechanisms in the marketplace. Second of all, and more importantly, it underscores that low wages may well be the product of a power imbalance between employers and workers. Still, the assumptions of the standard model may have some validity, especially in an increasingly global market place.

According to basic laws of supply and demand, an oversupply of low-skilled workers should have the effect of driving down wages, and if there are more low-skilled workers than available jobs, then their wage rates should be driven even lower. The reason that wages are so much higher at the top of the scale is that workers possess skills that are in short supply, and if employers demand those skills enough, they will be willing to pay for them. In other words, a shortage of highly skilled workers only drives up wages. This, however, has only led to perhaps what has increasingly become a highly controversial issue in recent years, which is whether increasing inequality is the result of what is known as the skills mismatch thesis—sometimes referred to as the skill-biased toward technical change hypothesis—or whether it is the result of deliberate public policy choices, such as anti-union legislation and maintaining a low minimum wage.

The standard model holds rising income inequality to be a function of a structural economic transformation. Technological change has tended to be biased toward those with higher levels of education and skills. As the economy has evolved from industrial-based manufacturing to postindustrial service, there has been a growing mismatch between good paying jobs and the skills available to workers. According to this school of thought, the labor market is divided into a primary market where high premiums are placed on skilled workers, and a secondary market with unskilled workers trapped in the lowest-wage service sector of the economy. Increasing skills differentials between the two labor markets have only led to the growth in wage inequality (Katz and Krueger 1992; Katz and Murphy 1992). The main culprit is technological change biased toward those with higher levels of education and skills (Juhn, Murphy, and Pierce 1993).

In a competitive market where the new and technologically advanced is always replacing the old and obsolete, it is a foregone conclusion that the wages of unskilled workers will be forced down while the wages of the skilled workers are driven up, thereby increasing the gap between the two. Nevertheless, this view has formed the basis for what Frank Levy and Peter Temin (2010) refer to as the "Washington Consensus" that maintains skills-biased technical change to be the source of inequality, stagnating wages for the average worker, and potentially long-term unemployment. This consensus also maintains that the economy could grow through a set of microeconomic policies of deregulation and privatization intended to achieve greater efficiency. Although the consensus has certainly affected wages and middle-class living standards, the emphasis on skills-biased technical change has also worked to shift responsibility for the plight of employees, and the policymakers who supported them, from employees, to the workers themselves. And yet, as much as this might be true, it misses the role that policy plays either in exacerbating or in hindering the so-called natural process. By adopting this consensus, policymakers only ended up supporting a policy tract that would in fact exacerbate the growing income inequality.

If, however, we don't accept that the source of low wages are the skills-mismatch thesis, then the source may be a set of policies that have effectively denied workers the type of voice necessary to drive up their wages. This is the view that policies that have resulted in the decline of labor market institutions are ultimately the source of low wages. This is not to say that public policy mandates low wages, rather the absence of institutions to countervail globalizing forces that on their own drive down wages. As part of the politicization of the issue, the focus has shifted from job creation, and wage rates, to job training. If the issue is no longer low wages, but the absence of skills, the onus is on workers to develop the necessary skills so that they can command higher wages. Job training becomes an alternative not only to a policy approach of generating jobs but also to the minimum wage itself. As Gordon Lafer (2002) observes, economic policy over the last couple of decades has been predicated on the assumption that more policy efforts, because of the dominance of the skills mismatch thesis, need to be focused on efforts to retrain workers rather than actually creating jobs. The skills mismatch thesis has become a convenient explanation for falling wages and rising inequality. And yet, the decline in unionism would appear to have played a greater role in determining wages of most workers than less education. Rather, a close examination of the mismatch argument appears to be driven by ideological conviction than empirical evidence. Mismatch theorists have asserted that the economy is undergoing a radical transformation in the way that the mundane tasks of factory workers, secretaries, and service workers are performed. But institutions that protected the wages of production workers have been eliminated while professional earnings have remain protected by an elaborate system of immigration control, business, educational credentials, and legal mandates. That is, the earnings of professionals have not been propped up by the rarity of their skills, but by their ability to exert institutional barriers to competition. The biggest blow to those at the bottom of the distribution has been the deterioration of unions. With this decline came a corresponding decline in wages because union wages were generally 28.4 percent higher than those of unorganized workers. What mismatch theories have effectively done is obscure the fact that it was the union premium that maintained higher wage rates for workers, not that workers receive wages equal to their marginal productivity according to traditional human capital theory. In other words, it is institutions that are key in setting wage rates and determining worth. This would also imply that some employers—non-unionized employers—are enjoying substantially greater profits. And yet focusing policy on job training allows us to obscure the reality that institutions that deliberately propped up wages have been targeted because they cut into profits.

Alternatives to Minimum Wage

If the basic idea behind a minimum wage is to boost income, not only of the poor, but of the middle class as well, the obvious question is: are there alternatives to the minimum wage? Remember that the minimum wage is specifically a wage floor that is legislated by either the U.S. Congress or state legislatures. In European countries it might be enacted through wage councils. Still, there may be other ways to guarantee those who work a minimum income. Three basic alternatives include the Earned Income Tax Credit (EITC), the idea of Employer of Last Resort (ELR), and the concept of a Universal Basic Income (UBI).

The EITC dates back to the 1970s and was in part a response to the failure of the Nixon administration to get the Family Assistance Plan (FAP) passed in Congress. The idea behind FAP was to create a minimum income floor. Families would receive a supplement regardless of whether there was a father present. Not only would it create a floor, but it would replace traditional public assistance cash transfer programs as well. It was to operate as a negative income tax. The favored FAP grant was $4,000. This meant that families with no income would essentially receive a guaranteed income from the government of that amount. To preserve the work incentive, the benefit had to be low enough that people would find it necessary to work, but high enough that their basic needs would also be met. The issue that ultimately doomed the proposal was how much to set the negative tax at. A negative tax proposed at about 50 percent of income meant that a family earning $4,000 would receive FAP money until they earned $8,000, and then no more. But if the negative tax was set at 25 percent, they would receive FAP money until they earned $16,000. This meant that those families with earnings of less than $16,000 would be eligible for FAP money. Conservatives in Congress opposed it on the grounds that it would reduce the incentive to work, and liberals in Congress opposed it on the grounds that it was not generous enough. But when the EITC was introduced in 1975, it was supported by conservatives, who saw it as a way for poor people on public assistance to have incentive to work without having to rely on the minimum wage. In fact, this was preferable to the minimum wage because workers indeed had to work in order to qualify, and because the additional money would be coming from the government, there would be no danger of adverse employment consequences.

The EITC is also a negative income tax that essentially supplements the low wages of those who work. Initially one had to have children in order to qualify for the credit. But in 2014, a family with one qualifying child would get a maximum credit of $3,305 while somebody with no qualifying children would get a credit of $496. If one had two children, the credit would be $5,460, and with three children, it would be $6,143. A family gets the maximum credit if the earned income is between the minimum wage and some percentage above that. The effect of an EITC for, say, a single mother with three children earning the federal minimum wage is to have an income of $21,223, of which 28.9 percent is being paid by the government. As one's income moves up the scale, the EITC then begins to phase out. The same single mother with three children would be eligible for an EITC until her income reaches $46,997, and $52,427 if she were married and filing jointly. Although conservatives tend to support the EITC because it rewards work, the idea is not without controversy. Prior to recent adjustments, it tended to penalize marriage, as the effect of a joint income would effectively lower the value of an EITC. But the EITC may also encourage employers to continue paying low wages because if employers know that a portion of their employees' wages are coming from the federal government, they have less incentive to raise wages on their own. Then workers may also have less incentive to work as hard for their employers as they could because their employers aren't paying their full income. Arguably, the failure to guarantee workers a living wage only passes a social cost onto society. Because workers are earning low wages, they are in more need of publicly provided subsidies. The EITC is but one way of subsidizing the profits of low-wage employers at their employees' expense.

Another approach is to simply create government jobs whereby the pay rate would effectively be the new minimum wage. Economist Randall Wray (2000) argues for government as employer of last resort to offer employment to those who are "ready, willing, and able" to work, but have not been able to find jobs. ELR would not replace traditional welfare, but would supplement private sector employment. ELR would not be workfare and would not replace existing social programs.

It would not pay starvation wages, nor would it provide union-busting low-wage labor. It would, however, eliminate the need for a minimum wage, as the ELR wage would effectively become the effective minimum wage. It could also establish the base package of benefits that private employers would have to supply. Although it could replace unemployment insurance, it could also just be added on to give workers who lost their jobs greater choices. The object here, through creating jobs for some of the unemployed, is to increase aggregate demand through the multiplier and thereby increase private sector employment. If it succeeds in doing this, it should also result in a reduction of the number of ELR jobs required. What it does not do is concede that increasing aggregate demand by increasing the living standards of those at the bottom must necessarily cause a demand-pull wage price spiral. Instead, with fixed prices, government's ELR wage is perfectly stable and sets a benchmark price for labor. Wray suggests, however, that if ELR were to be implemented, it is not likely that it will be inflationary in the sense of generating continuing pressure on wages and prices. Because it obligates government to make the initial investment into creating these ELR jobs, it certainly falls within the tradition of more expansive government programs. Again, instead of mandating a minimum wage that workers should be paid in the market place, we are creating an alternative program. But for the same reasons it is difficult to get Congress to act on the minimum wage and periodically raise it, it would be difficult to get them to authorize the type of public expenditure needed to get ELR going.

And the third approach is to simply have a guaranteed income or a universal basic income (UBI). On the surface, this might not appear to be different from a minimum wage, but it is actually intended to be more encompassing and, therefore, becomes more controversial. A broader conception of the minimum wage than the statutory minimum that has been prevalent in the United States is that of a basic income. Philosopher and political economist Philippe van Parijs (1992) puts forth the notion of what he calls Basic Income Capitalism, defined as a socioeconomic regime in which the means of production are for the most part privately owned, but where each citizen is entitled to substantial unconditional income over and above what s/he might earn through normal participation in the labor market. A basic income as such is essentially a pathway toward the achievement of a just society, which Van Parijs understands to be a free society in which all members are as free as possible. He defines it more precisely as a society that meets the following three conditions: "(1) There is some well enforced structure of rights (security condition). (1) This structure is such that each person owns herself (self-ownership condition). (3) This structure is such that each person has the greatest possible opportunity to do whatever she might want to do" (p. 467). To be truly free, one must possess the means to whatever one might want, and not just the "right" to do it. A basic income, then, especially if it is unconditional, and ideally if set at as high a level as possible, provides individuals with the means to be truly free. As Van Parijs (1995) explains, real freedom extends beyond formal freedom, which involves the ability to make choices among various goods that may be consumed. Rather, it involves the "real freedom to choose among the various lives one might wish to lead" (p. 33), or to be free of external controls. But without a basic minimum income, one's ability to take advantage of opportunity, that is, make choices, is indeed adversely affected. Real freedom, in other words, entails being able to effectively act on one's formal freedom. To earn an income that enables one to take advantage of opportunity is to effectively enable one to be autonomous.

Philosopher Stuart White (2003) also talks about a basic minimum as a vehicle for achieving what he defines as justice as fair reciprocity. According to this conception of justice, a good society is one of mutual concern and respect—it is one in which individuals exhibit what he calls *democratic mutual regard*. A society governed by democratic mutual regard is one in which "individuals seek to justify their preferred political and economic institutions to others by appealing to shared basic interests, and to related principles that express a willingness to cooperate with their fellow citizens as equals" (pp. 25–26). Each citizen has a basic interest in having adequate opportunity to reflect and deliberate critically about those matters that are essential to each's ethical agency. Therefore, the primary commitment of justice as fair reciprocity is the upholding of basic liberties and securities. In a society built around the ethos of democratic mutual regard, citizens must accept and affirm each other as equals, and consequently design a common set of institutions that will govern their lives together in a fundamental way. Justice as fair reciprocity, however, entails more than this give and take; it also involves a commitment to substantive economic reciprocity. That is, "if one willingly enjoys the fruits of one's fellow citizens' labours, then, as a matter of justice, one ought to provide some appropriate good in return" (p. 49). A society that derives benefit from the labor of low-wage workers ought to guarantee low-wage workers a minimum wage, as that minimum would constitute an "appropriate good in return." As individuals, we live in a cooperative enterprise known as the overall economy, and therefore we have a responsibility to ensure that all who participate, regardless of where one falls in the wage distribution, are in no way burdened by their participation. In other words, workers who do not earn wages sufficient to sustain themselves in dignity are indeed burdened. The concept of UBI, however, may not be viewed so much as an alternative to the minimum wage as an expansion of it. A minimum wage in the form of a wage floor merely adds to the employer's labor costs. It may well raise prices and, if set too high, lead to employment consequences. But a UBI carries a broader commitment. Neither author really addresses who pays for it. A UBI could, of course, be guaranteed through government programs. At the same time, the concept may be viewed as creating a set of rights that workers neither currently enjoy nor are entitled to. On a philosophical level, there is certain logic to it, but politically it is bound to run into the same types of problems that have always confronted the minimum wage in its minimal wage floor form.

Solutions?

Because American society is heterogeneous and politically pluralistic, it is not clear that an easy solution can be found to resolve the various controversies surrounding the minimum wage. For all those who support the minimum wage, there will always be those who oppose it. Still, there may be steps that could be taken. One approach is to re-conceptualize the issue. Noah Zatz (2009), for instance, raises the question of whether the minimum wage perhaps ought not to be considered a larger civil right. To a certain extent, the language of procedural democracy assumes that individuals as equals in standing before the law do enjoy certain basic civil rights. The implication being that without respect for the basic civil rights of voting, free speech, due process, and the right to pursue one's interests based on one's human agency, democracy is nonexistent, even if nominal elections are being held. Zatz asks the question of whether minimum wage law serves to protect the civil rights of workers. In other words, is it necessary to have a wage floor to protect their civil rights, and, if so, would a minimum wage be a necessary and sufficient condition? Defining the minimum wage as a civil rights issue might remedy an injury to workers' civil rights. As the lowest-paid workers tend to hail from groups central to anti-discrimination projects, it would appear that their status as low-paid workers means that they are not being treated on an equal footing with others, and certainly not with those with more resources.

One approach to justifying the minimum wage that has been obscured by a focus on anti-poverty arguments is that it offers a corrective to defects in the wage bargain between employers and employees. As Zatz puts it: "In its most stylized form, the minimum wage remedies employer theft. If an employer refuses to pay a worker the agreed-upon wage for work performed, the employer is a thief. The same is true if the employer forces the worker at gunpoint to agree to work for no wage at all or tricks her into the same. Furthermore, it can make no fundamental difference if what the employer steals is not the entire wage but only some fraction of it" (p. 7). Nevertheless, what matters most about the minimum wage is that it is no defense to show that the employer simply paid the going rate in a complex competitive market. The "inequality of bargaining power" provides the moderate alternative to the labor theory of value. What a minimum wage does is enact a presumption that when wages fall below a certain level, they are low for morally arbitrary reasons. Therefore, mandating a higher wage brings us closer to a world of fairness. Or at a minimum, it may serve to place some on an equal footing with others, and in this vein it becomes a civil rights issue in a broader sense. James Galbraith (1998) too has couched the minimum wage in terms of affording low-wage workers some monopoly power in the labor market, which, in the absence of either union coverage or a minimum wage, they otherwise lack.

During the early part of the twentieth century, when Sidney Webb (1912) argued that a minimum wage would increase efficiency, he, along with his wife Beatrice Webb, was also concerned about the social costs of paying low wages. Their case for the minimum wage was built on two main pillars: the doctrine of labor's *inequality of bargaining power* (IBP) and the *social cost of labor* (SCL) doctrine. IBP holds that employers individually and/or collectively enjoy a power advantage in wage determination, even in what we would consider a competitive labor market. The party benefiting from extra-low wages in labor markets is employers. But employers are not the only beneficiaries. Consumers, and especially affluent consumers who have a disproportionate share of income, also benefit from low wage labor in the form of lower prices. One social rationale for a legal minimum wage, as Bruce Kaufman (2009) points out, is that it offsets the workers' weak bargaining power in the labor market. Therefore, IBP creates a social rationale on efficiency and fairness grounds for state abridgement of freedom of contract. Added to the SCL doctrine, the argument for a legal minimum becomes stronger and the traditional neoclassical opposition to it becomes weaker. Neoclassical economists typically treat social costs arising from production processes where product prices are low and output as high as negative externalities arising from an absence of property rights for, in this case, the workers.

The innovation of the Webbs and American institutionalists was to apply the negative externality concept—missing property rights—to the employment relationship in order to develop a positive rationale for both legal minimum wages and collective bargaining. Their argument rests on the assumption that labor—human capital—as is the case with physical capital—requires some minimum ongoing expenditures for upkeep, repair, and depreciation. That is, if product prices were to cover the full costs of production, then firms must pay the workers a wage sufficient to cover individual and family subsistence costs, or provide in-kind compensation. But when the wage falls short of subsistence level, the social costs exceed the private labor costs borne by the firm and its customers. "In this case, either someone else bears this expense, or, socially viewed, the nation's stock of human capital starts to depreciate and wear out" (Kaufman 2009, p. 313). At a minimum each worker requires a minimum necessary level of healthcare to cover physical and mental wear and tear. A minimum wage, then, is seen as contributing to a solution of the social cost problem, and with far greater efficiency and fairness than can competition and laissez-faire. The idea is to use the minimum wage in the labor market that approximates the social cost of labor. Although a minimum wage can in effect be viewed as a tax on firms, firms paying low wages are nonetheless making a profit without paying the full social costs. A minimum wage, then, serves to end the social subsidy to otherwise parasitic firms. This would seem to suggest that the absence of a minimum wage, which effectively results in society bearing the social costs so that a few producers can derive benefit, is inherently antidemocratic. Society bears the costs for the benefit of a few. Establishing the floor, however, may not be enough.

Another solution, as alluded to by White, may be to redefine what society means by property rights. The concept of wage labor is the idea that the worker sells his labor services to an employer for wages. But what if those services were defined in terms of property rights? This would imply that paying workers below a specified wage would be tantamount to theft. In recent years, states have been passing right-to-work laws, which bar closed union shops. These laws make union organizing more difficult, which in turn may have the effect of suppressing workers' wages.

And yet, right-to-work laws rest on a fundamental assumption that has long permeated American labor law. That is, employers have property rights while workers do not, hence the asymmetrical balance of power between workers and their employers. When Congress passed the National Labor Relations Act (NLRA), which created the National Labor Relations Board (NLRB) in 1935, it was considered to be important because by requiring collective bargaining as a means to prevent labor strife and instability in labor markets, workers were effectively limiting the property rights of workers. Prior to passage of the NLRA, employers could easily assert their property rights and claim that unions and strikes were an infringement of those rights.

That is why the concept of collective bargaining and the right to it granted by the NLRA were so important. It effectively upended that assumption. If employers are required to recognize collective bargaining units and sit down and negotiate with their workers, workers are in effect being recognized as having a property right to their labor. To redefine workers' labor in terms of property rights is to also say that collective bargaining is not enough especially in an era when labor unions are in decline. In the absence of unions as an essential labor market institution, the minimum wage may take on even greater significance, as it is the only other major labor market institution left. Granting workers' property rights in their labor would only strengthen the minimum wage. By assaulting labor the way that right-to-work laws do, they effectively deny workers property rights in their labor. It is true that if workers were viewed as people with legitimate property rights in their labor, the property rights of employers would effectively be diminished. Measures taken by management that reduced the value of their workers' property in labor would essentially be akin to a "taking" worthy of some compensation. Still, it is highly unlikely that American labor law will go this far because it would rekindle many of the class warfare arguments and human relations battles that existed when the minimum wage first surfaced at the beginning of the twentieth century.

Politically, a step to take is to present the minimum wage as a middle-class issue. The issue should not be a partisan issue. Labor market institutions such as unions and the minimum wage do make a difference with regard to overall wage structure and achieving a more equitable distribution. The minimum wage, for instance, as Levin-Waldman (2011) argues, is not only about helping the working poor to earn a wage above the poverty line; it is also about shoring up the middle class through wage contour effects. A minimum wage that increases aggregate demand for goods and services because it enables more workers to have greater purchasing power is one that possibly expands the middle class because in the long term it will result in greater job creation (Levin-Waldman 2012). By presenting it as a middle-class issue, politicians would be able to remove it from the type of politics that have not only plagued the issue from the very beginning, but have effectively stunted its development as well.

Politics has famously been defined as who gets what, when, and how? Workers surely have an interest in getting higher wages while employers have an interest in limiting the wages that they are forced to pay. But this definition of politics concerns only the outcome of a political process. The process often requires restricting the size of the political universe affected by the issue. By marginalizing the issue and saying that it affects only a small segment of the labor market as minimum wage critics have been able to do, the minimum wage has effectively been relegated to a "trivial" matter affecting only a few. To successfully counter their efforts, supporters need to expand the universe of those affected by the issue, which means presenting it as a middle-class issue. In this regard, the issue would follow the same trajectory as Social Security in the 1930s. Because it was sold as a middle-class entitlement—something all were entitled to because they worked for rather than a program only for elderly people who were also poor—it was able to garner more political support.

Another solution, which is less of an alternative than another way of removing the issue from politics, is to index the minimum wage, whereby it would be tied to either the rate of inflation or productivity. As each increases, so too would the minimum wage, and it would do so automatically. Much of the opposition to the minimum wage stems from the fact that when Congress finally does get around to raising the minimum wage, the percentage increase may be viewed as so large that it represents a jolt. But if it were indexed, employers would be better able to plan for the increase. As indexation would mean an increase of only a percentage or two a year, they would know what to expect Although an argument for productivity may serve as a good justification for raising the minimum wage with appeal to the broader labor market, there perhaps needs to be a mechanism by which the minimum wage can be adjusted automatically on a regular basis. It doesn't solve the problem that the minimum wage at its current level isn't livable. To achieve a livable wage would require a drastic measure by Congress. As a political argument, productivity a least gets us to think about the minimum wage in a more positive way, even though it doesn't remove the fundamental political nature of the problem. Achieving a broader wage would require bold steps by Congress. Incremental steps of the type that have traditionally been taken wouldn't even bring the wage into lines with 50 percent of average annual hourly wages, let alone a so-called living wage. And yet, each year that Congress does nothing, the gap between the existing minimum wage and the poverty line only becomes that much larger, for a higher percentage increase is required for each year that Congress does nothing about the minimum wage. Herein lies the political problem that has been driving many of the economic consequences of a declining minimum wage. The larger the increase in the minimum wage, the more of a shock it is bound to be to that sector of the economy that hires most minimum wage workers. A mechanism for increasing the minimum wage in small increments on an annual basis would offer greater stability.

Under the current minimum wage regime, Congress shies away from being bold and voting for a "living wage" increase because of the immediate shock that would attend to such a large increase. The natural consequence of this is that the value of the minimum wage erodes even further. By the time Congress musters the political will to take action, it is inadequate to address the erosion in value, let alone the true needs of those working for the minimum wage. To have a minimum wage that enables individuals to support a family above the poverty line would require some mechanism for automatically adjusting the wage on an annual basis. Indexation would effectively take the politics out of the minimum wage. Moreover, indexation isn't only about poverty and keeping low-wage workers out of poverty, but about the maintenance of a more equitable wage structure.

Past calls for indexation have focused either on some percentage of average annual hourly earnings or the consumer price index (CPI) as a basis for indexation. Calls in the past for tying the minimum wage to a percentage of average annual hourly earnings have often focused on a rate of around 50 percent of the average annual hourly earnings in manufacturing.

The virtue of this approach is, of course, the historical precedent, because the minimum wage did hover around 50 percent of average annual hourly earnings for much of the history of the minimum wage program. Were the minimum wage to be set at that level based on the average for 2012 of $24.47, the minimum wage would be $12.23, as opposed to its current level of $7.25. Subsequently, whatever percentage the average annual wage increases by, the minimum wage increases by the same percentage.

The CPI is often favored because other programs, especially federal entitlements, are already tied to it. This has the obvious benefit of raising wages by whatever percentage increase there is in the CPI. The problem with the CPI, however, is that not only does it overstate the rate of inflation, it also does not accurately reflect market-caused price increases (Boskin et al. 1996). An index that increases wages at a rate greater than (or even different from) the actual inflation rate will exacerbate inflationary pressures. This then suggests the need to find some measure of productivity as the basis for an automatic adjustment mechanism. An argument can be made for a productivity-based index on both moral grounds and the standard model. According to the standard model, when productivity increases it is because of the marginal value each worker added to the enterprise. By theory, increases in productivity should justify increases in wages without any risk of inflation. Remember that George Stigler (1946) famously observed that a minimum wage that did not result in lower employment would result in greater efficiency because productivity would increase. There has perhaps been an expectation that as productivity increases the gains would be shared among workers in the form of higher wages. Since the end of the Great Recession in 2009, productivity has increased, but those gains have not been shared among the workers (Sum and McLaughlin 2010). Tying the minimum wage to productivity, especially through its wage contour effects, would ensure that those productivity gains are shared among the workers. This approach assumes that as productivity increases, and to the extent those increases yield higher wages in general, they can also be the basis for increases in the statutory minimum wage. A minimum wage that rises with increases in productivity would have its appeal both economically and politically.

Productivity, however, is difficult to measure. Elsewhere, I (1998) have argued that a productivity index could be created on the basis of the median wage of the lowest wage workers, who would in effect be regarded as low-skilled workers, many of whom work in retail sales, the low-wage service sector (cashiers, gas hands, etc.) and the fast-food industry. This focus doesn't require dealing with the different gradations of skills; rather, it assumes there are two kinds of workers: skilled and unskilled. The median of the lowest skilled workers serves as a reference point and, for all practical purposes, becomes the putative minimum wage. Then on the basis of changes made to the median of the lowest-wage sector, similar adjustments are made to the statutory minimum wage. Whatever percentage increase there was in the putative minimum wage would simply be applied to the statutory minimum wage. For instance, according to data from the CPS, the median wage of full-time workers below the 50th percentile was $3.74 in 1982 and it was $12.02 in 2012. Over the course of three decades median wages rose 221.4 percent. Had that same percentage increase been applied to the statutory minimum wage (then $3.35), it would have been $10.77 in 2012, which is actually more than the minimum wage being proposed by President Obama. The point is that it would have risen through incremental steps rather than the divisive politics that tend to characterize the current minimum wage regime.

To the extent that the putative minimum wage rises along with productivity increases, the effect is for the private sector to decide the rate of increase in the statutory minimum wage rather than the government. This would effectively create a public–private partnership type of relationship whereby government implements a new wage rate based on what is happening in the private sector of the economy. The decision effectively becomes a grassroots decision on the basis of a consensus arrived at through the collectivity of private decisions.

Critics of indexation schemes often allege such measures to be inflationary. And yet, because the statutory minimum wage is so far below the putative minimum wage of the lowest-wage sector, it is hard to see how the minimum wage increasing at the same rates as the others could exert much inflationary pressure. On the contrary, annual increases in the minimum wage would actually reduce much of the shock that many employers of minimum wage workers must experience each time Congress actually does implement a new minimum wage. These increases would be considerably less that those typically legislated by Congress, which at times have been as high as 25 percent.

Ultimately the whole question of indexation requires us to revisit the model of competitive markets. The assumption of the standard model is that rising wages will lead to lower employment, but it isn't clear whether that is a function of the increase per se or whether it is a function of the size of the increase. If the great concern of most minimum wage employers is the wage rates of those earning around the minimum wage, gradual increases would not have as great an impact as larger increases. Indexation, then, might also lessen the shock for those regions of the country where wage rates generally are lower. Moreover, automatic indexation would remove the issue from politics and ensure that those at the low end of the wage scale can continue to earn a wage that keeps up. This might also serve to reduce the level of turnover in minimum wage jobs. In as much as this might reduce turnover, employers would have greater incentive to invest in on-the-job training, which in turn will only lead to greater productivity.

Analysis

Overall, the minimum wage has been a controversial issue, revolving around ideas of measurement and definition. But at the end of the day, how the issue is defined is a matter of how different groups perceive the issue in relation to their respective interests. And yet, the minimum wage may at the core be about the type of society we would like to be. If the issue is about disemployment effects and how the minimum wage reduces employment for low-skilled workers, we need to ask whether there is value to simply creating low-wage jobs that don't enable people to support themselves. If the minimum wage is ultimately viewed as yet another form of redistribution—from managers to workers—then the question that has often been ignored has to be asked: are we as a society through low wages not redistributing from workers to employers? Are we not passing social costs onto all of society? Do we not all as taxpayers have to provide subsidies to low-wage workers who earn too little to subsist? And are those social costs not in effect subsidizing corporate profits?

References

Allegretto, Sylvia, Arindrajit Dube, and Michael Reich. 2011. "Do Minimum Wages Really Reduce Teen Employment? Accounting for Heterogeneity and Selectivity in State Panel Data." *Industrial Relations.* 50, 2 (April): 205–240.

Boskin, Michael J. et al. 1996. "Toward a More Accurate Measure of the Cost of Living." Washington: Advisory Commission to Study the Consumer Price Index, U.S. Senate.

Brown, Charles, Curtis Gilroy, and Andrew Kohen. 1982. "The Effect of the Minimum Wage on Employment and Unemployment." *Journal of Economic Literature* 20 (June): 487–528.

Brown, Christopher. 1992. "Commodity Money, Credit, and the Real Balance Effect." *Journal of Post Keynesian Economics.* 15, 1 (Winter): 99–107.

Budd, John W. 2004. *Employment with a Human Face: Balancing Efficiency, Equity, and Voice*. Ithaca, NY; London: ILR/Cornell University Press.

Burkhauser, Richard V. and T. Aldrich Finegan. 1989. "The Minimum Wage and the Poor: The End of a Relationship." *Journal of Policy Analysis and Management*. 8, 1: 53–71.

Burkhauser, Richard V. and T. Aldrich Finegan. 1995. *Myth and Measurement: The New Economics of the Minimum Wage*. Princeton, NJ: Princeton University Press.

Card, David and Alan B. Krueger. 1998. "A Reanalysis of the Effect of the New Jersey Minimum Wage Increase on the Fast-Food Industry with Representative Payroll Data." *Working Paper No. 6386*. National Bureau of Economic Research, Cambridge, MA.

Congressional Budget Office. 2014. "The Effects of a Minimum Wage Increase on Employment and Family Income." Congress of the United States. (February). Downloaded from http://www.cbo.gov/publication/44995.

Currie, Janet and Bruce C. Fallick. 1996. "The Minimum Wage and the Employment of Youth." *Journal of Human Resources*. 31, 2: 404–428.

Drazen, Allan. 1986. "Optimal Minimum Wage Legislation." *The Economic Journal*. 96 (September): 774–784.

Dube, Arindrajit, T., William Lester, and Michael Reich. 2010. "Minimum Wage Effects among State Borders: Estimates Using Contiguous Counties." *The Review of Economics and Statistics*. 92, 4 (November 2010): 945–964.

Dube, Arindrajit, Suresh Naidu, and Michael Reich. 2007. "The Economic Effects of a Citywide Minimum Wage." *Industrial and Labor Relations Review*. 60, 4 (July): 522–523.

Dunlop, John T. 1957. "The Task of Contemporary Wage Theory." In George W. Taylor and Frank C. Pierson, eds.

New Concepts in Wage Determination. New York: McGraw-Hill Book Co.

Ehrenberg, Ronald G. and Robert S. Smith. 1997. *Modern Labor Economics: Theory and Public Policy,* 6th ed. Reading, MA: Addison-Wesley.

Fairris, David. 2003. "The Impact of Living Wages on Employers: A Control Group Analysis of the Los Angeles Ordinance." University of California. Riverside, CA. (April 11–12).

Figart, Deborah M., Ellen Mutari, and Marilyn Power. 2002. *Living Wages, Equal Wages: Gender and Labor Market Policies in the United States.* London; New York: Routledge.

Figart, Deborah M., Ellen Mutari, Marilyn Power, and June Lapidus. 1995. "A Gender Analysis of U.S. Labor Markets for the Working Poor." *Feminist Economics.* 1, 3: 60–81.

Finegold, David. 1998. "Is the Fair Labor Standards Act Fair to Welfare Recipients?" *Journal of Labor Research.* 19, 2 (Sprung): 245–262.

Freeman, Alida Castillo and Richard B. Freeman. 1991. "Minimum Wages in Puerto Rico: Textbook Case of a Wage Floor?" *NBER Working Paper No. 3759.* (June).

Fried, Barbara H. 1998. *The Progressive Assault on Laissez Faire: Robert Hale and the First Law and Economic Movement.* Cambridge, MA: Harvard University Press.

Friedman, Milton. 2002. *Capitalism and Freedom.* Chicago, IL; London: University of Chicago Press.

Galbraith, James K. 1998. *Created Unequal: The Crisis in American Pay.* New York: Basic Books.

Glickman, Lawrence B. 1997. *A Living Wage: American Workers and the Making of Consumer Society.* Ithaca, NY; London: Cornell University Press.

Gordon, David M. 1996. *Fat and Mean: The Corporate Squeeze of Working Americans and the Myth of Managerial "Downsizing."* New York: The Free Press.

Gordon, Robert J. 1995. "Is There a Tradeoff between Unemployment and Productivity Growth?" *NBER Working Paper 5081* (April).

Houseman, Susan N. 1998. "The Effects of Employer Mandates." In Richard B. Freeman and Peter Gottschalk, eds. *Generating Jobs: How to Increase Demands for Less-Skilled Workers*. New York: Russell Sage Foundation.

Howes, Candace. 2002. "The Impact of a Wage Increase on the Workforce Stability of IHSS Home Care Workers in San Francisco Country." *Working Paper*. University of California Institute for Labor and the Economy and the University of California, Berkeley, Center for Education and Labor Research. November.

Juhn, Chinhui, Kevin Murphy, and Brooks Pierce. 1993. "Wage Inequality and the Rise in Returns to Skills." *Journal of Political Economy*. 101, 3: 410–442.

Katz, Lawrence and Alan B. Krueger. 1992. "The Effect of the Minimum Wage on the Fast-Food Industry." *Industrial and Labor Relations Review*. 46, 1 (October): 6–21.

Katz, Lawrence and Kevin M. Murphy. 1992. "Changes in Relative Wages, 1963–1987: Supply and Demand Factors." *Quarterly Journal of Economics*. 107: 35–79.

Kamolnick, Paul. 1993. "American Workers and the Future of Minimum Wage Politics." *Review of Radical Political Economics*. 25, 2 (June): 26–49.

Kaufman, Bruce E. 2005. "The Social Welfare Objectives and Ethical Principles of Industrial Relations." In John W. Budd and James G. Scoville, eds. *The Ethics of Human Resources and Industrial Relations*. Champaign, IL: Labor and Employment Relations Association.

Kaufman, Bruce E. 2009. "Promoting Labour Market Efficiency through a Legal Minimum Wage: The Webbs and the Social Cost of Labour." *British Journal of Industrial Relations*. 47, 2 (June): 306–326.

Kennan, John. 1995. "The Elusive Effects of Minimum Wages." *Journal of Economic Literature* 33 (December): 1950–1965.

Keynes, John Maynard. 1964. *The General Theory of Employment, Interest, and Money*. New York: Harvest/Harcourt.

Kosters, Marvin H. and Finis Welch. 1972. "The Effects of Minimum Wages on the Distribution of Change in Aggregate Employment." *American Economic Review*. 62, 3 (June): 323–332.

Kosters, Marvin H. ed. 1996. *The Effects of the Minimum Wage on Employment*. Washington: AEI Press.

Lafer, Gordon. 2002. *The Job Training Charade*. Ithaca, NY; London: Cornell University Press.

Lang, Kevin and Shulamit Kahn. 1998. "The Effect of Minimum-Wage Laws on the Distribution of Employment: Theory and Evidence." *Journal of Public Economics*. 69: 67–82.

Leamer, Edward E. 1999. "Effort, Wages, and the International Division of Labor." *Journal of Political Economy*. 107, 6, 1: 1127–1162.

Lester, Richard A. 1946. "Shortcomings of Marginal Analysis for Wage-Employment Problems." *The American Economic Review*. 36, 1 (March): 63–82.

Levin-Waldman, Oren M. 1998. "Automatic Adjustment of the Minimum Wage: Linking the Minimum Wage to Productivity." *Public Policy Brief No. 42*. Levy Economics Institute.

Levin-Waldman, Oren M. 2000a. "The Effects of the Minimum Wage: A Business Response." *Journal of Economic Issues*. 34, 3 (September): 723–730.

Levin-Waldman, Oren M. 2000b. "The Minimum Wage Can Be Raised: Lessons from the 1999 Levy Survey of Small Business." *Challenge* 43, 2 (March/April): 86–96.

Levin-Waldman, Oren M. 2000c. "Minimum Wage and Justice?" *Review of Social Economy*, 58, 1 (March): 43–62.

Levin-Waldman, Oren M. 2001. *The Case of the Minimum Wage: Competing Policy Models*. Albany: State University of New York Press.

Levin-Waldman, Oren M. 2011. *Wage Policy, Income Distribution, and Democratic Theory*. London; New York: Routledge.

Levin-Waldman, Oren M. 2012. "Wage Policy as an Essential Ingredient in Job Creation." *Challenge*. 55, 6 (November/December): 26.52.

Levy, Frank and Peter Temin. 2010. "Institutions and Wages in Post-World War II America." In Clair Brown, Barry Eichengreen, and Michael Reich, eds. *Labor in the Era of Globalization*. Cambridge, MA; New York: Cambridge University Press.

Meyer, Robert H. and David A. Wise. 1983. "The Effect of the Minimum Wage on the Employment Earnings of Youth." *Journal of Labor Economics*. 1, 1: 66–100.

Michl, Thomas R. 2000. "Can Rescheduling Explain the New Jersey Minimum Wage Studies?" *Eastern Economic Journal*. 26, 3 (Summer): 265–276.

Minimum Wage Study Commission. 1981 *Report of the Minimum Wage Study Commission Vol 1: Commission Findings and Recommendations*. Washington, DC: Government Printing Office.

Minsky, Hyman P. 1986. *Stabilizing an Unstable Economy*. New Haven, CT: Yale University Press.

Neumark, David, Mark Schweitzer, and William Wascher. 2004. "Minimum Wage Effects throughout the Distribution." *The Journal of Human Resources*. 39, 2: 425–450.

Neumark, David, and William Wascher. 1992. "Employment Effects of Minimum and Subminimum Wages: Panel Data and State Minimum Wage Laws." *Industrial and Labor Relations Review.* 46, 1 (October): 55–81.

Palley, Thomas I. 1998. *Plenty of Nothing: The Downsizing of the American Dream and the Case for Structural Keynesianism.* Princeton, NJ: Princeton University Press.

Partridge, Mark D. and Janice S. Partridge. 1999. "Do Minimum Wage Hikes Raise U.S. Long Term Unemployment? Evidence Using State Minimum Wage Rates." *Regional Studies.* 33, 8 (1999): 713–726.

Piore, Michael J. and Charles F. Sabel. 1984. *The Second Industrial Divide: Possibilities for Prosperity.* New York: Basic Books.

Prasch, Robert E. 1995. "Toward a 'General Theory' of Market Exchange." *Journal of Economic Issues.* 29, 3 (September): 807–828.

Reich, Michael. 2010. "Minimum Wages in the United States: Politics, Economics, and Econometrics." In Clair Brown, Barry Eichengreen, and Michael Reich, eds. *Labor in the Era of Globalization.* Cambridge, MA; New York: Cambridge University Press.

Reich, Michael, Peter Hall, and Ken Jacobs. 2003. *Living Wages and Economic Performance: The San Francisco Airport Model.* Institute of Industrial Relations. University of California, Berkeley. March.

Sen, Amartya. 1999. *Development as Freedom.* New York: Anchor Books.

Shapiro, Carl and Joseph E. Stiglitz. 1984. "Equilibrium Unemployment as a Worker Discipline Device." *American Economic Review.* 74, 3 (June): 433–444.

Spriggs, William E. and Bruce E. Klein. 1994. *Raising the Floor: The Effects of the Minimum Wage on Low-Wage Workers.* Washington: Economic Policy Institute.

Stigler, George J. 1946. "The Economics of Minimum Wage Legislation." *American Economic Review*. (June): 358–365.

Stigler, George J. 1986. "The Goals of Economic Policy." In Kurt R. Leube and Thomas Moore, eds. *The Essence of Stigler*. Stanford, CA: Hoover Institution Press.

Sum, Andrew and Joseph McLaughlin. 2010. "The Massive Shedding of Jobs in America." *Challenge*. 53, 6 (November/December): 62–76.

Van Parijs, Philippe. 1992. "Basic Income Capitalism." *Ethics* 102 (April).

Van Parijs, Philippe. 1995. *Real Freedom for All: What (If Anything) Can Justify Capitalism?* Oxford; New York: Claredon/Oxford University Press.

Volscho, Thomas W. Jr. 2005. "Minimum Wages and Income Inequality in the American States, 1960–2000." *Research in Social Stratification and Mobility*. 23: 347–373.

Webb, Sidney. 1912. "The Economic Theory of a Legal Minimum Wage." *The Journal of Political Economy*. 20, 10 (December): 973–998.

Weintraub, Sidney. 1978–79. "The Missing Theory of Money Wages." *Journal of Post Keynesian Economics*. 1, 2 (Winter): 59–78.

Weiss, Andrew. 1990. *Efficiency Wages: Models of Unemployment, Layoffs, and Wage Dispersion*. Princeton, NJ: Princeton University Press.

Welch, Finis. 1974. "Minimum Wage Legislation in the United States." *Economic Inquiry*. 12, 3 (September): 285–318.

Welch, Finis. 1978. *Minimum Wages: Issues and Evidence*. Washington: American Enterprise Institute for Public Policy Research.

White, Stuart. 2003. *The Civic Minimum: On the Rights and Obligations of Economic Citizenship*. Oxford; New York: Oxford University Press.

White, Stuart. 2007. *Equality*. Cambridge; Malden, MA: Polity Press.

Wray, L. Randall. 2000. "The Employer of Last resort Approach to Full Employment." Working Paper No. 9. Center for Full Employment and Price Stability: University of Missouri-Kansas City (July).

Zatz, Noah D. 2009. "The Minimum Wage as a Civil Rights Protection: An Alternative to Antipoverty Arguments?" *The University of Chicago Legal Forum*. Downloaded from: http://www.lexisnexis.com/ex-proxy.brooklyn.cuny.edu: 2048/Inacui2api/delivery/PrintDoc.

Introduction

The minimum wage is an issue that elicits strong emotion on all sides of the political aisle. It is an issue with varied opinion with regard to where it fits into the economy and whether it should be included in the policy toolbox. This chapter presents eight different perspectives on the minimum wage, mostly from economists, sociologists, think tank policy analysts and research directors, and a small business owner. What should become clear is that there is absolutely no correct way to approach the minimum wage, in large measure because the minimum wage affects different people differently. To the extent that this is true, it should be a given that whatever data is generated when studying the issue, along with the different perspectives, they should simply be used as information by policymakers, as part of their cost-benefit calculations to make policy. In other words, as is the case with all policy, when it comes to the minimum wage there is no right or wrong answer. Rather, every political community has to decide for itself what policies it wants to pursue and use the relevant information accordingly.

Molita Cunningham, right, and Ana Grant chant slogans supporting a $15 per hour minimum wage, as New York's wage board recommended for fast-food workers, at Government Center in downtown Miami on July 23, 2015. (AP Photo/Alan Diaz)

The Early Institutionalists and the Positive Case for a Minimum Wage
Bruce Kaufman

Richard Ely, lead founder of the American Economic Association (AEA, 1886), writes in *The Past and Present of Political Economy* (1884) that in America of his day economic thinking followed the doctrines of the English classical economists and their policy conclusion that "government should abstain from all interference in industrial life. *Laissez-faire* . . . was the oft-repeated maxim" (p. 13). He also observes that the laissez-faire doctrine "acquired the reputation of orthodoxy, and to be a heretic in political economy became worse than to be an apostate in religion" (p. 10).

Ely's first specialty area of study was labor, and he twice nearly lost his professor's job for the apostasy of supporting labor unions, protective labor law, and social insurance. The economic theory he appealed to was not classical British economics but historical-social economics from Germany, developed there by reform economists to give economic legitimacy to Bismarck's pioneering program of labor legislation. Ely and several other German-trained colleagues founded the AEA to promote a "new economics." In the USA the new economics evolved into institutional economics after the turn of the century and in the labor area, its center was at the University of Wisconsin with Ely, his student John Commons, and several other well-known colleagues. A similar movement coalesced in Britain and, in the labor area, was centered on Sidney and Beatrice Webb. The Webbs founded the London School of Economics (LSE) as a center for historical-social economics. Both the Wisconsin and LSE streams of labor studies later formed into the field industrial relations.

Ely says of the new economics (p. 64):

[T]his younger political economy no longer permits the science to be used as a tool in the hands of the greedy and avaricious for keeping down and oppressing the laboring classes. It does not acknowledge *laissez-faire* as an excuse for doing nothing while a person starves, nor allow the all-sufficiency of competition as a plea for grinding the poor.

In 1905 Ely, Commons, and several other economists formed the American Association for Labor Legislation (AALL). One of the groups' principal legislative objectives was enactment of state and federal minimum wage laws.

The Positive Case for a Legal Minimum

The labor institutionalists advanced four labor market justifications for a minimum wage (MW). They were quite similar to the four rationales listed in the Fair Labor Standards Act (FLSA, 1938), the nation's first federal MW law. Each justification is described in the following pages; for greater explanation and full citations to the literature, see Kaufman (2009, 2010, 2012).

The Worker's Bargaining Disadvantage

Commons and Andrews (1936: 42) state, "Minimum wage legislation marks a new stage in the long line of attempts to equalize the power of employer and employee in making the wage bargain." Based on data from local labor markets and in-depth fieldwork, the institutionalists saw that wage rates for people in the bottom strata of the labor market were shockingly low and far less than required for individual, let alone family, subsistence. They understood the idea behind the freedom of contract doctrine—that all sides gain from trade—but nonetheless believed the terms of trade in this case were so lop-sided, onerous, and negotiated under economic duress that the state had just cause to intervene. A minimum wage, therefore, helps level the playing field, protect the worker underdog, and prevent sweatshop pay. In addition, a minimum wage helps shift competition from labor cheapening to other more prosocial channels, such as improved management efficiency and product quality.

The worker's bargaining disadvantage arises from a number of complementary sources. One factor is that the worker needs the job more desperately than the firm needs the worker and, in addition, the worker cannot hold out as long because of limited job alternatives and scant financial resources. A second is that labor markets are typically overstocked with job seekers and their competition for work drives wages and conditions to a sweatshop level. A third is that labor markets suffer from a variety of imperfections and failures that give employers monopsony power over wages, some of which are inherent to the situation (e.g., only one or several firms in a local labor market) and others that are created by firms (e.g., wage collusion through local employer associations). A fourth is that labor markets are tipped by legal rules, such as employment-at-will, which come from employers' exercise of power in the political market place.

Social Costs of Labor and a Living Wage

A second rationale developed by the institutionalists for an MW is that it helps ensure market wages cover the social costs of labor and provide minimum sustainable income for workers and their families. Conventional microeconomics demonstrates that economic efficiency requires firms pay the full cost of the labor input or otherwise consumers and firms get a de facto subsidy. Social costs of labor include, for example, the expense of workplace injuries, maintaining workers and their families (the future workforce) during periods of slack production, and investments in education, health, and housing. Firms, however, are often able to dodge these costs and shift them back to workers, their families, and the community, thus making the private cost of labor less than the social cost. Ability to cost shift arises from a variety of factors: labor is rented and thus can be discharged when no longer needed (forcing maintenance costs onto workers or communities); market imperfections, such as worker immobility and poor job information, lead to market underpricing of workplace disamenities and hazards; and wages are pushed down below social cost by competition of the unemployed who are willing to work for wages that cover only day-to-day marginal cost. A rationale for an MW law is to prevent this kind of cost shifting and social subsidy by making firms pay the full long-run unit cost of labor. Of course, when forced to pay a higher wage, some firms may cut back employment but this loss of jobs, though regrettable, is in the interest of social efficiency and welfare, just as is loss of jobs from forcing firms to pay the full cost of environmental damage.

A Barrier to Destructive Competition

Orthodox economic theory evaluates a minimum wage through the theory lens of a competitive labor market, represented by the well-known demand-supply (DS) diagram, and reaches a negative conclusion because the MW distorts prices, reduces employment, and misallocates resources. The thrust of the institutional argument is that labor markets do not work this way in either theory or fact, such as for the bargaining disadvantage and social cost reasons just described, and the MW verdict may therefore shift from negative to neutral or positive.

Another justification for an MW is that flexible wage rates in labor markets do not automatically restore equilibrium as the DS model predicts, particularly in response to a negative demand shock, such as a stock market collapse or financial crisis. Rather, in a recession situation, once wage rates start to fall they lead to an economic implosion and deflationary race to the bottom. Wage cuts not only lower cost of production for firms (a plus for job creation) but also reduce household income and consumption spending (a minus for job creation). A result is that the aggregate labor market cannot regain an equilibrium—let alone a full employment equilibrium—because wage cuts cause demand and supply curves to spiral downward much as a dog chasing its tail. This disequilibrium story is a central part of Keynes's economics but was earlier anticipated by several labor institutionalists. A rationale for an MW, therefore, is that it creates a floor in labor markets and stops competition from turning into a destructive force that bankrupts firms and families. The fact that the FLSA was enacted in 1938 owes much to the destructive competition experience of the preceding decade.

Rising Income Inequality and Underconsumption

Enactment of the FLSA in 1938 also got a big push from another macroeconomic MW rationale developed by institutional economists, particularly the Webbs and Hobson. They argue a free-market economy has a built-in tendency to generate rising income inequality. With economic growth, demand curves for labor shift to the right but the wage rate for middle-to-lower class people only modestly increases because their labor supply curve is highly elastic. Since this group of the workforce saves little and spends most of its income on consumption, they are the principal force behind aggregate demand. Households at the top end of the income distribution, on the other hand, have relatively inelastic labor supply curves, and their wages substantially rise with economic growth. A significant share of their income, in turn, goes into saving, which expands capital investment and the economy's supply side.

The predicted secular trend, therefore, is growing maldistribution of income and wealth with slowdown in aggregate demand and stimulus to aggregate supply. Manifestations of the demand-supply imbalance are that wages lag behind productivity growth, the ratio of executive pay to production workers' pay climbs, and labor's income share falls and capital's share rises. The economy suffers from growing overproduction/underconsumption and susceptibility to collapse, such as when financial asset bubbles burst. The policy rationale for an MW, and a rise in the MW over time, is that it helps prop up the wage share of national income and keeps wages growing in line with productivity growth, thus helping maintain shared prosperity and demand-supply balance. Looked at it from an institutional perspective, both the destructive competition and income inequality functions of an MW maintain and expand the number of jobs, interpretable as a positive employment effect.

References

Commons, John and John Andrews. 1936. *Principles of Labor Legislation*, 4th ed. New York: Harper.

Ely, Richard. 1884. *The Past and Present of Political Economy*. Baltimore, MD: Johns Hopkins University.

Kaufman, Bruce. 2009. "Promoting Labor Market Efficiency and Fairness through a Legal Minimum Wage: The Webbs and the Social Cost of Labor." *British Journal of Industrial Relations*. 47, 2: 306–326.

Kaufman, Bruce. 2010. "Institutional Economics and the Minimum Wage: Broadening the Theoretical and Policy Debate." *Industrial and Labor Relations Review*. 63, 3: 427–453.

Kaufman, Bruce. 2012. "Wage Theory, New Deal Labor Policy, and the Great Depression: Were Government and Unions to Blame?" *Industrial and Labor Relations Review*. 65, 3: 501–532.

Bruce E. Kaufman is professor of economics in the Andrew Young School of Policy Studies at Georgia State University (Atlanta, USA). He is also a research fellow with the Centre for Work, Organization and Wellbeing at Griffith University (Brisbane AU) and, in addition, a visiting professor at Capital University of Economics and Finance (Beijing CH) and the University of Loughborough (Loughborough, UK). Professor Kaufman publishes across the disciplinary areas of the employment relationship, including labor economics, human resource management, industrial relations, labor and employment law, and business and labor history. Professor Kaufman has written or edited 18 books and over 100 journal articles and chapters.

Minimum Wages and Living Wages
Stephanie Luce

The federal minimum wage was established in 1938 as part of the Fair Labor Standards Act. A few states had begun enacting their own state minimum wages as early as the Massachusetts law in 1912, but there had been no consensus regarding a methodology or formula for setting the wage floor. The initial federal wage was set at 25 cents per hour, with no particular rationale for the rate and no provision for adjustment with inflation.

The term and concept of a "living wage" had already been in existence for many decades before then. (Stabile [2009] shows that the concept can be traced as far back as Plato and Aristotle.) While definitions vary, theorists and philosophers wrote of the need for workers to earn a wage sufficient to cover their basic expenses and to reproduce themselves and the future labor force. For some this was a moral argument about fairness, such as with Pope Leo XIII who in 1891 wrote in the *Rerum Novarum* that employers had a responsibility to pay a fair wage that was at least a living wage. In other cases, the argument was based on economic principles and the notion that workers needed to be able to sustain their labor power. The ILO Constitution, adopted in 1919, calls for workers to be paid a living wage, and in 1948, the United Nations adopted the Universal Declaration of Human Rights, which embraced the concept of a living wage in Article 23, which states, "Everyone who works has the right to just and favourable remuneration ensuring for himself and his family an existence worthy of human dignity, and supplemented, if necessary, by other means of social protection" (United Nations, 1948).

At least four countries have adopted the principle of a living wage in their national constitution: Mexico, India, Brazil, and Namibia (Anker 2011). Scholars and the ILO have been working to develop a common methodology for establishing a living wage but to date, no consensus exists, and the relationship between a "living wage" and minimum wage varies greatly by country.

In the United States, the modern "living wage" movement emerged in 1994, when a group of activists used the term to call on the city of Baltimore to find a way to raise wages for low-wage workers. At that time, the federal minimum wage was $4.25 per hour, and activists argued that workers should be paid at least the hourly wage necessary for a worker with a family of four to meet the federal poverty line. The federal government sets a poverty threshold every year, varying by family size and type, though not varying by geography. Most experts agree that the formula used for this is outdated and underestimates the actual income required to subsist in most parts of the country. Still, even with the outdated formula, the poverty threshold rate, converted to an hourly figure, was much higher than the minimum wage.

In the United States, states are allowed to set their own minimum wage rates but only cities in "home rule states" are allowed to do so. Baltimore is not such a city, and so it was not able to set a citywide wage. Instead, activists were eventually able to get the city to pass a "living wage ordinance" that mandated the employers receiving city contracts pay their workers a wage high enough to meet the federal poverty line. This idea spread throughout the country, and by the early 2000s, over 100 cities and counties had passed a version of a living wage ordinance. The ordinances varied in terms of which employers were covered, the wage levels, and other provisions, but most many set the higher wage for firms holding city service contracts, and some covered firms receiving economic development subsidies. Many ordinances included provisions for automatic indexing. Most also required employers to pay the base rate and provide health insurance, or to pay a higher wage without health insurance.

After awhile, activists were able to pass citywide living wage legislation in a handful of cities, and were successful in pressuring over 30 states to increase their state minimum wage, and, in some cases, to add in indexing.

Table 3.1 Comparison of Wage Rates for Selected Cities

	Boston, MA	New York, NY	San Francisco, CA	SeaTac, WA
Minimum wage[a]	$9 (up to $11 on 1/1/2017)	$8.75 (up to $9 by 12/31/2015).	$10.74 (up to $15 by 2018)	$15
Poverty Threshold, family of four[b]	$11.36	$11.36	$11.36	$11.36
City Living Wage ordinance rate	$13.89	$11.50 with health benefits, or 13.13 without	Same as minimum wage	Not applicable
Living Wage[c]	$22.40	$22.32	$25.44	$19.63

[a] Minimum wages for Boston and New York City set by state laws. Minimum wage in San Francisco and SeaTac are set by the city.
[b] Poverty thresholds are set by the U.S. Census. The rates are for 2013, family of four with two children. The Census provides an annual amount. To get an hourly wage, I divided by 2,080 hours of work.
[c] The rates are for a family of four (two adults and two children), and are from the MIT Living Wage calculator, http://livingwage.mit.edu/.

In 2012, after Occupy Wall Street and fast-food worker strikes helped raise a focus on inequality and low wages, activists launched more expansive campaigns to set citywide wages in more cities, and at much higher rates. In 2012 through 2014, 18 cities and counties passed municipal-wide minimum wages, ranging from $8.60 in Albuquerque, New Mexico, to $15 in Seattle and San Francisco. This activity has begun to narrow the gap between a minimum wage and a living wage.

Still, even with higher rates and indexing, the wages won are not high enough for a worker with a family to meet the basic costs of living. Table 3.1 shows an example of the wage levels in a few select cities.

Living Wage Research

Living wage opponents argue that such ordinances will result in job loss, higher costs for cities translated into higher taxes, and have a negative impact on firms' decisions to stay or move to the city. Some also argue that the ordinances will result in labor-labor substitution, causing employers to hire more educated or better-off workers to the detriment of disadvantaged workers.

To date, the majority of living wage research shows that the opponents' claims are unfounded. The research on living wage impact is not nearly as extensive as that found on minimum wage. Many living wage ordinances are small and cover few workers, and others have not been implemented or only weakly enforced, making it difficult to study their impact on firms and workers. However, a handful of studies by academics and city staff exist. These include employer and worker surveys, as well as contract evaluations and interviews with city staff in, at least, Baltimore, Boston, Cleveland, Detroit, Hartford, Los Angeles, New Haven, San Diego, and the San Francisco airports. They include prospective studies that attempt to estimate the impact of ordinances, and retrospective studies post enactment. I will focus only on retrospective studies here. [See studies by Brenner (2005); Brenner and Luce (2005); Elmore (2003); Fairris (2005);

Fairris, Runstein, Briones, and Goodheart (2005); Howes (2002); Howes (2005); Niedt, Ruiters, Wise, and Schoenberger (1999); Reich, Hall, and Jacobs (2005); Reynolds and Vortkamp (2005); Sander and Lokey (1998); and Williams (2004). Chapman and Thomson (2006) provide an extensive review of living wage impact studies through 2006.]

The studies vary but for the most part find little to no evidence of job loss caused by living wage ordinances. Employers report that with the living wage they experienced lower turnover and absenteeism. On the high end, annual turnover for baggage handlers fell from 95% to 19% at the San Francisco airport (Reich et. al. 2005). A study of Los Angeles estimates that lower turnover rates likely offset the higher living wage costs by approximately 16 percent (Fairris 2005). Most studies found no impact on employment, or little impact—for example, the Los Angeles airport survey suggests that job loss affected 1 percent of covered workers (Fairris 2005). Furthermore, a study of Boston employers found no evidence that employers replaced current workers with a new workforce (Brenner 2005).

Living wage impact studies also find that the wages primarily impact adult workers struggling to meet basic expenses. This suggests that the ordinances are well targeted to benefit the right workers.

A handful of studies evaluate the impact of ordinances on city budgets. For the most part, these have found that costs to the city are less than some predicted. For example, the San Diego City Manager's office predicted that city's ordinance would cost the city more than $3 million in the first year, but a later evaluation by city analysts showed the cost was $1.2 million (Hall 2007). Even living wage opponents Sander and Lokey (1998) found that 18 months after enactment of the Los Angeles law, there was "no significant positive or negative effect on the city's fiscal health or the local economy from the living wage ordinance." Elmore (2003) interviewed city staff and found some positive impacts for cities with a living wage, such as an increase in competitive bidding, which in turn lowered average contract costs.

A few studies conclude that living wage ordinances do cause harm. For example, Neumark (2002) and Adams and Neumark (2005) find that while living wage ordinances appear to alleviate poverty in cities, they result in modest job loss. These studies have been critiqued by Brenner, Wicks-Lim, and Pollin (2002) and Chapman and Thomson (2006). The critics point to several concerns, including the following: First, Neumark and Adams use the Current Population Survey (CPS) to estimate their results, but the CPS sample size is too small in most cities and unlikely capturing the workers and employers covered by the living wage ordinances. Second, Neumark and Adams's results show a particularly large impact from the provisions of the living wage laws that cover economic development assistance recipients. But research by Luce (2004) and others finds that few cities include this component, and even fewer have enforced it. Third, Neumark and Adams truncated their sample, focusing on only low-wage workers, which may have led to sample selection bias. Overall the majority of studies to date find overall net positive outcomes from living wage ordinances.

References

Adams, Scott and David Neumark. 2005. *A Decade of Living Wages: What Have We Learned?* San Francisco: Public Policy Institute of California.

Anker, Richard. 2011. "Estimating a Living Wage: A Methodological Review." *Conditions of Work and Employment Series No. 29.* Geneva: International Labor Organization.

Brenner, Mark D. 2005. "The Economic Impact of the Boston Living Wage Ordinance." *Industrial Relations.* 44, 1: 59–83.

Brenner, Mark D. and Stephanie Luce. 2005. *Living Wage Laws in Practice: The Boston, New Haven and Hartford*

Experiences. Amherst, MA: Political Economy Research Institute.

Brenner, Mark, Jeannette Wicks-Lim, and Robert Pollin. 2002. "Measuring the Impact of Living Wage Laws: A Critical Appraisal of David Neumark's How Living Wage Laws Affect Low Wage Workers and Low-Income Families." *Working Paper No. 43*. Amherst, MA: Political Economy Research Institute.

Chapman, Jeff and Jeff Thompson. 2006. "The Economic Impact of Local Living Wages." *Briefing Paper 170*. Washington, DC: Economic Policy Institute.

Elmore, Andrew J. 2003. *Living Wage Laws & Communities: Smarter Economic Development, Lower Than Expected Costs*. New York: Brennan Center for Justice.

Employment Policies Institute. 1998. *The Baltimore Living Wage Study: Omissions, Fabrications and Flaws*. Washington, DC: Employment Policies Institute.

Fairris, David. 2005. "The Impact of Living Wages on Employers: A Control Group Analysis of the Los Angeles Ordinance." *Industrial Relations*. 44, 1: 84–105.

Fairris, David, David Runstein, Carolina Briones, and Jessica Goodheart. 2005. *The Los Angeles Living Wage Ordinance: Effects on Workers and Employers*. Los Angeles: Los Angeles Alliance for a New Economy.

Hall, Matthew T. 2007. "Wage Law Costs Less Than Some Predicted." *Union Tribune*. October 21.

Howes, Candace. 2002. "The Impact of a Large Wage Increase on the Workforce Stability of IHSS Home Care Workers in San Francisco County." *Working Paper*. New London, CT: Department of Economics, Connecticut College.

Howes, Candace. 2005. "Living Wages and Retention of Homecare Workers in San Francisco." *Industrial Relations*. 44, 1: 139–163.

Luce, Stephanie. 2004. *Fighting for a Living Wage*. Ithaca, NY: Cornell University Press.

Luce, Stephanie. 2005. "The Role of Community Involvement in Implementing Living Wage Ordinances." *Industrial Relations*. 44, 1: 32–58.

Neumark, David. 2002. *How Living Wage Laws Affect Low-Wage Workers and Low-Income Families*. San Francisco: Public Policy Institute of California.

Niedt, Christopher, Greg Ruiters, Dana Wise, and Erica Schoenberger. 1999. "The Effects of the Living Wage in Baltimore." *Working Paper No. 199*. Washington, DC: Economic Policy Institute.

Reich, Michael, Peter Hall, and Ken Jacobs. 2005. "Living Wage Policies at the San Francisco Airport: Impacts on Workers and Businesses." *Industrial Relations*. 44, 1: 106–138.

Reynolds, David and Jean Vortkamp. 2005. "The Effects of Detroit's Living Wage Law on Nonprofit Organizations." *Economic Development Quarterly*. 19, 1: 45–61.

Sander, Richard and Sean Lokey. 1998. *The Los Angeles Living Wage: The First Eighteen Months*. Norcross, GA: The Fair Housing Institute.

Stabile, Donald R. 2009. *The Living Wage: Lessons from the History of Economic Thought*. Brookfield, VT: Edward Elgar.

United Nations. 1948. Universal Declaration of Human Rights (Article 23). Available online at http://www.un.org/en/documents/udhr/index.shtml#a23.

Williams, Dana. 2004. *Cleveland's Living Wage Law: A Three-Year Review*. Cleveland: Policy Matters Ohio.

Stephanie Luce, professor of labor studies at the Joseph S. Murphy Institute for Worker Education at SPS, received her B.A. at the University of California, Davis, and both her Ph.D. in sociology and her M.A. in industrial relations from the University of

Wisconsin at Madison. Best known for her research on living wage campaigns and movements, she is the author of Fighting for a Living Wage, *and coauthor of* The Living Wage: Building a Fair Economy, and The Measure of Fairness. *Her current research focuses on globalization and labor standards, labor-community coalitions, and regional labor markets. Her most recent book,* Labor Movements: Global Perspectives, *was published in 2014 by Polity Press.*

Minimum Wage: Good Intentions and Bad Results
Antony Davies

Those rightly concerned with helping the working poor naturally turn to wage controls as a tool for boosting workers' incomes. The claim that raising the minimum wage helps the working poor appears obviously true. In fact, the claim relies on four economic fallacies that, together, cause the minimum wage to hurt the very people it is intended to help.

First, minimum wage proponents get the causality of wages backward. A market price, of which a wage is one example, reflects the value of the underlying good or service. A worker with a particular skill set, experience, education, and work ethic can provide value to an employer. The employer who hires the worker produces a product that the employer sells to consumers. The more consumers value the employer's product, the more they will be willing to pay to obtain the product. The more consumers are willing to pay to obtain the product, the more the employer will be willing to pay to hire the workers who can produce the product. Increasing the minimum wage does not increase the value the consumer places on the product the worker produces. But it does increase the cost of employing the worker. The effect is to reduce the value of the minimum wage worker to the employer. A counterargument is that employers would like to pay their workers as little as possible, and that a minimum wage ensures that the employer will not be allowed to pay virtually zero. Yet, the data refute this counterargument. If the counterargument were true, then all employers would pay exactly the minimum wage, as there is no law requiring employers to pay more than the minimum. But this is not what we observe. In the United States, over 97% of workers earn more than the minimum wage (Bureau of Labor Statistics, 2013a). In 2013, the median wage in the United States was $16.87 per hour, meaning that more than half of U.S. workers were earning more than twice the minimum wage (Bureau of Labor Statistics, 2013b).

Second, minimum wage proponents claim that many employers can afford to pay the increased wage. Even if true, whether the employer is willing to pay an increased wage has less to do with what the employer can afford than it does with the value of the worker's labor and the difficulty of replacing the worker. Certainly major fast-food chains can afford to pay their workers more. But the managerial question is not whether the money exists to pay the workers more, but whether the money is best spent paying the workers more or paying for something else instead.

The recent trend of replacing cashiers in supermarkets and fast-food restaurants with machinery is an example. At $5 per hour, cashiers were less expensive than automated checkout machines. As the minimum wage rose to $7.25 per hour, supermarkets started to replace cashiers with machines. A counterargument is that the reason supermarkets added automated checkout machines was simply to speed up processing. But, supermarkets could also have sped up processing by adding more cashiers. What's noteworthy is that they chose to add machines. The increased minimum wage made the machines the lower-cost alternative. Similarly, as politicians push for a $10 per hour minimum wage, fast-food restaurants are experimenting with touchscreen consoles that will replace workers who take food orders. When the employer could obtain labor for $7.25 per hour, the touchscreen consoles were not cost-effective. But when labor costs $10 per hour, the touchscreen consoles become the lower-cost alternative. The minimum wage workers lose their jobs not because the employer can't afford them but because, by comparison, the machines have become the better investment.

Throughout, the issue is not whether the employer can pay the increased price but whether the employer is better off paying the increased price or paying for something else instead. Note that this choice is identical to the choice consumers face when deciding how to spend their money. Hybrid cars are more expensive than comparable gasoline-powered cars. The question a car buyer faces often isn't whether he can afford the more expensive hybrid, but whether he would rather buy a less expensive gasoline-powered car and spend the saved money on something else. As the price of gas rises, the hybrid becomes the more attractive choice. As the minimum wage rises, machines become the more attractive choice.

Third, minimum wage proponents often treat workers as homogeneous. There is no single "market for labor." There are many markets for labor. There is a market for unskilled labor, a market for skilled labor, a market-educated labor, a market for experienced labor, and markets for each type and combination of skill, education, and experience. But the minimum wage cuts across all these labor markets as if they were one. The result is that the minimum wage has quantitatively different effects in different labor markets. Increasing the minimum wage has little effect on employment in markets for experienced, skilled, and educated labor—high-productivity labor—because the wage rates in those markets are usually much higher than the minimum. But the minimum wage has a significant effect on employment in unskilled labor markets. Because higher productivity workers can do everything lower-productivity workers can do, plus more, competition for jobs across the two markets is not symmetric. If he had to, the engineer could compete with the janitor for the janitor's job, but the janitor cannot compete with the engineer for the engineer's job. The higher the minimum wage goes, the more costly workers become and so the less incentive employers have to hire workers. Because high-productivity workers can do everything low-productivity workers can do, plus more, the majority of the unemployment effects fall on the low-productivity workers.

The unemployment effects of the minimum wage across different labor markets are shown in Figure 3.1. The figure shows, for 1975 through 2012, unemployment among workers of various educational backgrounds compared to the relative minimum wage (the minimum wage as a fraction of the average hourly wage). Changes in the minimum wage appear to have no effect on unemployment among college-educated workers. An increased minimum wage is associated with a little more unemployment among high school–educated workers, much more unemployment among workers without high school diplomas, and more unemployment still among young workers without high school diplomas.

Fourth, minimum wage proponents often portray minimum wage jobs as dead ends. The argument is that low-productivity

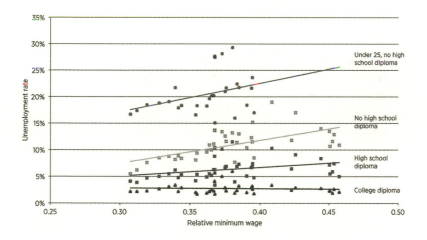

Figure 3.1 Minimum wage (relative to the average hourly wage) as compared to the unemployment rates for workers with different levels of education (1975–2012; data for workers under 25 with no high school diploma, 1985–2012). (Davies, A., 2013. *Unintended Consequences of Raising the Minimum Wage*, Mercatus Research.)

workers can't acquire education and training because, at the minimum wage, they have to devote all their time to working just to stay alive. If only they could earn more, they could afford to devote some time to acquiring valuable skills. But this argument ignores the fact the minimum wage job itself increases the value of the worker's labor. Simply by establishing a track record of showing up for work and performing the job's tasks, the worker increases the value of his labor. This is borne out in the data. Of workers who start out working for the minimum wage, almost 50% end up earning more than the minimum wage within one year. Within three years, 97% are earning more than the minimum wage (Carrington and Fallick, 2001). Certainly, there are some workers who are perpetually stuck in minimum wage jobs. But those workers are a very small minority. For almost all workers, the minimum wage job is a stepping-stone from which the worker gains experience that increases the value of his labor and the wage his labor commands in the market. Conversely, raising the minimum wage makes the worker more expensive and so discourages employers from giving that first chance at a job to untried workers. In a very real sense, the minimum wage removes the first rungs in the income ladder the worker will spend his career climbing.

Yet, the minimum wage is not entirely bad. The minimum wage helps some workers. Because workers with more skills and experience are more valuable to employers, as the minimum wage rises, employers will tend to lay off less skilled and less experienced workers and use the cost savings to pay the increased wage to the more skilled and experienced workers. In the end, the minimum wage does not help workers at the expense of employers but helps more productive workers at the expense of less productive workers.

References

Bureau of Labor Statistics. 2013a. Characteristics of Minimum Wage Workers: 2013, US Department of Labor. (www.bls .gov/cps/minwage2013.pdf)

Bureau of Labor Statistics. 2013b. May 2013 National Occupational Employment and Wage Estimates United States, Occupational Employment Statistics, US Department of Labor. (www.bls.gov/oes/current/oes_nat.htm)

Carrington, W. J. and B. C. Fallick, 2001. "Do Some Workers Have Minimum Wage Careers?" *Monthly Labor Review*, May. (www.bls.gov/opub/mlr/2001/05/art2full.pdf)

Antony Davies is associate professor of economics at Duquesne University and Mercatus Affiliated Senior Scholar at George Mason University. His primary research interests include econometrics and public policy. Davies has authored over 100 op-eds in over 30 newspapers, including the Wall Street Journal, Los Angeles Times, New York Daily News, *and* Philadelphia Inquirer, *and is a regular columnist for the* Pittsburgh Tribune-Review. *He is a frequent lecturer at policy conferences on Capitol Hill. In addition to teaching at the undergraduate, masters, and Ph.D. levels, Dr. Davies was chief financial officer at Parabon Computation, president and cofounder of Paragon Software (now Take-Two Interactive), and cofounder and chief analytics officer at Repliqa (now indiePub Games). Dr. Davies earned his B.S. in economics from Saint Vincent College, and Ph.D. in economics from the State University of New York at Albany.*

Policymakers Should Exercise Maximum Caution on the Minimum Wage
Michael Saltsman

Economics may not be the oldest profession, but the minimum wage is surely one of the longest-studied topics in the discipline.

Researchers have been theorizing about the effects of minimum wage since before the federal minimum wage was even established in 1938 by the Fair Labor Standards Act. Today, the wage floor is as much a political flashpoint as it is an empirical one, with candidates for office using their support for raising it as a campaign platform.

Both proponents and opponents of a minimum wage increase share the same goal: reducing poverty. The question, then, is whether a higher minimum wage is the best means to achieve it. After decades of empirical research and much debate, the answer to that question is a resounding "no."

Admittedly, it seems counterintuitive: Requiring a higher hourly wage for employees living in poverty should leave them better off than they were before. But this strategy runs into problems early on, starting with the employment status of impoverished Americans. According to data from the U.S. Census Bureau, nearly 60 percent of working-age adults in poverty aren't working. That means a minimum wage of $10.10 or even $15 won't benefit them—it just makes them more expensive for a prospective employer to hire.

Among those who would be affected by a minimum wage increase, the targeting isn't much better. For example, consider the $10.10 federal minimum wage supported by President Obama: Data from the CPS shows that the average family income of a beneficiary is nearly $55,000 per year. That's because less than 10 percent of beneficiaries are single parents supporting children. By contrast, 60 percent of the affected employees are either dual-earners in a married couple, or they're living at home with family or relatives.

It wasn't always this way: In 1939, 85 percent of low-wage employees lived in a poor household. (In other words, there was a relatively direct relationship between earning a low wage and living in an impoverished household.) Over time, this relationship has changed dramatically, as more low-wage earners were second- or third-earners in households far above the poverty line. By 2003, economists Richard Burkhauser (Cornell University) and Joseph Sabia (University of Georgia) found that just 17 percent of low-wage earners lived in poor households.

These facts—on who lives in poverty, who earns the minimum wage, and what kind of household they live in—help explain why past attempts to use a mandated wage increase to reduce poverty levels have fallen short. Economists from Cornell University and American University, writing in a study published in the *Southern Economic Journal*, found no associated reduction in poverty in the 28 states that raised their minimum wages between 2003 and 2007.

If poor targeting were the only problem with a higher minimum wage, it might still be worth pursuing as one of many policy options to reduce poverty. But there are unintended consequences of a minimum wage increase that policymakers also need to keep in mind—the loss of entry-level jobs being the foremost among them.

The business argument is straightforward: If a labor-intensive business with small profit margins (e.g., a restaurant or grocery store) is presented with higher mandated wages costs, they have to find a way to offset it in order to maintain their relatively small profit per employee. Some businesses may be able to raise prices on their customers without too harmful a drop in sales.

But other employers, facing a price-sensitive customer base, aren't so lucky. Instead of raising prices, they have to provide the same product or service, by investing in business model changes to where the customer serves themselves. (If you've ever checked out your own groceries at a supermarket or pumped your own gas, you've experienced this trend firsthand.)

Some advocates for a higher minimum wage deny that these impacts exist, or suggest that the benefits of a wage mandate offset the costs. And indeed, the question of minimum wages and their impact on employment has been fiercely debated. But two separate neutral reviews of the economic literature—one from economists at the University of California-Irvine and the Federal Reserve Board, another from the nonpartisan Congressional Budget Office (CBO)—conclude that a minimum wage increase does indeed reduce job opportunities. In the case of a $10.10 federal minimum wage, the CBO's mid-range estimate was that a half-million jobs would be eliminated.

The job losses aren't equally distributed—rather, they tend to affect younger, less-educated, and lower skilled job seekers. (The magnitude of the measured job loss varies based on the time and place, but one "consensus" range places the impact at a 1 to 4 percent drop in employment for affected youth following each 10 percent minimum wage increase.)

Research suggests that policymakers can't afford to dismiss these lost opportunities as acceptable collateral damage: Economists at the University of Virginia and Middle Tennessee State University found that high school students who worked part time during their senior year had higher wages than their unemployed peers six to nine years after graduation.

These young people, along with other minimum wage earners, aren't waiting on the government to give them a raise. Economists from Miami and Trinity University found that two-thirds of minimum wage earners receive a raise within one to twelve months on the job. (A subsequent study from a separate team of economists confirmed these results.)

Yet neither these market-driven wages nor the immense shortcomings of the U.S. minimum wage policy have stopped legislators from pursuing them. Better alternatives for poverty reduction are necessary—and indeed, they already exist. The earned income tax credit (EITC), for instance, is a refundable federal tax credit that boosts employees' wage through the tax code rather than a mandate on employers. (Twenty-five states and Washington, DC, have their own supplement to the federal credit.) Thanks to these credits, the minimum wage for a single parent with two children is already above $9 or even $10 an hour depending on the state.

True, a campaign to expand a tax credit doesn't work nearly as well at a campaign rally. But unlike a higher minimum wage, it will provide tangible benefits to those families that are truly in need of help, instead of just sounding good.

Michael Saltsman is the research director at the Employment Policies Institute (EPI), where he manages the institute's work on public policies that impact the entry-level job market. His writing and research have appeared in the New York Times, Wall Street Journal, *and* Washington Post, *among other publications, and he's been a guest on numerous national television and radio programs. Prior to his work at EPI, Saltsman worked as a field economist for the Bureau of Labor Statistics. He has degrees in Economics and Political Science from the University of Michigan.*

A Strong National Wage Floor Is Essential to Protecting Workers, Fighting Inequality, and Maintaining a Growing U.S. Economy
David Cooper

In the debate preceding passage of the Fair Labor Standards Act, the law that established the federal minimum wage in 1938, President Roosevelt declared, "No business which depends for existence on paying less than living wages to its workers has any right to continue in this country." It was a populist sentiment born out of the horrendous working conditions of that time: Americans, facing limited options in the wake of the Great Depression, toiled for long hours in factories and sweatshops for wages impossible to live on. Those dire conditions made clear the need to set standards that would protect workers against exploitation, including a minimum wage that set a strong national wage floor. That need has not diminished. If anything, years of neglect have shown that a rising wage floor is essential to improving living standards and maintaining the health of the national economy.

The minimum wage is a labor standard in the same way that we have labor standards prohibiting child labor, setting the number of hours in a normal workweek, and establishing safe working conditions. It ensures that no matter an individual's personal circumstances, the nature of the job, or the overall macroeconomic conditions, someone willing and able to work must be paid at least a reasonable amount for each hour of labor. Society may debate what constitutes a "reasonable amount," but clearly the creators of the law thought that the minimum wage should be high enough that someone working a regular job at that wage could live off his or her earnings. It is hard to believe that today's minimum wage would meet that standard; at $7.25 it is so low that someone working full time, year-round at the minimum wage falls below the federal poverty line if they have just one child.

This need to set a basic standard of pay comes from the fundamental imbalance, in any employment situation, in bargaining power between the employer and employees. Periods of economic distress and high unemployment exacerbate that imbalance, leaving workers with little bargaining power to demand decent pay. Even under more stable economic conditions, this lack of bargaining power is acute in low-skill, low-wage industries whose workers likely have fewer job options. Traditionally, unions counteracted some of this imbalance. But as collective bargaining has all but disappeared over the past half century, policies like the minimum wage have become all the more important—not only as a backstop for preventing exploitive working conditions but also as the only foreseeable means of making improvements in job quality and raising living standards.

Through regular increases, a rising minimum wage also helps ensure that the benefits of economic growth and technological progress are broadly shared. From the time of its inception until roughly the early 1970s, the minimum wage was increased at roughly the same rate as growth in overall labor productivity. In other words, as workers' ability to generate goods and services for their employers increased, so did the minimum amount that society deemed should be paid to workers for each hour of work. Yet beginning in the 1970s, increases to the minimum wage became smaller and less frequent, such that the real value of the wage floor began to erode even as productivity continued to rise. Adjusting for inflation, the minimum wage at its high point in 1968 was equal to roughly $9.50 in 2014 dollars.[1] Thus, today's minimum wage workers, earning $7.25 per hour, are paid 24 percent less than their counterparts over

45 years ago—despite being older and having higher levels of education on average than workers at that time.

In fact, average labor productivity in the United States has more than doubled since the late 1960s. Had the minimum wage been raised in line with productivity since 1968, it would have been about $19 per hour in 2014. Some may argue that productivity for low-wage work has not gone up as much as average overall U.S. productivity. While that is true, it does not negate the underlying purpose of the minimum wage as a lever against rising inequality. For example, barbers today cannot cut significantly more hair than they could 100 years ago, yet most would likely agree that barbers today should be paid more than they did in the previous century. If we believe that the benefits of economic growth and technological progress should improve the living conditions of all workers, then we need to have mechanisms to ensure rising wages for all.

The minimum wage is a critical piece of this effort. The failure to adequately raise the minimum wage since the 1970s has been a key contributor to the growth in wage and income inequality since that time. The gap between wages for workers at the 10th percentile (i.e., workers earning more than 10 percent of all workers but less than 90 percent) and wages for workers at the median (those earning more than half of all workers but less than half) grew by 25 percent between 1979 and 2014. Research has shown that between one-half and two-thirds of that increase can be attributed entirely to the declining value of the minimum wage (see Mishel 2013).

What this means is that we have let workers at the bottom fall further and further away from those at the middle. In 1968, the minimum wage was equal to 55 percent of the median wage. The minimum wage in 2014 was worth only 37 percent of the median wage (Cooper, 2013). This is the furthest from the median that the federal minimum wage has ever been, and it puts the United States in the dubious place of having the third-lowest minimum-to-median ratio of all modern developed countries.

This erosion in the wage floor has consequences for the broad middle class. First, the minimum wage is the foundation upon which the entire wage structure is built—if that foundation is left to erode, over time the entire structure is weakened. Indeed, government data show that hourly wages for the vast majority of American workers—the bottom 70 percent of wage earners—were essentially stagnant from 1979 to 2013, despite large improvements in labor productivity over that time (see Bivens et al., 2014). Policies beyond the minimum wage facilitated this problem, but the lack of a rising wage floor certainly contributed to it. Second, business owners may generate extra profit by paying wages too low to live on, but often at the expense of taxpayers, as low-wage workers turn to public assistance to supplement their inadequate earnings. Roughly half of workers in the bottom-fifth of the wage distribution rely on some form of public assistance (see Cooper, 2014). We need strong safety-net programs to protect individuals and families from undue material hardship, but without a rising wage floor to ensure that businesses are paying decent wages, these programs serve as taxpayer subsidies to profitable companies that can afford to pay more.

Finally, a growing body of evidence suggests that countries with higher levels of inequality experience slower rates of growth. There is an intuitive sense to this: If a growing share of the population cannot afford to buy basic necessities, then consumer demand falls and overall growth slows down. In the United States, consumer spending accounts for about 70 percent of the economy. For a growing and stable economy, we need a base of consumers with rising incomes who can purchase goods without relying on public aid or consumer credit. Regularly raising the wage floor helps keep this virtuous cycle in motion.

For all our growth and technological improvements since the 1960s, there is no reason that workers today should be paid less than workers a generation ago, but they are, and our country suffers for it. As the United States once again faces levels of inequality not seen since the eve of the Great Depression, policymakers need to remember the lessons learned from that era and restore the basic labor protections that ensured decent wages, enabled broadly shared prosperity, and created a thriving middle class.

References

Bivens, et al. 2014. *Raising America's Pay: Why It's Our Central Economic Policy Challenge*. Economic Policy Institute Briefing Paper #378. http://www.epi.org/publication/ raising-americas-pay/.

Cooper, David. 2013. *Raising the Federal Minimum Wage to $10.10 Would Lift Wages for Millions and Provide a Modest Economic Boost*. Economic Policy Institute Briefing Paper #371. http://www.epi.org/publication/ raising-federal-minimum-wage-to-1010/.

Cooper, David. 2014. *Raising the Federal Minimum Wage to $10.10 Would Save Safety Net Programs Billions and Help Ensure Businesses Are Doing Their Fair Share*. Economic Policy Institute Issue Brief #387. http://www.epi.org/ publication/safety-net-savings-from-raising- minimum-wage/.

Mishel, Lawrence. 2013. *Declining Value of the Federal Minimum Wage Is a Major Factor Driving Inequality*. Economic Policy Institute Issue Brief #351. http:// www.epi.org/publication/declining-federal-minimum- wage-inequality/.

David Cooper is a senior economic analyst at the Economic Policy Institute, a nonprofit, nonpartisan research organization in Washington, D.C. He conducts national and state-level research on a variety of issues, including the minimum wage, employment and unemployment, poverty, and wage and income trends. He also coordinates and provides technical support to the Economic Analysis and Research Network (EARN), a network of state-level research and advocacy organizations. David has been interviewed and cited for his research on the minimum wage, poverty, and U.S. economic trends by numerous local and national media, including the New York Times, *the* Washington Post, *the* Wall Street Journal, *the* Associated Press, USA Today, U.S. News and World Report, *and* NPR. *He holds a Bachelor of Arts and Master of Public Policy from Georgetown University.*

Raising the Minimum Wage Would Help, Not Hurt, Our Economy
David Madland

Raising the minimum wage would be good for our economy. A higher minimum wage not only increases workers' incomes—which is sorely needed to boost demand and get the economy going—but also reduces turnover, cuts food stamps, and pushes businesses toward a high-human-capital model.

Despite these positive benefits, and the sad fact that the minimum wage is worth far less today than it was in the late 1960s, opponents continue to trot out the same unfounded argument that the minimum wage reduces employment. The evidence, however, is clear: Raising the minimum wage does not have the harmful effects that critics claim. A significant body of academic research finds that raising the minimum wage does not result in job losses, even during periods of economic weakness.

Critics of the minimum wage, however, often hold on to the claim that raising the minimum wage will lead to significant job losses and ultimately hurt the overall economy. The argument that raising the minimum wage will increase unemployment is somewhat far-fetched, since the minimum wage impacts a relatively small share of the overall workforce, which is itself concentrated in certain industries such as restaurants and demographic groups such as teenagers. Still, political opponents of the minimum wage often make such claims, so it is important to rebut them.

To see how little effect the minimum wage has on overall employment levels, I reviewed more than two decades' worth of minimum wage increases in U.S. states from 1987 through 2012 and examined unemployment rates one year later. I found no evidence that the minimum wage impacts aggregate job creation. Indeed, the majority of states that raised the minimum wage actually saw a decrease in their unemployment rate over the next year and also saw their unemployment rate fare better than the national average.

Researchers at Goldman Sachs as well as the Center for Economic and Policy Research performed similar analysis of state minimum wage increases and came to similar results: states that raised the minimum wage had faster employment growth compared to states that didn't raise their minimum wage.

While these kinds of comparisons of what happens to unemployment and aggregate employment after a minimum wage increase are far too simplistic to prove the minimum wage is good for employment, they do indicate that claims of significant harm are wildly off the mark. They also suggest instead that one must dig deeper to look for the real causal effects of the minimum wage.

To understand the effects of the minimum wage, it is important to understand that there are wide regional variations in economic trends across states. These regional growth differentials are unrelated to minimum wage policy and are driven rather by deeper structural forces, including decades-long industrial restructuring processes and divergent population trends, to name a few—all of which may obscure the impact of minimum wage changes.

Fortunately, there are at least five different academic papers that utilize a research design that controls for precisely such regional trends. Specifically, these papers collectively find that an increase in the minimum wage has no significant effect on employment levels. These five academic studies also cover different geographical areas and different time periods, and use a range of methodologies—from small case studies to large econometric analysis—lending great credibility to their findings. In addition, they focus on highly impacted groups such as restaurant workers and/or teenagers, where minimum wage increases actually result in wage increases and where we might actually observe some impact. Furthermore, these academic studies are considered significant improvements over previous studies because of the methodologies employed. Specifically, these studies accurately control for confounding regional trends by either controlling for heterogeneous trends across Census or examining all U.S. counties along state borders that had different minimum wages. This research design combines the detailed analysis possible in case studies with the generalizability of a nationally representative sample. In short, a number of the highest-quality academic studies find that raising the minimum wage had no effect on employment levels.

Certainly, there are some academic studies that find increases in the minimum wage reduce employment among certain groups, such as teenagers or restaurant employees. But, generally academic studies find no or only minimal employment effects. Not surprisingly, over 600 economists—including eight Nobel Prize winners—recently signed a letter in support of an increase in the federal minimum wage, arguing: "In recent years there have been important developments in the academic literature on the effect of increases in the minimum wage on employment, with the weight of evidence now showing that increases in the minimum wage have had little or no negative effect on the employment of minimum wage workers, even during times of weakness in the labor market."

The results of these studies should not be surprising because workers are far more complicated than the simplistic economic models that opponents rely on. Workers are not widgets. They are human beings. And human beings benefit from being paid more, while widgets do not. Unlike widgets, workers can spend their wages, work harder and chose to stay with an employer. That's why the research indicates that raising the minimum wage boosts demand, increases worker effort, and reduces turn-over, which can counteract the higher wage costs.

What's more, there may be another factor that comes into play, especially during hard times: economic power. Low-wage workers have very little of it, particularly during periods of high unemployment.

When the economy is doing poorly, employers have less incentive to raise wages, while workers, especially those mak-ing near minimum wage, have little ability to demand a raise because there is a ready supply of unemployed labor available to take their job. Even though these workers likely become more productive—labor productivity has generally increased over time, and productivity growth during the past two reces-sions was especially strong—they have less economic power to share the gains of their increased productivity. This suggests that especially during hard economic times, there is a critical role for government to raise the minimum wage to ensure that workers are being paid for their economic contributions.

In short, policymakers should feel confident that raising the minimum wage would not hurt employment. Instead, it would provide the kind of boost in consumer demand that our economy sorely needs.

David Madland is the Managing Director of the Economic Policy team and the Director of the American Worker Project at American Progress. He has written extensively about the economy and American politics on a range of topics, including the middle class, economic inequality, retirement policy, labor unions, and work-place standards such as the minimum wage. His recent book, Hollowed Out: Why the Economy Doesn't Work without a Strong Middle Class, *was published by the University of California Press in July 2015.*

Madland has appeared frequently on television shows, includ-ing "PBS NewsHour" and CNN's "Crossfire"; has been cited in such publications as the New York Times, *the* Wall Street Jour-nal, *the* Washington Post, *and* The New Yorker; *and has been a guest on dozens of radio talk shows across the United States. He has testified before Congress on a number of occasions, as well as several state legislatures.*

Madland has a doctorate in government from Georgetown University and received his bachelor's degree from the University of California, Berkeley. His dissertation about the decline of the U.S. pension system was honored as the best dissertation of the year by the Labor and Employment Relations Association. Madland is the coauthor of Interest Groups in American Campaigns, *a book about the role and influence of interest groups in American democracy, and is the author of several academic articles. He has worked on economic policy for Rep. George Miller (D-CA) and has consulted for several labor unions.*

Molly Moon's Minimum Wage Perspective
Molly Moon Neitzel

When I first decided to open an ice-cream shop, I knew that one of my goals would be to pay my employees a living wage. So I wrote that decision into my business plan, along with other things that were important to me, like paying 100% of the health insurance premiums for my employees and making sure all my product and packaging was compostable. I had my share of critics; there were plenty of people who said I was crazy, and that I would never be able to make a profit this way.

Seven years later, my company has grown from one shop with seven employees in 2008 to six ice-cream shops, with just under 100 employees during our busiest months. What I've learned is that taking care of my employees and paying a living wage is absolutely the right thing to do, and it's also good business strategy.

In 2013, a small grassroots campaign started in Seattle to increase the local minimum wage to $15 an hour. I joined the effort and worked with local leaders and other business owners to help make this happen. That year I also decided to pay all of my non-tipped employees at least $15 an hour. Our company is currently working to get all of our tipped employees to $15 with increases over the next five years.

Other employees in our company make about $8 an hour in tips, on top of the $11 Seattle minimum wage as of April 1, 2015. We are planning to get all of our employees to $15 an hour within five years, two years sooner than the law requires.

Along the path to a minimum wage increase in Seattle, it became clear to me that a consumer-driven economy can seriously benefit from an increase in low-wage earners' pay. More money in low-wage workers' pockets will result in more money spent in all businesses. It's estimated that 100,000 workers in Seattle are already benefiting from this increase, which also means they will have more money to go out to eat—and to buy ice cream. I predict this increase will ultimately result in more sales for my company. Workers all over Seattle will have more money to spend on things that may have been a rare treat for them previously.

It's also good for my own team. Offering living wages, and generous benefits like free healthcare, paid maternity leave, subsidized bus passes, and paid vacation time helps us recruit top talent, and makes for a more loyal workforce. After raising our back-of-house wages from $11 to $15 in 2013, we saw a significant change in the kind of candidate we can attract. We now hire kitchen employees with pastry degrees from top culinary schools, and the very competitive compensation gives us our pick of candidates. Companywide, our people stay with us much longer than industry average. Our turnover rate is around 24%, while the industry standard in our area is closer to 64%. The savings on replacement and retraining are exciting, and the morale in our company is a palpable excitement to be here.

Having a healthy, robust group of employees has a great impact on our community, and allows Molly Moon's to be an employer that does more than just write paychecks. We recently added maternity and paternity/family leave policies and now offer all employees who have worked at least 500 hours in the previous year 12 weeks of fully paid maternity leave.

We also offer employees who meet this same threshold 12 weeks of 70% paid leave for paternity leave and all other FMLA-qualifying family leave.

Incorporating values into business strategy can also help your marketing plans. I know that, as a customer, I choose to spend money with businesses that share my values and I think my customers do, too. When we announced our new family leave policy via social media, the response was huge. The story reached 25,000 people on Facebook, Twitter, and Instagram, earning more than 800 likes with lots of comments supporting what we're doing and letting us know they are excited to continue to support our business because of this.

And then there's the fact that many people working full time on today's minimum wage aren't able to support themselves. I believe that as a community, we have to be willing to make some changes so that everyone can have a chance to thrive.

But in order for this to work, it's important for business owners to be aware of the additional costs and rewards that come with raising the minimum wage. I know this may cost me more in the short term, with significant increases in payroll. But the investment will yield significant rewards for my workers, community, and my business's bottom line. Not to mention my customers—many of whom will also be getting raises, and celebrating with more trips to the ice-cream shop.

What we're doing here in Seattle is seen as cutting edge, maybe even outside of the mainstream. But I believe the success of the business community here will help influence the hearts and minds of the rest of the country and show other business owners that this is not only the right thing to do but is also great for business. The national minimum wage needs to be raised to give low-wage workers a much-needed boost, and a shot in the arm to our economy.

Molly Moon Neitzel is the owner and CEO of Molly Moon's Homemade Ice Cream. With six ice-cream shops and around 100 employees during the company's busiest months, Molly Moon's has experienced rapid growth since opening in 2008. Neitzel supports a living minimum wage and argues that, in the long run, paying higher wages can decrease costs for business owners and increase sales in a consumer-driven economy.

Minimum Wages and Economic Inequality
Thomas Volscho

At a time of very high inequality, many naturally look to the minimum wage as a potential mechanism for redistributing income. In recent years, the minimum wage rates of the federal and state governments have been supplemented by some cities and other localities who have attempted to pass more radical "living wage" ordinances. These laws stipulate a minimum compensation for labor performed. To the extent that a substantial share of the population derives income in exchange for labor, then a minimum wage has the potential to shape the distribution of wages and household income. Institutionalist economists have argued that higher minimum wage rates will produce a more equitable distribution of income, while economists working from the traditional textbook model have argued against the minimum wage for reducing income inequality.

Neoclassical and neoliberal economic theorists suggest minimum wages will distort labor markets and possibly increase economic inequality. This stems from their assumption that workers are paid according to their marginal productivity coupled with the supply and demand for a specific skill set possessed by workers. The minimum wage instead sets a nonmarket price on labor, according to the neoclassical perspective (e.g., Stigler, 1946). By artificially raising the price of labor, there should be a decrease in the demand for such labor. As George Stigler (1946) stated, "The higher the minimum wage, the greater will be the number of covered workers who are discharged" (p. 361). An increase in the share of unemployed workers could increase inequality as the wage income of the unemployed is cut and the wages of currently employed workers are bid down due to an increase in the labor supply. Another possible consequence is that the imposition of a minimum wage compels employers to substitute laborsaving technology in place of workers. Employers might also pass the increased wage cost to consumers, resulting in a decrease in demand and layoffs or cuts in workers' hours. Stigler summarized the neoclassical position on how minimum wages may impact inequality: "The manipulation of individual prices is neither an efficient nor an equitable device for changing the distribution of personal income" (1946, p. 362).

Institutionalist economists have long argued that minimum wages do not have the disemployment effects that neoclassical and neoliberal economists claim. This is an important precondition for institutionalist claims that minimum wages can impact the distribution of income. If disemployment effects are nonexistent or minimal (see, for example, Card and Krueger, 1995; Levin-Waldman, 2001; Belman and Wolfson, 2014), then higher and broadly applied minimum wage rates may reduce the level of income concentration. There are various ways the minimum wage might alter the income distribution. The minimum wage may redistribute income by lowering profits and increasing the wage share of income (Levitan and Belous, 1979). The imposition of a wage floor may elevate the incomes of low-income families (Webb, 1912; Freeman 1996; Levin-Waldman, 2001). At the firm level, minimum wages may make low-paid jobs more valuable to workers and lead to a decline in the need for supervisory personnel (Webb, 1912; Calvo and Wellisz, 1979). During the Progressive Era, Webb (1912) also noted that higher minimum wages may allow better nutrition and health among workers, thereby increasing their productivity on the job. Contrary to neoclassical notions that higher minimum wages compel employers to *substitute* technology in place of wage labor, some institutionalists have argued that employers might *supplement* workers with better capital, thereby increasing productivity and increasing the value of output per hour (Lavoie, 1992). As the potential mechanisms may vary, empirical research suggests that higher minimum wages may compress inequality of wages and income.

A significant body of research has emerged that looks at how minimum wage rates impact income inequality. The inflationary deterioration of the statutory federal minimum wage in the 1980s was estimated to explain 25 percent of the rise in male wage inequality and about a third of the increase in women's wage inequality between 1973 and 1988 (DiNardo, Fortin, and Lemieux, 1996). Lee (1999) found lower federal minimum wage rates relative to state mean and median wage rates could explain 70 percent of the growth in earnings inequality between middle- and low-income women and men, and 25 percent of the growth in inequality between the 50th and 25th percentile of men's wages. Even stronger results, studying the period between 1972 and 2003, were found by Lemieux (2006)—that changes in the minimum wage accounted for 80 percent of the change in inequality among male workers and 90 percent of the change in inequality among women workers. Weaker, yet substantial, evidence is reported in Autor, Manning, and Smith (2014). Volscho (2005) found that states with higher real minimum wages, net of a battery of economic and demographic control variables, had a lower Gini index of family income inequality using panel data on states over the period 1960 to 2000. The most significant evidence was found for a threshold effect in that the minimum wage had its strongest impact when set to values above $5.35 (in 2014 dollars). A careful review of existing evidence on a broad range of minimum wage effects on employment, inequality, and poverty may be found in Belman and Wolfson (2014). It is important to recognize, as Levin-Waldman notes, "the nature of the research done so far has . . . effectively legitimated a particular set of power relations and constrained a range of policy choices" (2001, p. 164). Taken as a whole, most research suggests that increases in minimum wages may reduce the level of income inequality and federal minimum wage deterioration can account for a significant portion of the growth in wage inequality observed since the 1970s.

Note

1. Dollars adjusted using the Research Series of the Consumer Price Index for Urban Consumers (CPI-U-RS).

References

Autor, David H., Alan Manning, and Christopher L. Smith. 2014. "The Contribution of the Minimum Wage to U.S. Wage Inequality over Three Decades: A Reassessment." MIT Working Paper.

Belman, Dale and Paul J. Wolfson. 2014. *What Does the Minimum Wage Do?* Kalamazoo, MI: W. E. Upjohn Institute for Employment Research.

Calvo, Guillermo A. and Stanislaw Wellisz. 1979. "Hierarchy, Ability, and Income Distribution." *Journal of Political Economy.* 87: 991–1010.

Card, David and Alan B. Krueger. 1995. *Myth and Measurement: The New Economics of the Minimum Wage.* Princeton, NJ: Princeton University Press.

DiNardo, John, Nicole M. Fortin, and Thomas Lemieux. 1997. "Labor Market Institutions and the Distribution of Wages: 1973–1992." *Econometrica.* 64: 1001–44.

Freeman, Richard B. 1996. "The Minimum Wage as a Redistributive Tool." *Economic Journal: The Quarterly Journal of the Royal Economic Society.* 106, 436: 639–649.

Lavoie, Marc. 1992. *Foundations of Post-Keynesian Economic Analysis.* Brookfield, VT: Edward Elgar Publishing Co.

Lee, David S. 1999. "Wage Inequality in the United States during the 1980s: Rising Dispersion or Falling Minimum Wage?" *Quarterly Journal of Economics* 114: 977–1023.

Lemieux, Thomas. 2006. "Increasing Residual Wage Inequality: Composition Effects, Noisy Data or Rising Demand for Skill." *American Economic Review.* 96: 461–498.

Levin-Waldman, Oren. 2001. *The Case of the Minimum Wage: Competing Policy Models.* Albany, NY: State University of New York Press.

Levitan, Sar A. and Richard S. Belous. 1979. *More Than Subsistence: Minimum Wages for the Working Poor.* Baltimore, MD: Johns Hopkins University Press.

Stigler, George J. 1946. "The Economics of Minimum Wage Legislation." *The American Economic Review.* 36: 358–365.

Volscho, Thomas W. 2005. "Minimum Wages and Income Inequality in the American States, 1960–2000." *Research in Social Stratification and Mobility.* 23: 343–368.

Webb, Sidney. 1912. "The Economic Theory of a Legal Minimum Wage." *Journal of Political Economy.* 20: 973–998.

Thomas Volscho is assistant professor of sociology at the City University of New York-College of Staten Island. His research areas are in social stratification, political sociology, and racism studies. He has published research on how state-level minimum wages impact family income inequality and recent time-series research (with Nathan Kelly) on the determinants of the income share of the top 1 percent in the United States (published in the American Sociological Review*). He is currently studying the impact of the decline of mental hospitals and the rise of prisons as it relates to suicide rates. In this essay Volscho argues that minimum wages actually have an effect for reducing inequality, and that certainly this should be a consideration in policy discussions.*

4 Profiles

Introduction

*In this chapter I present profiles of different individuals and orga-
nizations that have held prominent positions in the establishment
and subsequent evolution of the minimum wage debate, as well as
those who have been vocal in subsequent debates over the minimum
wage. Essentially, there are four main groups of profiles. The first
group consists of the early Progressive thinkers who were prominent
in formulating some of the earliest and most serious arguments for
the minimum wage, as well as some of those who voiced their opposition to it. Among the organizations profiled are the AFL-CIO,
the American Federation of Labor and the Congress of Industrial
Organizations. The AFL-CIO is an interesting case because it
flipped from opposition to the minimum wage during the early part
of the twentieth century to being supportive during the post–World
War II years. Therefore, on one level, it fits into the first group
of Progressive thinkers, but on another level it fits into the group
of important institutions. The second group consists of the legislative group during the 1930s that secured passage of the Fair Labor
Standards Act (FLSA) in 1938. This group includes prominent
figures like Franklin Delano Roosevelt, the 32nd president of the
United States, and the legislative leaders, William Connery in the
House of Representatives and Hugo Black in the U.S. Senate, who*

Sen. Elizabeth Warren (D-Mass.) speaks about raising wages during the
forum AFL-CIO National Summit at Gallaudet University in Washington
on January 7, 2015. (AP Photo/Jose Luis Magana)

introduced the Connery–Black Bill, which ultimately became the FLSA. The third group consists of academic voices on both sides of the minimum wage debate, most prominently from the 1970s until today. And the fourth group could be said to consist of contemporary activist organizations and individuals who have been able to present their positions in language with somewhat populist appeal.

The Progressives

Louis Brandeis (1856–1941)

Louis Brandeis was a lawyer who would be appointed in 1916 as an associate justice of the U.S. Supreme Court, where he would serve until 1939. A graduate of Harvard Law School, Brandeis was very much involved in progressive causes, most notably defending the workplace and labor laws. Because of his involvement in such causes, he was often dubbed the "People's Lawyer." Brandeis is often viewed as a symbol of the little guy's fight against big centralized firms that were dominating the nation's economic life at the time. Brandeis, who lived through the great wave of mergers between 1897 and 1904, where 4,237 firms merged into 237 combinations, was convinced that big business only became big through illegitimate means. For Brandeis and his contemporaries, opposition to big business was based on their perception of its political implications—that centralization and the consolidation of economic power into the hands of only a few represented a threat not only to competition in the market place but political democracy as well (Lustig 1982). He was among the early Progressive reformers supporting workman's compensation, and was instrumental in the Supreme Court's ruling in 1908 that a minimum wage constituted a legitimate form of government regulation in order to protect the rights of women, specifically their maternal function.

Brandeis's contribution to the early minimum wage debate lies mostly in his argument before the Supreme Court in *Muller v. Oregon* in 1908 and his presentation of what has come to be known as the "Brandeis Brief." The *Muller* case involved the state of Oregon's passage of a statute limiting the working hours of women to 10 hours a day. Previous attempts by states to limit the hours of men were held to be unconstitutional on the grounds that they violated their liberty of contract. At issue in this case was whether women working in excess of the limit might constitute a threat to the community's health and welfare. If there was a threat, it was not because of the nature of their work per se, but because of their socially and sexually defined roles, specifically their roles as mothers. In *Muller* the Court acknowledged that there were differences that would justify regulation in this case—an infringement of the women's liberty of contract—whereas it had rejected it in the past. The Court actually asserted that protecting women's maternal function and society's future generations was a compelling public interest that the liberty of contract for women could be abridged. At the same time, the Court appeared to be establishing the precedent for a minimum wage on the grounds that it would be necessary to protect the most vulnerable groups in society from exploitation, which in this case were women.

Aside from the legal precedent that *Muller* created, it also introduced the concept of empiricism through the Brandeis Brief, which detailed extensively the working conditions of women in a variety of industries. It was perhaps the first time that the Court was presented with statistics or "proof" detailing the detrimental impact of long hours on the lives of women. This was important because in the absence of empirical evidence all the Court had to rely on were theoretical presuppositions of what types of arrangements were conducive to the public interest. In the Brandeis Brief, the Court was able to find a causal relationship between means and ends that could truly justify interference with individual liberty. For social reformers during the Progressive period, there now was a group that warranted special protection, namely, women in sweated industries. The Brandeis Brief, in short, created the basis for what were regarded as "essentialist arguments," that protective labor legislation like maximum hours and ultimately minimum wages were in fact essential to protect women from exploitation (Figart, Mutari, and Power 2002).

John Bates Clark (1847–1938)

John Bates Clark was an American economist who very much was a proponent of the neoclassical school of economics and an opponent of institutionalists. A graduate of Amherst College in Massachusetts and the University of Heidelberg in Germany, he spent most of his career teaching political science at Columbia University in New York City. He was among those who were considered to be instrumental in the marginalist revolution—the idea that an additional unit of labor that adds to the marginal revenue of the firm is ultimately the basis for paying workers more. And yet, he supported a legal minimum wage for the same reasons that Webb did: it would lead to greater efficiency. He argued that the absence of one essentially triggered a process whereby employers chose from the ranks of the most necessitous men and women. Trade unions would, of course, go a long way toward removing this evil, but in the absence of unions, the law might remove it. Clark (1913) took the position that even though the state wasn't responsible for its citizens' poverty, they nonetheless had a valid claim against the state simply by virtue of their need and helplessness. He understood that the basis for minimum wage laws was that poorly paid workers were regarded as victims of social arrangements beyond their control. Because there were social defects in the economic system that resulted in low pay, they had valid claims.

Still, Clark wasn't suggesting that the core problem was the capitalist system. On the contrary, Clark was a strong proponent of capitalism. He fervently believed in the competitive market place. He believed that what a social class received was under natural law proportionate to what it contributed to the general output of industry. Arguably, this would imply that workers not making a contribution to the output are not entitled to higher wages. But it might also imply that a firm would really have no output without the effort of workers, and therefore, they were entitled to at a least a livable wage. Though he started out as a social reformer, he gradually shifted toward conservatism. He believed that each input contributed its marginal product. This meant that under competitive conditions, each factor of production is paid according to its "value added" to the total revenue of the product, or its marginal product. Clark called this theory of competitive distribution a "natural law" that was just. Under a competitive system, labor gets what it creates, capitalists get what their capital creates, and entrepreneurs get what their coordinating function creates. Therefore, if workers become more productive and add greater value to the company's long-term profitability, their wages will then tend to rise. Then if their wages rise in one industry, competition will only force other employers to raise their workers' wages, with the result being that wages will then be equal to the marginal product of labor. Based on this marginal productivity theory, Clark justified American wage rates and criticized labor unions for attempting to raise wages above his otherwise natural law. At the same time, he also opposed the power of monopolies and big business that attempted to exploit workers by forcing wages below labor's marginal product. As he saw it, a competitive environment in both labor and industry was thus essential to legitimate wage and social justice. In fact, Clark wrote a book in 1914 titled *Social Justice without Socialism*. Although his justification of a legal minimum wage would appear to be a contradiction of his theory of marginal productivity, it might also be viewed as a corrective to the lack of true competitive conditions in the market place that resulted in workers receiving wages less than the value of the marginal physical product of labor (Skousen 2009, pp. 234–237).

John R. Commons (1862–1945)

John R. Commons is considered to be among the most prominent Progressives, as one who essentially founded the school

of institutional economics, out of which progressive legislation emerged. Born in Hollansburg, Ohio, in 1862, Commons
graduated from Oberlin College and then earned a Ph.D. from
Johns Hopkins University. A strong and passionate advocate
for social justice, he was often considered to be too radical.
After teaching at Oberlin and Indiana University, he secured an
appointment to Syracuse University in 1895 but was dismissed
from there in 1899 because he was considered to be too radical. Following his dismissal from Syracuse, Commons wound
up at the University of Wisconsin at Madison, where he would
spend the rest of his career, having a profound influence on
leading scholars to come out of there, as well as progressive
legislation.

Commons took the view that modern economic theory
needed to be understood in its social context; otherwise, it
was mechanical. Therefore, there was to be no distinction
between industrial life and social life (Miller 1998). In his
classic *Institutional Economics* (1998), Commons sought to
show how individuals, and their individuality for that matter,
were shaped by institutions. Commons made it clear that we
did not begin as isolated individuals, but that as individuals we were the creatures of the larger society. The basis for
economic activity was the "transaction," which he defined as
the "means, under operation of law and custom, of acquiring
and alienating *legal* control of economic quantities, including
legal control of the labor and management which will after-
wards produce and deliver commodities towards the ultimate
consumers" (p. 45). What Commons understood was that
custom played a role in economic transactions. This was an
important point because it meant that transactions were not
based on price alone, as postulated in the standard model,
but that economic phenomena had to be understood within
a larger social context.

Commons's greatest influence was on labor unions. Reject-
ing the neoclassical economics position that labor contracts
are negotiated between employers and employees as equals,

Commons developed the more institutional position that the two were really unequal with regard to bargaining position. On the contrary, there was a great deal of power imbalance between workers and employers, and as a result, workers were often forced to accept whatever wages and working conditions they were offered. Otherwise, they would starve. Therefore, labor unions provided a corrective to this power imbalance because they effectively offered workers a measure of bargaining power they otherwise lacked. The implications for the minimum wage, then, were enormous because Commons was suggesting that, contrary to the assumptions of the standard model that wage rates are a natural process set by the market place, institutions really matter. If workers in unionized factories relied on the collective bargaining power of unions to bolster wages of workers so that they could earn a respectable wage, it then followed that workers in non-unionized industries—what economists would typically refer to as the "covered" sector as opposed to the uncovered sector—would similarly need an institution to bolster their wages, and that institution would be the minimum wage.

It had been the prevailing view at the time that a decline in prices and wages during recessions and depressions would lead to a restabilization of the market. Commons took the view that a decline in prices and wages during recessions and depressions would only aggravate them by reducing purchasing power and in turn lead to bankruptcy. The answer lay in redistributing income from profits to wages through collective bargaining agreements. Collective bargaining would prevent both profiteering and underconsumption, thereby assisting in the maintenance of purchasing power and aggregate demand. Commons no doubt recognized that unions did indeed have defects that might hinder economic efficiency in various ways; he also maintained that in most cases their benefits to society outweighed their costs (Kaufman 2003). The same argument would have to apply to the minimum wage. Although Commons hadn't been directly involved in the minimum wage debate, his contributions to institutional economics provided a fundamental foundation upon which minimum wage legislation would rest. That foundation being that institutions are necessary in a market economy where there is unequal power to enable workers to obtain fair and livable wages. Moreover, by pushing up workers' wages, they in turn will have purchasing power that will enable them to demand goods and services in the aggregate, and it is this aggregate demand for goods and services that ultimately drives the economy. Commons would go on to draft workers' compensation legislation in Wisconsin, the first of its kind, and ultimately the model for what would develop into unemployment insurance, again resting on the assumption that institutions that maintain worker purchasing power are ultimately what maintain aggregate demand for goods and services.

Edward Filene (1860–1937)

Edward Filene was an American businessman and philanthropist best known for the Filene's Department store chain. Born in Salem, Massachusetts, in 1860, Filene was admitted to Harvard University, but didn't attend when his father became seriously ill and he took over the family business—the department store started in Boston in 1881. But Filene also played a role in the passage of workman's compensation and the minimum wage. In his own business, Filene sought to implement Frederick Winslow Taylor's principles of scientific management and improve not only the efficiency of the business but also the overall quality of his workers. While many in the business community were opposed to a minimum wage, Filene actively supported it. On the pages of the *American Economic Review*, Filene wrote that one way of increasing efficiency was for employers to pay wages that would command higher-quality employees. A higher wage would be more cost-effective because employers would not have to spend as much time providing direction and correcting the errors of those who were less well trained. Low wages simply resulted in employers having cheap standards, which only produced inefficient employees. These workers wouldn't be productive because they wouldn't earn enough to maintain themselves properly. Employers would not be able to get effective organization out of those who were unintelligent, and they could not be intelligent if they did not have enough to live on properly. A legal minimum wage would then help employers as well as employees, by enabling them to compete on an even playing field with other employers, and preventing employers from paying employees insufficiently to be consumers of their business. Moreover, employers would be more likely to take an interest in their employees by educating them to a level that would make them worth the wage. Ultimately, Filene reasoned that the state would assume the function of providing education and training to future workers. To this extent, the minimum wage would serve to enhance public efficiency (Filene 1923). Filene would play a pivotal role in passing the nation's first workman's compensation law in 1911.

Samuel Gompers (1850–1924)

Samuel Gompers has gone down in history as a seminal figure in American labor history. Born in London in 1850, he was removed from school shortly after his 10th birthday and sent to work as an apprentice to a cigar maker to help his impoverished family. In 1863, Gompers immigrated to the United States with his family and settled on the lower east side of New York City. There for a brief time he assisted his father in manufacturing cigars at home, and in his spare time he had formed a debate club with his friends. The club was to grow into a contact for upwardly mobile young men in New York City. When he was 14, he joined and became active in the Cigarmakers' Local Union No. 15, which was the English-speaking union of cigar makers in New York City. In 1873, Gompers moved to the cigar maker David Hirsch & Company, which was considered to be a high-end establishment where only skilled workers worked. In 1875 Gompers was elected president of the Cigar-makers' International Union Local 144, which almost collapsed in 1877. Skyrocketing unemployment and the large pool of desperate workers willing to work for subsistence wages only put pressure on gains in wages and the shortening of hours that union shops had already achieved. Gompers along with a friend then used the Local 144 as a base to rebuild the Cigarmakers' Union, introducing a high dues structure and implementing programs to pay out-of-work benefits, sick benefits, and death benefits for union members in good standing. Gompers told the workers they needed to organize because wage reductions were almost a daily occurrence, and that the capitalists were interested only in profits. He was elected second vice president of the Cigarmakers' International Union in 1886, and first vice president in 1896.

In 1881 Gompers helped found the Federation of Organized Trades and Labor Unions as a coalition of like-minded unions. It was then reorganized in 1886 into the American Federation of Labor with Gompers as president, which for the exception of 1895, he would remain as president until his death in 1924. Because Gompers saw the future of labor lying in collective bargaining agreements, he was not actually in favor of the min-imum wage in its earliest days. Under Gompers's leadership the labor movement shied away from using legislation as a tool to improve wages and other working conditions, but rested on voluntarism. This reflected the classical laissez-faire tradition that working conditions and wages could best be obtained through firm-level negotiations with trade unions. Labor unions also chose a cautious approach to the establishment of a legal mini-mum because of the unions' experience with the courts and the use of the conspiracy doctrine (Hattam 1993). Gompers's philosophy of labor unions centered on economic ends for workers, such as higher wages, shorter hours, and safe working conditions so that they could enjoy an "American" standard of living—a decent home, decent food and clothing, and money enough to educate their children. For him, collective bargaining was the most direct way to achieve these improvements. His fear of legislating these improvements, like a minimum wage, was that it would undermine efforts to organize workers into unions. Among his famous quotes was: "We want a minimum wage established, but we want it established by the solidarity of the working men themselves through the economic forces of their trade unions, rather than by any legal enactment. . . . We must not, we cannot, depend upon legislative enactments to set wage standards. When once we encourage such a system, it is equivalent to admitting our incompetency for self-government and our inability to seek better conditions" (Thurber 2013).

Oliver Wendell Holmes (1841–1935)

Oliver Wendell Holmes was an associate justice of the U.S. Supreme Court, appointed in 1902 by President Theodore Roosevelt after having served many years on the Massachusetts Supreme Judicial Court. During his time on the Massachusetts Supreme Judicial Court, Holmes rose to be chief justice and also held the position of Weld Professor of Law at the Harvard Law School, from which he also graduated. Holmes has often been considered to be a judicial restraintist, taking the position that courts and judges should defer to the will of legislative bodies who represented the democratic will of the people. In his view, the Supreme Court should not declare a law unconstitutional "unless it can be said that a rational and fair man necessarily would admit that the statute proposed would infringe fundamental principles as they have been understood by the traditions of our people and our law" (Holmes quoted in Pohlman 1984, p. 81). He believed in deference to the sovereign, which held monopoly power for the existence of a legal order. He also assumed that as a practical matter that law must be found in the dominant forces in society, which he believed were reflected in the legislature. Therefore, judges should generally defer to their wishes. So when it came to the early cases concerning the constitutionality of minimum wage legislation, Holmes often found himself to be in dissent as the majority of the Court tended to hold both maximum hours and early minimum wage legislation to be an unconstitutional violation of individual liberty of contract. In the famous *Lochner v. New York* decision in 1905 the Supreme Court held that the state of New York could not interfere with bakers' liberty of contract by restricting their hours to 10 hours a day and 60 a week because the Court could see nothing in what they did that constituted a threat to their health and well-being. In a rather caustic dissent, Holmes stated: "The 14th Amendment does not enact Mr. Herbert Spencer's Social Statics." In other words, there was no basis for restricting legislative actions because it violated judges' social Darwinistic notions of society. He then went on to say that "I think that the word 'liberty,' in the 14th Amendment, is perverted when it is held to prevent the natural outcome of a dominant opinion, unless it can be said that a rational and fair man necessarily would admit that the statute proposed would infringe fundamental principles as they have been understood by the traditions of our people and our law. It does not need research to show that no such sweeping condemnation can be passed upon the statute before us. A reasonable man might think it a proper measure on the score of health. Men whom I certainly could not pronounce unreasonable would uphold it as a first instalment of a general regulation of the hours of work" (U.S. 1905).

The clearest example of this was in *Children's Hospital v. Adkins* decided in 1923. This case involved the constitutionality of the District of Columbia's minimum wage for women. Here the Supreme Court rejected the earlier argument made in *Muller* and asserted that women no longer needed special legislative protection because things had changed. What changed? The Constitution was amended in 1920 to give women the right to vote. Therefore, there was no reason to offer special protection if it meant violating her liberty of contract. Whatever biological differences that existed between men and women that the Court asserted that society had a compelling interest in protecting seemed to disappear on the basis of the Nineteenth Amendment. While acknowledging the ethical right of every worker to a livable wage that was the purpose of a trade organization, in his dissent, Holmes raised the question of whether maximum hours was not also an interference with liberty if the minimum wage was. Were they not opposite sides of the same coin? He could see no difference in either the kind or the degree of interference with liberty. Moreover, he asserted, the law did not compel anyone to pay anything. Rather it only established a minimum floor. Later on in the 1937 case of *West Coast Hotel Co. V. Parrish* (1936), which involved a minimum wage statute in Washington State that had been on the books since 1913, the Court reversed itself and held that minimum wages were necessary to preclude the possibility of wage disputes that would result in a disruption of normal business activity, thereby creating an inconvenience to all concerned. Here the Court used Holmes's dissent in *Adkins* to form the core of its argument in *West Coast Hotel*. As Holmes put it:

> This statute does not compel anybody to pay anything. It simply forbids employment at rates below those fixed as the minimum requirement of health and right living. It is safe to assume that women will not be employed at even the lowest wages allowed unless they earn them, or unless the employer's business can sustain the burden. In short the law in its character and operation is like hundreds of so-called laws that have been upheld. (pp. 396–397)

Again, Holmes was merely making it clear that there was nothing in a minimum wage law that most rational people would not find to be reasonable forms of regulation. His dissent in *Adkins*, which was now the core of the majority opinion in *Parrish,* was essentially echoing the same reasonable man standard that he set forth in *Lochner*. That is, if reasonable people, and by extension the community at large, as they act through their elected legislative bodies, believe that maximum hours and minimum wage legislation to be a reasonable interference with liberty of contract because it promotes the larger public interest, then courts have no basis for invalidating such actions. This decision would be a milestone in the history of the minimum wage because it would be recognized from this point forth that the minimum wage was a legitimate governmental policy tool.

Richard A. Lester (1908–1997)

Richard Lester was a prominent labor economist who could in many respects be said to fall into the category of latter-day institutionalists. Born in Blasdell, New York, in 1908, he received his BA degree from Yale in 1929 and his PhD from Princeton in 1936. After briefly teaching at Princeton, he went on to the University of Washington and then Duke University. During World War II, he served in the Labor Division of the War Production Board, the War Manpower Commission in 1942, and then the Office of the War Secretary from 1943 to 1944. In 1945 he returned to Princeton, where he would spend the rest of his professional career. He assisted in drafting the New Jersey Unemployment Compensation Act and would serve as chairman of the New Jersey Employment Security Council from 1955 to 1965. In 1962 he published *The Economics of Unemployment Compensation*. But his best-known work addressed the issue of wage determination and the minimum wage. During the 1940s, he developed the "range theory of wages," which recognized that individuals in similar jobs were often paid differently. Using this theory, he was able to explain why the minimum wage often did not have the dire consequences predicted by the standard model.

In a survey of business executives during the 1930s and 1940s, Lester observed that business executives, unlike economists, tend to think of costs and profits as dependent upon the rate of output, not the other way around. For these executives, employment levels were not determined by wage rates, but by rate of output (Lester 1946). Institutionalists had been arguing that wage differentials were very much a product of culture, power, and tradition (Lester 1947a). On the contrary, in his studies of North–South wage differentials during the 1930s and 1940s, Lester argued that in the absence of unions, real wage differentials existed and persisted because of employer policies and characteristics of the labor market. Because labor organizations were nonexistent, employers, especially in the South, tended to dominate the labor market. For Lester, the spread of unionism in 1932 resulted in a reduction in wage differentials (Lester 1947b). It then followed that a uniform minimum wage across the country would have the same effect.

Sidney Webb (1859–1947)

Among the most prominent figures in the early minimum wage debate was Sidney Webb. Webb was a British socialist and an early member of the Fabian society, which was a British socialist organization whose purpose was to advance socialism through gradualist and reformist means. The Fabian society would lay the groundwork for the development of the British Labor Party and also have influence on the policies of those states emerging from decolonization of the British Empire. He came to economics gradually. While holding a clerical job, he studied law in his spare time at the Birkbeck Literary and Scientific Institute at the University of London. He also studied at King's College London prior to being called to the bar in 1885. Webb would also be one of the founders of the London School of Economics in 1895, where he served as professor of public administration from 1912 until 1927. He, along with his wife Beatrice Webb, a fellow Fabian, would go on to found the *New Statesman* magazine in 1913. By 1929, he was Baron Passfield and would go on to become British colonial secretary in Ramsey McDonald's labor government in 1929. His seminal book was the *History of Trade Unionism*, but for the Fabian Society he wrote on poverty in London and the eight-hour day.

In the "The Economic Theory of a Legal Minimum Wage," published in the *Journal of Political Economy* in 1912, Webb put forth the concept of an efficiency wage, which would also come to be known as the Webb effect. Webb argued that people who are paid better are able to work harder because they have greater energy, due in large measure to their ability to better sustain themselves. Moreover, the greater morale among employees deriving from higher wage rates also leads to greater loyalty to their employers. Because a legal minimum wage would have the positive effect of increasing productivity, a wage floor would be beneficial to employees and employers alike. Employers would most appreciate the security a minimum wage would provide them against being undercut by dishonest or disloyal competition, and employees would be able to better maintain themselves, thus enabling them to be better workers. As a result of higher wages, productivity would increase naturally. Rather than eliminating competition for employment, it would transfer pressure from one element in the bargain (employers) to the other (employees). Moreover, the aggregate efficiency of the nation's industry would be promoted as the best available candidates are hired. A legal minimum wage, then, would positively increase the productivity of the nation's industry by ensuring that those who are left unemployed would be the least productive members of the workforce. Not only would employers be forced to look for the best workers so as to increase their overall productivity, employees also would be forced to develop their skills so that they could be counted among the better class of workers (Webb 1912).

Webb based his conclusions on his observations of the effects of the minimum wage in Australia, where the first minimum wage laws took effect during the 1890s. He based his conclusions on his observations in Australia following passage of the first minimum wage in the 1890s. Webb, along with his wife Beatrice, was also concerned with the social costs of paying low wages. Their case for a minimum wage was built on two main pillars: the doctrine of labor's *inequality of bargaining power* (IBP) and the doctrine of social cost of labor (SCL). IBP holds that employers individually and/or collectively enjoy a power advantage in wage determination. Employers make up one group that benefits from extra-low wages in labor markets, but they aren't the only beneficiaries. Consumers, and especially affluent consumers who have a disproportionate share of income, also benefit from low-wage labor in the form of low prices. Therefore, one social rationale for a minimum wage is to offset the weak bargaining position of labor in the market place. When the SCL doctrine is added to this, however, the argument for a minimum becomes even stronger because it illustrates the negative externalities arising from the payment of low wages, or what could be considered the absence of a property right for workers in their jobs. What the Webbs and other American institutionalists did was to apply the negative externality concept, or missing property rights, to the employment relationship. Their argument rests on the assumption that labor, or human capital, is just like physical capital in that it requires a minimum ongoing expenditure for upkeep, repair, and depreciation. If product prices are to cover the full costs of production, then firms must pay their workers a wage sufficient to cover the individual and family subsistence costs, or provide in-kind compensation. But when the wage falls short of subsistence level, the social costs exceed the private labor costs borne by the firm and its customers. At a minimum, each worker requires a level of healthcare sufficient to cover physical and mental wear and tear. A minimum wage, then, solves the problem of social costs, as it approximates the social costs of labor. With a minimum wage, then, there should be no need for social subsidy to otherwise parasitic firms. Otherwise, the public is subsidizing the profits of businesses at the expense of workers by providing low-wage workers the social supports they need because their wages are too low (Kaufman 2009).

The Legislators

William Connery (1888–1937) and Hugo Black (1886–1971)

William Connery was a member of the House of Representatives representing Massachusetts from 1923 until his death in 1937. A graduate of the College of the Holy Cross, his first profession was acting and then theater manager. In Congress, however, as Chair of the House Committee on Labor, he would cosponsor the Connery–Black Bill, which would ultimately become the FLSA. Hugo Black, then a member of the Senate from Alabama, would be the other cosponsor in the Senate. Black represented Alabama in the Senate from 1927 until 1937, and then served as associate justice on the U.S. Supreme Court from 1937 until his death in 1971, where he had a reputation as a strong defender of liberal policies and civil rights.

Hearings on the Connery–Black bill began during the summer of 1937 before a joint committee of Congress. The bill contained essentially three objectives: First, to put an end to child labor and other oppressive labor practices. Second, to establish fair wage and hour standards that would take into account the concerns of respective industries. And third, to create a board that would be responsible for fixing fair minimum wages and reasonable workweeks for those industries where workers had been lacking in sufficient bargaining power. Initially conceived, the FLSA was not intended to create a uniform wage floor but to establish a system for fixing wages on an industry-by-industry basis. In this vein, it bore similarity to the NIRA. The bill would essentially require the Fair Labor Standards Board to determine the minimum wage and maximum hours for particular occupations on the basis of the board's findings that such occupations otherwise lacked effective facilities for collective bargaining.

What was being proposed was considerably more cumbersome than a simple wage floor, and it no doubt arose out of a desire to placate the concerns of organized labor, that the enactment of such legislation wouldn't undermine their efforts to organize workers and achieve living wages through collective bargaining. But it also reflected a desire to be sensitive to the variation among industry due to the specifics of a particular industry. It specifically sought to return value for the mandated minimum wage that would have to be paid, which had initially been an issue in the *Adkins* case. Among the reasons for why the *Adkins* court struck down the minimum wage was there was no expectation that women would return anything of commensurate value for the wages being paid. Later in *Tipaldo,* the state of New York tried to separate the state's new minimum wage law from the earlier one in the District of Columbia by claiming a commensurate relationship between the state's minimum wage and the value of services exchanged. It will be recalled that in trying to defend the minimum wage, the plaintiffs in *Tipaldo* claimed that they were going to offer value for the minimum wage.

Franklin Delano Roosevelt (1882–1945)

Franklin Roosevelt was the 32nd president of the United States, having served from 1933 until 1945, when he died in office shortly after being sworn into his fourth term. Though a cousin of Republican Theodore Roosevelt, Franklin Roosevelt was a Democrat and had served as assistant secretary of the navy under President Woodrow Wilson, who defeated both Republican incumbent William Howard Taft and Progressive candidate Theodore Roosevelt seeking a third term in 1912. Prior to being elected president in 1932, Roosevelt would serve as governor of New York, and be responsible for the enactment of reform legislation. Two of his advisors, Frances Perkins and Harry Hopkins, would go on to serve in his cabinet as secretaries of labor and commerce respectively. As president during the depths of the Great Depression, which began with the stock market crash of 1929, Roosevelt would offer what came to be known as the New Deal.

The New Deal was a package of legislation intended to get the economy going through a variety of different stimuli. Because prices were depressed, they needed to be raised. In agriculture, farm prices could be raised by paying farmers to plant less. Because prices were low due to low demand, demand could be increased and prices raised by providing people with purchasing power. For workers, labor legislation, most notably the Wagner Labor Relations Act in 1935, and the minimum wage in 1938, would serve to bolster wages. For the elderly, Social Security would provide retirement income, thereby enabling them to purchase items. For the poor, new public assistance programs would enable them to purchase goods and services. And for the unemployed, public works programs would put them to work, thereby allowing them to demand goods and services through increased purchasing power.

The first federal minimum wage legislation, however, did not come from the FLSA. First the National Industrial Recovery Act (NIRA) and later the National Recovery Act (NRA) contained codes that established minimum wages on an industry-by-industry basis. Both these pieces of legislation were signed into law by Roosevelt. The NIRA, passed in early 1933, was designed to maintain price and market stability by adopting industry codes that would safeguard against unfair competition. The codes contained provisions on wages, hours, working conditions, union membership, and collective bargaining. Essentially Congress delegated authority to the executive branch, for a federal administrator to supervise the making of codes, which often was a collaborative venture with representatives from industry. And in many cases, the codes were written by trade associations. Section 3 (a) of the act specifically authorized the president to approve codes of "fair competition" after making certain prescribed findings (Kirkendall, 1974, pp. 41–42). Section 7 dealt with issues of collective bargaining, maximum hours, and minimum wages. With this section it was established that as a matter of fair competition that (1) employees were to have the right to organize and bargain collectively with representatives of their choosing; (2) they were not to be coerced into joining a company union; and (3) their employers were to comply with maximum hours and minimum wages as they were approved and prescribed by the president (*Statutes at Large* 1933). Although maximum hours and minimum wages were to be prescribed, they were not uniform but would vary from industry to industry. The underlying purpose behind the NIRA was to prohibit those practices regarded as unfair by industry because they might have the effect of destroying the price structure without justification. The codes were also intended to prohibit the unfair practice of exploiting workers by cutting their wages and increasing their hours of labor.

The NIRA was ruled unconstitutional in *Schechter Poultry Corp vs United States* on the grounds that the codes were a violation of the Separation of Powers in that the Executive Branch was effectively writing legislation through them. With regard to the maximum hours and minimum wage components, the Court merely asserted that there was no real relationship to interstate commerce. By 1935, however, the National Labor Relations Act, or Wagner Act, of 1935 was passed. Although the Wagner Act did no more than codify a series of federal regulations protecting the rights of workers to organize and bargain collectively, it was, for the time, a revolutionary piece of legislation. Opponents viewed it as a revolutionary break from America's constitutional tradition, for it appeared to enlarge the powers of the national state and intrude on purely private economic transactions. They also saw it as a conscious effort on the part of the state to strengthen trade unionism because it implied a government endorsement of unionizing. But for Senator Joseph Wagner of New York, the bill's sponsor, trade unionism was essential to ensuring an equitable distribution of the rewards of the economy. And through unionism, income could be redistributed to workers, thereby maintaining their purchasing power and ensuring that this type of depression does not occur again (Dubofsky 1994). What the new law implied was that in the development of a capitalist system, generally biased in favor of employers and other property owners, there was a need for labor market institutions that could give workers effective voice and in so doing maintain stability. By 1938, after the Supreme Court reversed its position in *West Coast Hotel* in 1937 and upheld the constitutionality of the minimum wage at the state level, Congress passed, and Roosevelt signed into law, the Fair Labor Standards Act, thereby creating the nation's first national minimum wage. It is perhaps worth noting that in the face of vitriolic criticism, Roosevelt called minimum wage critics "hopelessly reactionary." In his State of the Union Address in January 1938, Roosevelt actively promoted the minimum wage. He took note that "millions of industrial workers receive pay so low that they have little buying power . . . hence suffer great human hardship." These workers were "unable to buy adequate food and shelter, to maintain health or to buy their share of manufactured goods," and this was effectively putting a drag on the nation's economy. To counter some of the reactionary claims made by some that the minimum wage was a step in the direction of bolshevism and communism, he dismissed this as absurd in a fireside chat where he stated that the American people should

> not let any calamity-howling executive with an income of $1,000.00 a day, who has seen his employees over to the Government relief rolls in order to preserve his company's undistributed reserves, tell you—using his stockholders' money to pay the postage for his personal opinions—tell you that a wage of $11.00 a week is going to have a disastrous effect on all American industry. Fortunately for business as a whole, and therefore for the Nation, that type of executive is a rarity with whom most business executives most heartily disagree.

Roosevelt went onto remind the nation that if the nation wanted "resolutely to extend the frontiers of social progress, we must . . . ever bear in mind that our objective is to improve and not to impair the standard of living of those who are now under-nourished, poorly clad and ill-housed" (quoted in Woolner 2013).

The Academicians

The academic debate over the minimum wage has by and large been divided into two warring camps. The first group, faithful to the standard model that there are employment consequences, has sought to show that the minimum wage does indeed cause unemployment, particularly among teenagers. Two representatives from this camp are David Neumark and William Wascher. On the other side of the debate has been David Card, especially in work he did with Alan Krueger on the fast-food industry, who has been demonstrating that the minimum wage has not had the dire effects predicted by the standard model. In more recent years, the work of Card has been added onto by Arindrajit Dube and Michael Reich, who similarly have been demonstrating that the minimum wage has not had the dire effects predicted by the standard model.

Richard V. Burkhauser

Richard Burkhauser is the Sarah Blanding Professor of Policy Analysis in the College of Human Ecology at Cornell University. He received his BA in economics from Saint Vincent's College in 1967, his MA in economics from Rutgers University in 1969, and his PhD in economics from the University of Chicago in 1976. His research tends to focuses on how public policies affect the economic behavior and well-being of vulnerable populations, such as low-income households. So when it comes to the minimum wage, he is raising the question of whether the minimum wage is necessarily the best approach for assisting the poor, or whether other types of policies might not be better targeted. He certainly has been among those economists that have argued that the minimum wage as an anti-poverty measure is poorly targeted. In a paper with T. Aldrich Finnegan (1989), he maintained that most minimum wage workers simply were not poor. Because only a small fraction of the labor market actually earned the statutory minimum wage, the potential benefits were presumed to be so small that they could not possibly offset the more likely larger costs to employment. Moreover, the benefits were presumed to be smaller still because most minimum wage earners were not the primary earners in their households. Rather, they were secondary earners and, by and large, teenagers. Therefore, because their incomes were not considered to be as consequential as the income of primary earners, the potential benefits given the costs were considered to be even smaller still.

In a 2004 report for the Employment Policies Institute, he, along with Joseph Sabia, argued that an increase in the minimum wage to $7 an hour, as was then being proposed by then-senators John Kerry and Ted Kennedy, was a poor way to help the poor. The report claimed that only 15 percent of an increase would go to families in poverty and that 60 percent of the benefits would go to families earning more than twice the poverty line. They also found that the majority of beneficiaries are not the primary earners in their households. Only 12.6 percent of beneficiaries were unmarried women with children, and that more than 82 percent were either not the highest earner in their households (secondary earners), single adults, or were married without children. Since the majority of these people were not struggling to get by on low wages, an increase in the minimum wage was not only poorly targeted but also highly inefficient and not at all effective in combating poverty. Moreover, the effect of a minimum wage increase would even be worse when considering the well-documented job loss that could be expected from such an increase.

In a later paper (2010) Burkhauser and Sabia on the basis of data from the Current Population Survey (CPS) found that state and federal minimum wages between 2003 and 2007 had no effect on poverty. Using the March CPS for 2008, they estimated that those workers who would directly benefit from an increase in the minimum wage were already earning between $7.25 and $9.49 an hour while the minimum wage was still $5.85 an hour. While 17.7 percent of all workers earning between $5.70 and $9.49 an hour stood to benefit from an increase in the minimum wage, 80.3 percent of all workers were earning a wage of $9.50 or more. They argued that the then proposal to raise the minimum wage to $9.50 an hour would not be well targeted toward poor workers, and that it would be even less target-efficient than the last increase, which took effect in 2009. Therefore, they concluded that any further increases in the minimum wage would do little to reduce poverty and would be a poor substitute for the EITC as a mechanism for reducing poverty. On the contrary, because employment was considered to be an important anti-poverty mechanism and that wage subsidies can increase the working poor's income, the EITC would indeed be a more effective means of assisting the poor than an increase in the federal minimum wage.

In a more recent paper for the Institute for the Study of Labor in Germany, Burkhauser (2014) reiterated his position that minimum wages are an ineffective mechanism for reducing poverty. Why is this so? Because most minimum wage workers who gain from an increase in the minimum wage simply are not poor. They do not live in poor or even near-poor families. Some workers who do live in poor families have wages above the proposed minimum wage. They just don't work full time. The EITC is a more effective mechanism because it only raises the wage rates of those workers living in low-income families and the size of the credit is dependent on the number of children. He suggests that we could dramatically improve the lives of low-income families if we were to use the real economic costs of increasing the minimum wage to finance an expansion of the EITC. Expanding the EITC would have a far less negative

effect on the employment of low-skilled workers and the positive macroeconomic benefits would be even greater still because
the working poor are more likely to consume. And because the
EITC is paid through the tax code rather than the employer,
the negative macroeconomic effects on employment would
also be less.

Burkhauser has also become a favorite of the right that wants
to dispute claims of rising income inequality. In an article in
the *National Tax Journal* that he coauthored with Jeff Larrimore and Kosali Simon, he offers a "second opinion" on the
extent to which the middle class has failed to benefit from economic growth of the last three business cycles between 1979
and 2007. Rather, using cross-sectional data to capture the
economic resources available to individuals at the same point
in the income distribution over time, they find evidence that
the decline of the middle class is far less certain. Using CPS
data, more than simply wage income, they consider tax credits
and liabilities along with the ex-ante value of in-kind benefits
like health insurance benefits. They impute the ex-ante value
of employer contributions to health insurance as well as the
value of public health insurance from outside sources. They
argue that taxes and transfers have a real impact on the well-
being of those paying taxes and receiving transfers. Therefore,
by considering post-tax, post-transfer income, including the
value of health insurance, we can gain a better understanding
of the effect of program change on people's economic resources.
When using the most restrictive definition of income—pre-tax,
pre-transfer tax unit cash income—the resources of the middle
class have stagnated over the last three business cycles. But
once the definition of income is broadened to include post-tax,
post-transfer, size-adjusted cash income, middle-class Americans are then found to have made substantial gains and these
increases are even larger when considering the ex-ante value of
health insurance. In turn, this means that the gap between the
top and the bottom is not nearly as great as some would have
us believe.

David Card (1956–)

David Card is a Canadian labor economist and Professor of Economics at the University of California at Berkeley. He received his BA degree from Queen's University in Canada in 1978 and his PhD in economics from Princeton University in 1983. In 1995 he received the John Bates Clark Medal, which is awarded to economists under the age of 40 who are judged to have made the most significant contribution to economic thought and knowledge. Prior to coming to the University of California, he was on the faculty of Princeton from 1983 to 1996. From 1988 to 1992, he was co-editor of the *Journal of Labor Economics*, and the co-editor of *Econometrica* from 1993 until 1997. Card came to prominence with his studies of the minimum wage in the fast-food industry that he coauthored with his then Princeton colleague Alan Krueger, who would serve as chief economist in the Department of Labor under President Clinton and then first as Assistant Secretary of the Treasury for Economic Policy and second as Chairman of the Council of Economic Advisors under President Obama. These studies were widely cited as being supportive of the minimum wage.

Their principal studies, which appeared revolutionary at the time, were of the fast-food industry in both California and New Jersey. Until then, it had been the conventional wisdom, in lines with the standard model, that increases in the minimum wage lead to decreases in unemployment. Employers would either lay off workers or substitute technology for them, thereby creating a disemployment effect or they would not create new jobs in the future. In New Jersey, Card and Krueger (1995) found that when the state minimum wage was raised from $3.35 to $4.25 during July of 1988, and from $4.25 to $5.05 in 1992, there was no disemployment effect. With Pennsylvania serving as the control group for the New Jersey study, they also found there to be no substitution effect. Although the minimum wage increase did lead to price increases for meals, suggesting that the costs of the increase were simply passed onto the consumer, there was no evidence that prices rose faster among stores in New Jersey that were most affected by the rise in the minimum wage. Moreover, the raise in the minimum wage didn't negatively affect the number of store openings. In a follow-up study several years later, Card and Krueger only confirmed their earlier results (1998). These studies were important because they challenged the reigning orthodoxy and ultimately ushered in a new political economy of the minimum wage.

In more recent years, Card's work has focused on U.S. labor market comparisons to Canada on a variety of labor market issues, most notably the minimum wage, the impact of the decline of institutions on income inequality, and immigration. Card along with coauthor John DiNardo (2002) attributed the rise in overall wage inequality during the 1980s to trends in the minimum wage and declining unionization. Then in a study written with Thomas Lemieux and Craig Riddell (2008), Card noted that at least until the 1970s, it had been the dominant view that unions tended to increase wage inequality, but that it was increasingly becoming clear that it was declining unionism that contributed to a steep increase in wage inequality in both the United States and the United Kingdom during the 1980s. The fraction of workers covered by collective bargaining agreements in the United States, the United Kingdom, and even Canada had been relatively modest. Collective bargaining in these countries also tended to be conducted at the industry or sectoral level. Therefore, within narrowly defined groups, wage inequality was always lower for union workers than nonunion workers.

On the basis of longitudinal data, Freeman found there to be low-wage inequality in the union sector. He found that the dispersion tended to fall when workers left nonunion jobs for union jobs, and that it rose when they moved in the opposite direction. Card, Lemieux, and Riddell (2008) also found that in both Canada and the United States between 1984 and 2001 there was low-wage inequality in the union sector. Male unionization rates declined 14 percentage points in Canada, whereas in the United States they declined by only 9 percentage points over the same time period. Union wage compression effects help explain a reasonable fraction of secular growth in male wage inequality and of cross-country differences in male wage inequality. But unlike the United States and the United Kingdom, overall inequality in Canada remained very stable. And yet, overall wage inequality would have declined had union wage impacts remained at their 1984 levels. In other words, had there not been a decline in unions, inequality would have been less. Card et al. suggest that there may have been several developments to offset the pressure toward increased inequality associated with the decline in union strength, at least in Canada. The real minimum wage in Canada rose from the mid-1980s to the late 1900s, while in the United States it was approximately constant over the same period. Again, these findings are important because they undermine the standard model's assumption that wage setting is a natural process and reinforces the idea that institutional economists earlier made clear, which was that institutions did indeed matter.

Just as Card's work on the minimum wage has demonstrated that it does not have a detrimental impact on the labor market, his work on immigration has also shown that increased immigration would not pose a threat to the labor market. In a study with Ian Preston and Christian Dustmann (2012), Card asked the question of why there was strong public opposition to immigration across Europe. On the basis of data for 21 countries from the European Social Survey (ESS), which included questions on the labor market, social impacts of immigration, and the desirability of increasing or reducing immigration inflows, they found that variation in individual attitudes toward immigration policy could be attributed more to compositional concerns than concerns over wages and taxes. In fact, immigration appeared to have no real impact on wages and taxes. By compositional concerns, they meant how immigration would affect the composition of neighborhoods, schools, and workplaces. They specifically found a 70 percent gap between the most- and least-educated respondents on the issue of whether immigration should be either increased or reduced was attributable to intensity of concerns over compositional amenities. Meanwhile, differences in economic concerns accounted for only 10–15 percent.

Arindrajit Dube

Arindrajit Dube is a labor economist based at the University of Massachusetts at Amherst. He received his BA in economics from Stanford University and his PhD in economics from the University of Chicago. Prior to joining the faculty at the University of Massachusetts, he was a Research Economist at the Institute for Research on Labor and Employment at the University of California at Berkeley. Dube's work on the minimum wage could be said to fall into the new political economy of the minimum wage, and, along with Michael Reich and others, addresses the issue of heterogeneity that Wascher and Neumark are skeptical of. But within the scheme of considering trade-offs, Dube's work makes it clear that there aren't the dire employment consequences predicted by the standard model, and that the benefits to society may actually outweigh the costs. His work certainly continues what Card and others started.

Along with Suresh Naidu and Michael Reich, Dube (2007) looked at the effects of a minimum wage law that was enacted by a public ballot measure for the city of San Francisco in 2003. While the federal minimum wage was still $5.15 an hour, San Francisco's was now $8.50, which was still 26 percent higher than California's minimum wage of $6.70. Looking at primarily the restaurant industry because it was considered to be the primary employer of fast-food workers, they found that the benefits to the increases did outweigh the costs. The city wage floor did significantly raise the wages of those at affected restaurants and compressed the wage distribution among restaurant workers, and increased the average wages of fast-food workers twice as much as those at sit-down restaurants. And yet, there was no increase in business closure or employment loss detected. To the extent that such findings undermine the traditional orthodoxy, they also add to the ambiguity surrounding the effects of the minimum wage. Moreover, they reinforce some of the evidence that suggests that we may know very little about the minimum wage or its actual effects.

Then with Lester and Reich, Dube (2010) argues that a major problem with the data is that economists have been taking two different methodological approaches. Traditional national-level studies use all cross-state variation in the minimum wage over time to estimate the effects. Meanwhile, case studies typically compare adjoining local areas with different minimum wages around the time of the policy change. They specifically compare all contiguous county pairs in the United States that are located on opposite sides of a state border, in an attempt to generalize the case study approach by all local differences in minimum wages in the United States over a 17-year period from 1990 to 2006. Because the restaurant industry is the most intensive users of minimum wage workers, it is the prime focus, although other low-wage industries are considered too. In 2006, they employed 29.9 percent of all workers paid within 10 percent of state or federal minimum wages, thus making them the single largest employer of minimum wage workers. Also the proportion of workers at or close to the minimum wage is similar among all restaurant workers. What they found was that employment effects vary substantially among specifications. The estimated earnings effects were positive and significant for both limited-service and full-service restaurants, with the earnings effects being somewhat greater among limited-service restaurants than among full-service restaurants. For cross-state contiguous counties, they found strong earnings effects and no employment effects. When looking at local comparisons while also controlling for heterogeneity in employment growth, they found no detectable employment losses from the types of minimum wage increases that have been taking place over the years in the United States.

In a subsequent study, Dube, along with Reich and Sylvia Allegretto (2011), examined whether minimum wages really reduced teen employment. Using CPS data from 1990 to 2009 they controlled for both heterogeneity and selectivity. Here their central argument concerns confounding effects of heterogeneity patterns in low-wage employment that are coupled with selectivity of states that have implemented minimum wage increases. There was little difference in employment effects between male and female teens. Rather, many minimum wage studies probably overstate their precision due to the use of conventional standard errors, which may also lead them to incorrectly reject a hypothesis of no employment effect. But minimum wage studies that have used local employment data generally don't find disemployment effects. In this particular study, they focus their estimates on the effects of minimum wage increases on wages, employment, and hours of work for teenagers. Their evidence does not support disemployment effects associated with minimum wage increases, although there may still be an effect on hours. Although firms may not decrease their demand for workers, they may nonetheless decrease their demand for the number of hours that are worked by teenagers. Or teenagers themselves may opt to work less following minimum wage increases, thereby supplying fewer hours of their labor services. All in all, their findings added to those of the previous study that minimum wage increases, again in the range that have been implemented in the United States, do not reduce employment among teens.

Dube's voice, however, has not only been that of a serious scholar looking at the issue critically, but also of an expert attempting to have an impact on the public debate. In March 2013, for instance, Dube testified on whether the nature of the changing economy required indexation before the U.S.

Senate Committee on Health, Education, Labor, and Pensions in support of the Harkin–Miller Bill to raise the minimum wage to $10.10 an hour. He made it clear that while top pay and corporate profitability grew rapidly, the minimum wage failed to keep pace with rising productivity. Meanwhile, the declining minimum wage had contributed to rising inequality, and accounted for half the rise in inequality in the bottom half of the pay distribution, and this was even more so among women. Therefore, an increase in the minimum wage and its indexation thereafter would reduce the gap between those at the bottom and the rest of the workforce. He noted that the high watermark of the minimum wage was in 1968 when the minimum wage was $10.60 an hour in 2013 dollars. The next highest peak was in 1978 when the minimum wage reached $9.37 an hour in 2013 dollars. Therefore, the Harkin–Miller Bill to raise the minimum wage, with full adjustment by 2016, would most likely restore the minimum wage to its 1978 value at $9.38. Still, it would be lower than its 1968 value. He then went on to show that a single parent with just one child earning the minimum wage was below the poverty line, and that reality only served to widen the gap in inequality.

In November 2013, he published an op-ed piece in the *New York Times* in which he argued that raising the minimum wage was indeed something that the nation could do. He argued that it was a matter of fairness in a country where the minimum wage population was no longer composed mainly of teenagers, but was becoming older and perhaps more educated over time. In making this claim, he was taking aim at the standard criticism of the minimum wage that most minimum wage earners are teenagers and lacking in skills. The changing nature of the economy made it clear that we could no longer make this assumption. Not only had the minimum wage in the United States failed to keep pace with inflation because of legislative failures but also that relative to other OECD countries, it was the third lowest. He noted, "The social benefits of minimum wages from reduced inequality have to be weighed against possible costs. When it comes to minimum wages, the primary concern is about jobs. The worry comes from basic supply and demand: When labor is made more costly, employers will hire less of it." Although it was a valid concern, the evidence from the type of minimum wage increases that have occurred in the United States had shown the impact on jobs to be small. He further argued that minimum wage increases have helped lift families out of poverty—that a 10 percent increase in the minimum wage results in a 2 percent reduction in poverty. Moreover, it actually enhanced the efficacy of the EITC that critics often tout as an alternative to the minimum wage. Finally, he made it clear that he supported the Harkin–Miller Bill that would raise the minimum wage to $10.10 an hour and index it to inflation. Indexation was important, Dube argued, because it would replace politics with economics as the adjustment mechanism, thereby making change predictable (Dube 2013).

David Neumark (1959–) and William Wascher

David Neumark is a labor economist currently at the University of California at Irvine. He received his BA from the University of Pennsylvania in 1982 and his PhD from Harvard in 1987. After serving as an assistant professor at the University of Pennsylvania from 1989 until 1994, he became a professor at Michigan State University in 1994 and remained there until 2004. Since 2005, he has been at the University of California at Irvine. William Wascher is deputy director of the Program Direction Section, Research and Statistics of the Board of Governors of the Federal Reserve System. He received his BA in economics and mathematics from the University of Delaware in 1978 and his PhD in economics from the University of Pennsylvania in 1983. He has been with the Federal Reserve Board since 1983. From 1989 to 1990, he was a Senior Staff Economist at the Council of Economic Advisors in the

Executive Office of the President and from 1998 to 1999 he was Visiting Economist at the Bank of International Settlements in Basel, Switzerland. Together Neumark and Wascher have written several studies, first showing the disemployment effects on the minimum wage, and then in response to Card and Krueger, who were actually refuting them.

In their earlier work, they studied the effects of state minimum wage laws using panel data. They found that a 10 percent increase in the minimum wage resulted in a 1–2 percent decrease in employment among teenagers, and a 1.5 to 2 percent decrease in employment among young adults. And yet, they also found that a subminimum wage in those states that enacted them tended to moderate them (Neumark and Wascher 1992). In reporting these findings, they were only supporting the conventional findings that had initially been reported in the 1981 federal Minimum Wage Study Commission. In later work, Neumark and Wascher (2000), using administrative payroll records obtained from fast-food restaurants in both New Jersey (where there were increases) and Pennsylvania (where there were no increases) and (more of which will be said in the next profile), found that, contrary to Card and Krueger's findings that there were no disemployment effects, there were indeed effects. First they found that there was much less variability in the payroll data over the period between Card's and Krueger's surveys than there was in their data. Secondly, they found that different data effectively led to opposite conclusions. Card's and Krueger's data had suggested that the New Jersey minimum wage increase of 18.8 percent actually led to an 11 to 16.8 percent employment increase in New Jersey relative to Pennsylvania where there had been no increase. But simply replicating Card and Krueger's differences-in-differences estimate on the basis of payroll data, they found that employment really decreased by 3.9 to 4.0 percent in fast-food employment. Therefore, they argued that the payroll data was consistent with standard model predictions that increasing the minimum wage will indeed reduce the demand for low-wage workers.

Despite their conclusions that there were adverse employment consequences, not all their studies have necessarily been anti-minimum wage. In Chapter 2, I suggested that there are potential middle-class benefits to the minimum wage through wage contour effects. In a later study along with Mark Schweitzer (2004), they took a look at the issue. Although they acknowledged there to be wage contour effects, particularly for those earning immediately above the minimum wage, they still concluded the minimum wage to have negative effects for those throughout the distribution, because low-wage workers were bound to be hurt through a reduction in hours. In other words, even if they were earning more, employers would compensate by reducing their hours. In more recent work, they (2011) they estimated the effects of the interaction between the minimum wage and the earned income tax credit (EITC) on labor market outcomes. They found that for single women with children, the EITC actually boosted employment and earnings. When the EITC was combined with an increase in the minimum wage, the positive effect on employment and earnings was only enhanced. And yet, they also found the effects to vary for other groups. For less skilled minority men and women without children, the EITC adversely affected their employment and earnings when the minimum wage was high. But for very poor families with children, higher minimum wages increased the positive effects of the EITC on their income. Still as to whether the combination of a high EITC and a high minimum wage was good policy, it was really a question of whom policymakers were trying to help.

In sum, Neumark and Wascher's work could perhaps be summed up as stressing the trade-offs that need to be considered in policy, especially the minimum wage. It is not a question of good or bad, but costs and benefits that need to weighed against each other. In the face of the political economy of the minimum wage that has presented new evidence on the minimum wage, Neumark and Wascher along with J. M. Ian Salas (2014) recently revisited the issue. In Chapter 2, we noted that

Reich and Dube (who will also be profiled later in the chapter) observed that the problem with much of the empirical work on the minimum wage is a failure to take into account spatial heterogeneity, and that when taken into account minimum wages in the United States have not reduced employment. Here Neumark and Wascher sought to test the untested assumptions about the construction of better control groups. Using methods that let the data identify the appropriate control groups, Neumark and Wascher still found evidence of disemployment effects, particularly for teens. In other words, the minimum wage still posed a trade-off of higher wages for some against some job losses for others.

Michael Reich (1945–)

Michael Reich is a labor economist at the University of California at Berkeley, where he is also director of the Institute for Research on Labor and Employment, A graduate of Swarthmore College, he received his PhD in economics from Harvard. In 1968 while still in graduate school, he helped found the Union for Radical Political Economics (URPE). Being of the Vietnam generation he became heavily involved in activist causes and movements and was a subscriber to the New Left movement. As one of the founders of URPE, he subscribed to the view that there needed to be an American version of socialism with public ownership of the means of production and a government-planned economy in order to meet the social needs of all, rather than the private profit needs of a few. After teaching for a short time at Boston University, he joined the faculty at Berkeley in 1974 and became a full professor there in 1989. And for many years he taught courses in Marxist economics, political economy, and the history of economic thought. A strong supporter of progressive causes, it would come as no great surprise that he would be a supporter of the minimum wage. And yet, his support for the minimum wage, at least at the academic level, hasn't necessarily assumed the form of a

Marxist critique of the capitalist system stressing the exploitation of low-wage workers. Rather, it has found voice in studies with Dube and others demonstrating that the minimum wage does not have the predicted employment consequences of the standard model. On the contrary, when factoring heterogeneity into the equation, the minimum wage can be said to have more positive benefits on the whole than costs. In this vein, Reich too falls into the new political economy of the minimum wage.

In June 2013, Reich also testified before the U.S. Senate Committee on Health, Labor, and Pensions in favor of a minimum wage increase, where he also defended his work on the minimum wage and labor market outcomes against other contradictory research. He was testifying on the history of the minimum wage and noted that in the decades immediately following World War II, the wage floor brought the minimum wage up to a value of $10.60 in 1978 in 2013 dollars, which was 46 percent higher than the current minimum wage of $7.25 an hour. He noted that in addition to reversing the downward spiral in wages brought on by the Great Depression, the federal minimum wage helped transform many low-wage industries. These effects were mostly evident in the South, which had been much poorer than the rest of the nation and had been poorly integrated with the national economy. And yet following passage of the FLSA, a more prosperous South began to emerge with more employment growth and higher wages. Moreover, an equally dramatic upsurge in the South's fortunes occurred following extensions of the FLSA during the 1960s and the Civil Rights revolution. Through a review of the minimum wage effects since 1938, Reich was confirming President Roosevelt's view that the FLSA was both far-reaching and far-sighted—that it removed one of the forces that deepened and prolonged the Great Depression. During the postwar years, minimum wage increases were important in creating a shared prosperity. If it was the case that minimum wage employment once provided young workers with work experience that would enable them to progress to better paying jobs, Reich was making it clear that the economy had sufficiently changed that minimum wage jobs could no longer be seen as stepping-stones into middle-class employment. Moreover, middle-class workers were looking at minimum wage rates as reference points for their own levels of economic security. Therefore, the new context alone makes a compelling case for increasing the minimum wage, which he fully supported.

Contemporary Activist Organizations and Individuals

The nature of the American political system is such that the minimum wage would most likely never be increased were there not organizations and/or individuals lobbying for their increase. Because of the diversity of opinion on any public policy issues, as well as power differentials between groups, it has become a truism in American politics that all policy issues need a constituency behind them, and for the minimum wage that constituency has primarily been organized labor, as well as other community and public interest organizations. At the same time, there have been writers, mainly journalists, who have called attention to the issue in the popular press.

AFL-CIO

The American Federation of Labor and the Congress of Industrial Organizations is essentially a confederation of the nation's labor unions. It is a national trade union center. Initially separate organizations, the two merged in 1955 to become the AFL-CIO. From 1955 until 2005, the AFL-CIO represented nearly all unionized workers in the United States. In 2005, several of the large unions split away from the AFL-CIO to form the Change to Win federation (CtW). The CtW, a coalition of American labor unions, was formed as an alternative to the AFL-CIO. The split represented a debate over how best to

spend union funds. One group, amid declining union membership, thought that increasingly more money and effort should
be directed toward organizing more nonunion membership,
while the other group thought that more money and effort
should be directed toward legislative activity on matters of concern to working people, regardless of whether they were union
members or not. The coalition was founded on two basic principles: First, that working people, including union members,
cannot consistently win in the legislative arena without uniting
or organizing millions more workers into unions. And second,
every worker in America has the right to a union that has the
focus, strategy, and resources to organize their workers in their
respective industries and win. Then in 2009, several of the
CtW unions sought to re-affiliate with the AFL-CIO. Today,
the largest member of the AFL-CIO is AFSCME, the American Federation of State, County and Municipal Employees,
which boasts a national membership of 1.6 million workers.

Although the AFL-CIO has been a major constituency
behind increases in the minimum wage since passage of the
FLSA, it was not always supportive. In fact, in the early years,
the AFL, in particular, opposed the minimum wage because
it feared that protective legislation would undermine efforts
to organize men and achieve contracts through collective bargaining. The AFL initially opposed all legislation that might
improve working conditions out of a fear that it would undermine the impulse to organize. Under Gompers's leadership the
labor movement shied away from using legislation as a tool to
improve wages and other working conditions, but rested on
voluntarism, which reflected the classical laissez-faire tradition that working conditions and wages could best be obtained
through firm-level negotiations with trade unions (Hattam
1993). Over time, however, the AFL-CIO came to support
protective legislation for women, mainly because women were
barred from joining unions.

Organized labor, however, was not of a single voice. There were
indeed differences between the AFL and CIO (Burns 1956).

The AFL had traditionally sought to obtain either shorter hours or better pay through collective bargaining. The CIO, formed from newly emerging industrial unions, was considerably more militant and often ready and willing to use the strike as a weapon (Bernstein 1969). Despite the boost that unions got from the Wagner Act, the AFL still clung to a more voluntary approach, whereas the CIO opted for greater militancy. Whereas the AFL was willing to give Connery–Black its unqualified support, the CIO had its reservations. For the AFL, support stemmed from its longtime crusade for a living wage and its belief that the measure represented a step in that direction. For the CIO, however, reservations stemmed from the fact that the measure involved more than a simple wage floor.

The issue dividing them was the extent, if any, to which this bill might interfere with unions' traditional functions of organizing and negotiation over wages and other conditions of employment. AFL president William Green was convinced that it did not deal with the "fixing of general minimum wage standards," because if it did, as he testified, it "would be strenuously opposed by the American Federation of Labor as contrary to our conceptions of democracy, and as violating the cardinal principles of self-government in private industry prevailing in this country" (U.S. Congress 1937, p. 219). John L. Lewis, president of the CIO and the United Mine Workers, however, felt that there was one area where it did, which was easily corrected with the elimination of section 5. Overall, he was willing to pledge his support for it on the grounds that it would increase mass purchasing power, an essential ingredient in economic recovery, and ultimately further the aims of industrial democracy. But at the same time, he proposed amending it so that in the end it would amount to no more than a wage floor.

Under section 5 of the bill, a two-tiered minimum wage would be created. The first tier was to create the floor of 40 cents an hour and the second would allow the Labor Standards Board to establish a range from 40 cents an hour to 60 cents an hour to a maximum yearly earnings of $1,200. The second tier was to apply to those industries where it was determined that there were insufficient collective bargaining opportunities. It was on this point that the bill was considered to be blurring the line between establishing a simple wage floor, which Lewis believed would go a long way toward establishing industrial democracy, and bargaining on behalf of workers who otherwise lacked that monopoly power. This was the point where the bill had the potential to undermine the efforts of the unions. And from Lewis's point of view, the elimination of section 5 would go a long way toward making it more democratic.

Despite disagreements between the AFL and CIO prior to passage of the FLSA, the merged organization was fully on board with its support for extensions of coverage and increases to the minimum wage. Unions in particular began to play the important role of a constituency and source of information. No sooner were the amendments passed to the FSLA in 1955, than was the AFL-CIO pressing for a higher wage. In May of 1956, AFL-CIO president George Meany appeared before the Senate Labor subcommittee asking for Congress to increase the minimum wage for what he termed the "forgotten America." Acknowledging that these people were unorganized and lacked other labor protections, Meany emphasized the need to broaden coverage and to so amend the FLSA that more workers would be protected (AFL-CIO News 1956). Then in 1961 when it was being debated to extend coverage more and raise the minimum wage to $1.25, the AFL-CIO was again calling for both. But it wasn't just a matter of being supportive, the AFL-CIO actually formed a Joint Minimum Wage Committee, made up of 22 unions, to spearhead efforts to improve the wage hour law (AFL-CIO News 1960). In legislative rankling over amendments to the FLSA in 1961, the AFL-CIO was actually unwilling to sacrifice expanded coverage for a higher minimum wage. This had actually been an issue dividing the House of Representatives from the Senate. The AFL-CIO's Joint Minimum Wage Committee viewed the House

Committee's action as a "substantial breakthrough" (AFL-CIO News 1960). When the full House voted, it passed a bill raising the minimum wage to $1.25 but with a limited expansion of coverage, while the Senate sought to expand coverage even further. In the end, though, it was the issue of coverage that ultimately brought the bill to defeat. The House bill would have added only an additional 500,000 to 700,000 to the 23.7 million workers already covered, while the Senate bill would have covered an additional 4 million workers. The chair of the conference committee and sponsor of the Senate bill, then-senator John Kennedy, indicated a willingness to yield on some issues so long as the House yielded. But a major factor in the impasses that ultimately resulted in the bill's death in committee was the AFL-CIO's refusal to sacrifice increased coverage for a higher hourly wage (*Congressional Quarterly Almanac* 1960). Still, the AFL-CIO, through its Department of Legislation, continued to provide invaluable information on the effects of the minimum wage and the benefits to workers.

Economic Policy Institute

The Economic Policy Institute (EPI) is a progressive think tank that at times may get confused with the Employment Policies Institute because it shares the same initials. If the Employment Policies Institute exists to demonstrate the ill effects of raising the minimum wage, the EPI is there to show in detailed terms the state of America's economy, especially for middle-class and low-wage workers. To a certain extent, the EPI has been a friend of organized labor, and has been very supportive of the same causes. Founded in 1986 as a nonpartisan think tank, it was created to include the needs of low-income and middle-income workers in economic policy decisions. The EPI believes that every person deserves a good job with fair pay, affordable healthcare, and retirement security. It is therefore the mission of EPI to conduct research and analysis on the state of working America, make policy proposals, and attempt to affect the

policy debate in favor of those policies that will benefit low-
and middle-income workers.

As a think tank it conducts a wide range of research on a
variety of issues. Among its most important research projects is
its encyclopedic *State of Working America,* published 12 times
since 1988. This work gives a detailed account of the nation's
labor market, by age group, educational attainment, occupa-
tion, and industry. With regard to the minimum wage, EPI puts
out studies that (1) make it clear that there aren't the employment consequences claimed by the standard model, and certainly not claimed by the Employment Policies Institute, and
(2) the minimum wage population is not nearly as narrow as
that claimed by those who typically oppose the minimum wage.
Their studies make it clear that most minimum wage workers
are really adults with children, not teenagers who are merely
secondary earners. They also make it clear that the benefits of
minimum wage increases to the economy would outweigh the
costs, and that millions of American workers, especially those
at the lower rungs of the economic ladder, would benefit from
increases in the minimum wage. As a think tank, however, it
sees its role as larger than simply providing information that
can be used by policymakers and progressive activists alike. It
often jumps into the political fray. In January 2014, it released
a letter to both President Obama and Republican Speaker
of the House, John Boehner, signed by over 600 economists
(including this author), calling for an increase in the minimum
wage to $10.10 an hour. The letter made it clear that at least
five years had passed since the federal minimum wage was last
increased and that its value eroded significantly. More to the
point, the letter asserted that close to 17 million workers would
benefit directly from an increase in the minimum wage and
that an additional 11 million workers earning just above the
minimum would also see wage increases through "spillover"
effects as employers would then have to adjust their internal
wage ladders. The vast majority of workers who would benefit
would be adults in working families, and disproportionately

women who work a minimum of 20 hours a week and are dependent on these earnings to make ends meet. Whereas the standard model would counter that an economy with high unemployment is the wrong time to increase wages, the EPI letter asserted the opposite. In an economy with persistently high unemployment, an increase in the minimum wage was necessary to counter the already downward pressure on wages from the recession. Moreover, a minimum wage increase would have a stimulative effect on the economy because low-wage workers would spend their additional earnings in the economy, thereby increasing aggregate demand for goods and services, which in turn would have a positive effect on the job front. This letter was signed by economists from around the country including, several Nobel laureates in economics, and also including many economists who are strict adherents to the standard model.

The EPI's concern about wages, however, isn't restricted only to low-wage workers but also all middle-income workers who have seen their wages eroded. Aside from the fact that declining wages for low-wage middle-income workers suggest the decline of the American dream and perhaps the disappearance of the middle class, it also has been a contributing factor to the rise of wage inequality. In many of the EPI's studies on the minimum wage, it has made clear that an increase in the minimum wage and its subsequent indexation would represent an important step in narrowing the gap in inequality. That is, the increase in the ratio between the top 20th and the bottom 20th percentiles of the income distribution would be narrowed.

Barbara Ehrenreich (1941–)

Barbara Ehrenreich is an author and journalist who is known for doing in-depth work on a variety of different social causes. As a political activist, she considers herself a "myth buster by trade." A graduate of Reed College in 1963 with a degree in chemistry, she went on to earn a PhD in cellular immunology from Rockefeller University in 1968. Electing not to pursue a career in science, Ehrenreich first worked with the Bureau of the Budget in New York City and with the Health Policy Advisory Board. Later she took a position as an assistant professor at the State University of New York at Old Westbury. In 1972, Ehrenreich began co-teaching a course on women and health with feminist journalist and academic Deirdre English. Through the rest of the 1970s, Ehrenreich worked mostly in health-related research, advocacy, and activism, including co-writing, with English, several feminist books and pamphlets on the history and politics of women's health. During this period she began speaking frequently at conferences staged by women's health centers and women's groups, by universities, and by the U.S. government. She also spoke regularly about socialist feminism and about feminism in general. Throughout her career, she also worked as a freelance writer and is perhaps best known for works of nonfiction and social commentary. The work that she is perhaps best known for, and most relevant to the minimum wage debate, is *Nickeled and Dimed: On (Not) Getting By in America,* published in 2001.

In *Nickeled and Dimed,* Ehrenreich writes from the perspective of an undercover journalist who is trying to understand the impact of the 1996 welfare reforms on the working poor, many of which we would associate with minimum wage work. But it isn't a book filled with interviews with low-wage workers; rather, it is a personal journey into the lives of low-wage workers who work in a variety of different jobs. During the course of a year she decides to live the life of a low-wage worker and works in different settings across the country. She begins her journey by taking a job in Florida serving tables not far from Key West, Florida, where she actually lives. Shunning her home, she sought housing on the basis of what she would be able to afford on a low-wage worker's pay, which turned out to not be very much. From there she moves onto Portland, Maine, where she works for a maid service scrubbing a nursing home and a residential facility. There she discovers that the cost of an efficiency apartment is too expensive given her low wages, so she is forced to live in a low-end motel. From there she goes on to Minnesota, where she works at Wal-Mart. Aside from having to go to a chiropractor's office for a drug test, and sit through a session where she is to internalize the philosophy of Sam Walton and the Wal-Mart culture, she is also made to endure a session on the evils of labor unions and why they are particularly harmful to low-wage workers. She details one of the sessions:

> Once, long ago, unions had a place in American society but they "no longer have much to offer workers," which is why people are leaving them "by the droves." Wal-Mart is booming; unions are declining: judge for yourself. But we are warned that "unions have been targeting Wal-Mart for years." Why? For the dues money of course. Think of what you would lose with a union: first your dues money, which could be $20 a month "and sometimes much more." Second, you would lose "your voice" because the union would insist on doing your talking for you. Finally, you might lose even your wages and benefits because they would all be "at risk on the bargaining table." You have to wonder— and I imagine some of my teenage fellow orientees may be doing so—why such friends as these union organizers, such outright extortionists, are allowed to roam free in the land. (pp. 144–145)

She investigates the challenges faced by low-wage workers, making it clear that these workers really cannot get by on the low wages they earn, many of which are slightly higher than the statutory minimum wages. For many low-wage workers, they are forced to live in hotels because they cannot afford the security deposits, first month's fees and last month's fees. The daily cost of hotels is certainly more than they would have to spend were they able to obtain apartments. Because they are living in hotels, they are then forced to purchase food that is more expensive and less healthy than they otherwise would if they had access to refrigeration.

Among the myths that she attacks is that low-wage work is necessarily unskilled work, which in many's mind-set might also be the same as easy work. On the contrary, Ehrenreich finds manual labor to be taxing, uninteresting, and degrading. She claimed that the work, like hamburger flipping, required stamina, focus, quick thinking, and fast learning. She argues that constant and repeated movement creates a risk of repetitive stress injury, but these workers don't have the luxury of taking off sick days because they are in pain. Rather, they often have to work through their pain just to hold a job in a market with constant turnover. Many low-wage workers are forced to fill their days with degrading and uninteresting tasks such as mopping and cleaning toilet bowls. At the same time, she calls attention to managers who served mainly to interfere with worker productivity, in order to force employees to undertake pointless tasks, and to make the entire low-wage work experience even more miserable. Her larger point, however, is that these low-wage workers are not the teenagers that the standard model claims are hurt by minimum wage increases. Rather, they are adults who in many cases are trying to provide for themselves and their children, and that they are truly being harmed by low wages. In some cases, when she needed a break from the difficulty of a low-wage existence, she would return to her comfortable suburban life style. As this is an undercover investigation, she concedes that she had that luxury, which most minimum wage workers did not. Rather, this is their life from which there is no escape, and even small adjustments to the minimum wage, as much it may help, aren't really going to end their misery. In many respects, her work that represents the best traditions of ethnographic studies to be found in anthropology points out the utter irrelevance of most of the social science literature on low-wage workers generally and the minimum wage labor market particularly. While policymakers seek to buttress their arguments both for and against minimum wage increases with the latest studies, Ehrenreich is effectively giving voice to those who have all but been ignored.

Employment Policies Institute

The Employment Policies Institute was founded in 1991 as a nonprofit research organization dedicated to the study of public policy issues surrounding employment growth. This institute claims that its primary focus is on issues affecting entry-level employment. When it comes to the minimum wage, the Employment Policies Institute has been at the forefront in opposing increases on the grounds that minimum wage increases harm employment prospects specifically for low-skilled workers. While the Employment Policies Institute claims to sponsor nonpartisan research that is conducted by university economists around the country, it has often been alleged that this institute in particular is a front for the fast-food industry, with findings that show how much the minimum wage will hurt fast-food workers. In fact, much of its research and other projects are associated with the minimum wage, particularly in those states with plans to increase their minimum wages above the federal minimum wage. It is, in short, a bad idea.

As they have in the past, the Employment Policies Institute has weighed in on President Obama's call for a $10.10 minimum wage. Citing work by Neumark and Wascher, they argue that a hike in the minimum wage will reduce employment for low-skilled workers while having little or no effect on poverty rates. In fact, they claim on the basis of new data from researchers at Miami University and Trinity University that up to 1 million jobs would be lost and these findings are consistent with the findings of the Congressional Budget Office in 2014. They also cite others' research that the minimum wage is particularly detrimental to the interests of unskilled workers. In a study they sponsored, by William

Even at Miami University and David Macpherson at Trinity University, the message was that the minimum wage harms black male unskilled workers more than it does white male unskilled workers. Employment for white males between the ages of 16 and 24 decreased by 2.5 percent, while employment for black males in this age group decreased by 6.5 percent. The report also notes that in the 21 states fully affected by the federal minimum wage increases in 2007, 2008, and 2009, the employment consequences were staggering for black males. While 13,200 black males lost their jobs due to the recession directly, 18,500 black males lost their jobs as a direct result of the federal minimum wage mandate. From this institute's standpoint, the debate on the employment consequences of minimum wage increases has been settled conclusively, and the research proves that the burden is shouldered disproportionately by young black men.

Naquasia LeGrand (1992–)

Naquasia LeGrand is simply a young low-wage worker who would stand to benefit from an increase in the minimum wage from its current rate of $7.25 an hour to $10.10. She works at a Kentucky Fried Chicken in Brooklyn, New York. She shares a two-bedroom apartment with her grandmother in the Canarsie section of Brooklyn. As presented in the *Huffington Post*, she was frying chicken, sweeping floors, and serving customers for 7.25 an hour when she was recruited by union organizers to join a campaign for higher pay. Her grandmother was initially opposed to her joining a union for fear that she would lose her job. After participating in five strikes backed by Service Employees International Union and the local NT Communities for Change Group, she became the face of a growing movement. Over the next 15 months, she had become one of the most visible faces of the movement staging strikes around the country for a $15 minimum in fast-food restaurants. Among her accomplishments was that she had the opportunity to promote her cause on "The Colbert Report," and to join in on a strategy session with congressional Democrats. She even got to meet President Obama at the White House. She then began organizing daylong fast-food strikes in New York City, and eventually in more than 100 cities. While she spends a good deal of her time as an activist, she still works about 15 hours a week at a KFC (Matthews 2014).

In an interview with the *International Business Times,* she was asked how she responded to critics who accuse unions of creating moles and unrest among a small number of unsatisfied workers, to which she responded:

So, yeah, they say I'm pretty much a clone, like they're cloning me. This is what I say to that: No. Because at any given time, I could have said, "Forget this campaign; I don't want to do this." It wasn't up to the union. What they gave us workers was a foot to get in the door. We didn't know how to get a foot in the door. The union gave us the light to see what was really going on behind the counter. Single moms and single fathers are struggling while these companies make money, and we're not really paying attention as workers because we're too busy working and not thinking about these things.

And these things that are coming to light are true. And that's why these companies are mad and calling us moles. They don't want us to know the truth. They want us to be stuck in the dark, living in poverty. That's not right. What I say is I'm standing up as a hard worker who appreciates her job, who is grateful for my job, but who is also standing up for me and other workers who believe that we deserve better pay and the right to unionize without retaliation. (Young 2014)

National Association of Manufacturers

The National Association of Manufacturers (NAM) is the largest manufacturing association in the United States and represents both small and large manufacturers in every industrial sector in all 50 states. It claims to be the voice of manufacturers and the leading advocate for a policy agenda that helps manufacturers compete in the global economy and create jobs across the country. It also claims to be on the frontlines of policy battles ranging from immigration reform and labor relations to energy and the environment, trade policy, and taxes. It has also historically been opposed to any and all types of regulations, claiming that they harm economic efficiency and infringe individual liberty. And when it comes to the minimum wage, NAM has always been a prominent voice in the business community opposing increases. It was certainly a voice early on, fiercely opposing any type of governmental regulation. In hearings over the initial Connery–Black Bill, a representative from the National Association of Manufacturers referred to it as a step in the direction of bolshevism and fascism. Even in more recent hearings and debates over minimum wage increases, those opposed to increases still cite that claim in the direction of bolshevism that was originally made in 1938.

By the 1960s, however, NAM was no longer offering the fascism argument against the minimum wage; rather, it was expressing its concern for low-skilled workers, that what was important was for low-skilled workers to get education and training so that they would be able to produce services of a greater value. As far as wage setting was concerned, the government had no business to get itself involved. NAM now accepted that the minimum wage was the law of the land but was questioning the wisdom for further increases in the minimum wage, claiming that it would create a hardship to those employing unskilled and inexperienced workers. When questioned in Senate hearings over amendments to the FLSA during the 1960s, one senator pointed out that workers in the market place, especially low-skilled workers, tended to be exploited in the absence of governmental regulations, including minimum wages, and that the federal government had a moral obligation to say to employers in this country that they either employ with a minimum wage of health and decency or become employees yourself. To this, the NAM representative made it clear that he believed that the government had no such obligation.

Although most minimum wage workers are not in manufacturing, the NAM still opposes increases in the minimum wage, and it is still considered to be a powerful player in the larger corporate lobby. In 2014 when the Senate took up the measure to raise the minimum wage to $10.10 an hour, NAM came out against even allowing the measure to proceed to an up or down vote. While the language of the opposition to the minimum wage may have changed since the 1930s, its opposition still remains strong.

National Employment Law Project

The National Employment Law Project (NELP) is an organization that assumes that all workers have rights, and certainly should have a fair share in the national economy. The organization was formed, in part, in response to declining opportunities for American workers over the last three decades. On its website it states that its core mission is to ensure that work serves as both a ladder to economic opportunity and an anchor of security for working families. Too many low-wage jobs, instead of good ones, have been created due to globalization, domestic policy choices, and lax enforcement of workers' rights. Moreover, this has increased inequality to levels that only imperil the middle class. Therefore, the NELP seeks to restore the promise of opportunity in the twenty-first century by entering into partnerships with national, state, and local groups. The NELP seeks to promote policies and programs that create good jobs, strengthen upward mobility, enforce worker rights, and assist unemployed workers through improved benefits and services. In this vein, the NELP has certainly been a voice for low-wage workers and has become a key constituency for increases in the minimum wage. For the NELP, livable wages aren't only a matter of fairness and justice but also of workers' rights. Workers are entitled to earn livable wages—wages that enable them to support themselves and their families in dignity because that is the essence of a fundamental human right.

NELP is a national organization providing a variety of services to low-wage workers and their communities. It provides in-depth legal and policy analysis for the purpose of improving working conditions and bolstering economic security. It also conducts empirical research on low-wage labor markets and documents key trends in the economy for the purpose of establishing a foundation for effective policy solutions. It offers expert legal and technical assistance in order to assist advocates in their fight against legal restrictions. It provides strategic leadership in coalitions and brings together diverse constituencies behind a common goal. It seeks to educate the public on the plight of working families. And, finally, it seeks to build community capacity by disseminating policy and research reports, conferences, and the training of students.

The NELP has been involved in a variety of efforts to raise the minimum wage. It has made clear that it has a long history of supporting grassroots campaigns to raise state minimum wages. In efforts to raise state minimum wages, they work with community groups across the country, coalitions of community organizations, worker centers, advocacy groups, and labor unions to raise statewide minimum wages. They do this either through legislative campaigns or by putting the issue to voters on statewide ballot initiatives. Not only have they attempted to design policies that raise minimum wages, but which also provide worker protections to workers in low-wage industries. The NELP, for instance, supported successful ballot initiatives in 2004 and 2006 that raised minimum wages and also created automatic adjustment mechanisms for the minimum wage in Arizona, Colorado, Florida, Michigan, Missouri, Montana, Nevada, and Ohio. At the federal level, the NELP has sought to restore the value of the minimum wage to its historic purchasing power, which had been achieved in 1968, and believes that such a wage would be at least $10 an hour in today's dollars.

It has also sought to get minimum wage increases for tipped workers and to get annual cost-of-living increases for the minimum wage legislated into law so as to arrest its erosion in value.

U.S. Chamber of Commerce

The U.S. Chamber of Commerce (the Chamber) is perhaps the world's largest business organization representing the interests of more than 3 million businesses of all types, sizes, and sectors. Its stated overarching mission is to strengthen the competitiveness of the U.S. economy. Therefore, a fundamental activity of the Chamber is the development and implementation of policy on major issues affecting business. Historically the Chamber has not been supportive of increases in the minimum wage. The Chamber believes that a minimum wage, especially one that bites, will cause job loss. If given a choice for the purposes of boosting low-wage pay between an increase in the minimum wage and the earned income tax credit, the Chamber appears to opt for the latter. Although the Chamber officially went on record opposing an increase in the minimum wage as proposed by President Obama, surprisingly the Women's Chamber of Commerce, most of whose 500,000 members are small business owners, came out in favor of the increase.

Still, the Chamber has a record of working toward efforts that undermine minimum wage increases. In 2014, for example, the Chamber signed onto a lawsuit filed by the International Franchise Association against Seattle, Washington's, minimum wage law. Specifically, they were challenging what they considered to be a discriminatory provision of the law. Under the law, small businesses with more than 500 employees are granted up to seven years to implement the $15 an hour minimum, while franchised food chains, categorized as large employers, are given only three to four years to implement the law. In its amicus brief, the Chamber asserts: "By saddling franchises with increased labor costs that non-franchised small businesses are not required to bear, the Ordinance will make it difficult—if not impracticable—for franchisees to compete. Not only does it impose the largest minimum-wage increase in the history of the United States, but it does so by targeting franchisees for disparate treatment because of their affiliation with out-of-state franchisors and fellow franchisees" (Ashtari 2014).

References

Allegretto, Sylvia, Arindrajit Dube, and Michael Reich. 2011. "Do Minimum Wages Really Reduce Teen Employment? Accounting for Heterogeneity and Selectivity in State Panel Data." *Industrial Relations.* 50, 2 (April): 205–240.

Ashtari, Shadee. 2014. "U.S. Chamber of Commerce Loins Lawsuit against Discriminatory Seattle Minimum Wage Hike." *Huffington Post.* (August 14). Downloaded from http://www.huffingtonpost.com/2014/08/14/chamber-of-commerce-Seattle-minimum-wage_n_5680004.html.

Bernstein, Irving. 1969. *Turbulent Years: A History of the American Worker 1933–1941.* Boston, MA: Houghton Mifflin Co.

Burkhauser, Richard V. 2014. "Why Minimum Wage Increases Are a Poor Way to Help the Working Poor." *IZA Policy Paper No. 86.* (June). Downloaded from http://ftp.iza.org/pp86.pdf.

Burkhauser, Richard V., and T. Aldrich Finnegan. 1989. "The Minimum Wage and the Poor: The End of a Relationship." *Journal of Policy Analysis and Management.* 8, 1: 53–71.

Burkhauser, Richard V., Jeff Larrimore, and Kosali I. Simon. 2012. "A 'Second Opinion' on the Economic Health of the American Middle Class." *National Tax Journal.* 65, 1 (March): 7–32.

Burkhauser, Richard V. and Joseph J. Sabia. 2004. "Why Raising the Minimum Wage Is a Poor Way to Help the Working Poor: An Analysis of Senators Kerry and Kennedy's Minimum Wage Proposal." Employment Policies

Institute. (July). Downloaded from https://www.epionline
.org/wp-content/studies/burkhauser_07–2004.pdf.

Burns, James MacGregor. 1956. *Roosevelt: The Lion and the Fox 1882–1940*. New York: Harcourt, Brace & World, Inc.

Card, David, and Alan B. Krueger. 1995. *Myth and Measurement: The New Economics of the Minimum Wage*. Princeton, NJ: Princeton University Press.

Card, David, and Alan B. Krueger. 1998. "A Reanalysis of the Effect of the New Jersey Minimum Wage Increase on the Fast-Food Industry with Representative Payroll Data." Working Paper no. 6386. National Bureau of Economic Research.

Card, David, and John DiNardo. 2002. "Skill Biased Technological Change and Rising Wage Inequality: Some Problems and Puzzles." *Working Paper No 8769*. National Bureau of Economic Research (February).

Card, David, Thomas Lemieux, and W. Craig Riddell. 2008. "Unions and Wage Inequality." In James T. Bennett and Bruce E. Kaufman, eds. *What Do Unions Do?: A Twenty-Year Perspective*. New Brunswick, NJ: Transaction Publishers.

Card, David, Ian Preston, and Christian Dustmann. 2012. "Immigration, Wages, and Compositional Amenities." *Journal of the European Economic Association*. 10, 1 (February): 78–119.

Clark, John Bates. 1913. "The Minimum Wage." *The Atlantic Monthly*. 112, 3 (September): 289–297.

Commons, John R. 1998. *Institutional Economics: Its Place in Political Economy*. Vol. 1. New Brunswick: Transaction Publishers.

Congressional Quarterly Almanac. 1960. Vol. 16, 86th Congress, (2nd session): 309–319.

Dube, Arindrajit. 2013. "The Minimum Wage We Can Do." *The New York Times*. (November 30). Downloaded

from http://opinionator.blogs.nytimes.com/2013/11/30/
the-minimum-we-can-do/#more-150801.

Dube, Arindrajit, T. William Lester, and Michael Reich. 2010. "Minimum Wage Effects among State Borders: Estimates Using Contiguous Counties." *The Review of Economics and Statistics*. 92, 4 (November 2010): 945–964.

Dube, Arindrajit, Suresh Naidu, and Michael Reich. 2007. "The Economic Effects of a Citywide Minimum Wage." *Industrial and Labor Relations Review*. 60, 4 (July): 522–523.

Dubofsky, Melvyn. 1994. *The State & Labor in Modern America*. Chapel Hill: The University of North Carolina Press.

Figart, Deborah M., Ellen Mutari, and Marilyn Power. 2002. *Living Wages, Equal Wages: Gender and Labor Market Policies in the United States*. London; New York: Routledge.

Filene, Edward A. 1923. "The Minimum Wage and Efficiency." *American Economic Review*. 13 (September): 411–415.

Hattam, Victoria C. 1993. *Labor Visions and State Power: The Origins of Business Unionism in the United States*. Princeton, NJ: Princeton University Press.

Kaufman, Bruce E. 2003. "John R. Commons and the Wisconsin School of Industrial Relations Strategy and Policy." *Industrial and Labor Relations Review*. 57: 3–30.

Kaufman, Bruce E. 2009. "Promoting Labour Market Efficiency through a Legal Minimum Wage: The Webbs and the Social Cost of Labour." *British Journal of Industrial Relations*. 47: 306–326.

Kirkendall, Richard. 1974. *The United States 1929–1945: Years of Crisis and Change*. New York: McGraw-Hill Book Co.

Lester, Richard A. 1946. "Shortcomings of Marginal Analysis for Wage-Employment Problems." *The American Economic Review*. 36, 1 (March): 63–82.

Lester, Richard A. 1947a. "Marginalism, Minimum Wages, and Labor Markets." *The American Economic Review.* 37, 1 (March): 135–148.

Lester, Richard A. 1947b. "Reflections on the 'Labor Monopoly' Issue." *Journal of Political Economy.* 55, 6 (December): 513–536.

Lochner v. New York. 1905. 198 U.S. 45.

Lustig, R. Jeffrey. 1982. *Corporate Liberalism: The Origins of American Political Theory, 1890–1920.* Berkeley: University of California Press.

Matthews, Karen. 2014. "Meet the 22-Year-Old KFC Employee Taking the Minimum Wage Fight to the White House." *Huff Post Business.* (3/2). Downloaded from http://www.huffingtonpost.com/2014/03/02/naquasia-legrand-kfc_n_4885937.html.

Miller, Edythe S. 1998. "Veblen and Commons and the Concept of Community." In Waren J. Samuels, ed. *The Founding of Institutional Economics: The Leisure Class and Sovereignty.* London; New York: Routledge.

"National Industrial Recovery Act." 1933. *Statutes at Large* 73rd Congress, Session 1 Chs, 89, 90 (June 16).

Neumark, David, J. M. Ian Salas, and William Wascher. 2014. "Revisiting the Minimum Wage—Employment Debate: Throwing Out the Baby with the Bathwater?" *Industrial and Labor Relations Review.* 67 (Supplement): 608–648.

Neumark, David, Mark Schweitzer, and William Wascher. 2004. "Minimum Wage Effects throughout the Distribution." *The Journal of Human Resources.* 39, 2: 425–450.

Neumark, David, and William Wascher. 1992. "Employment Effects of Minimum and Subminimum Wages: Panel Data and State." *Industrial and Labor Relations Review.* 46, 1 (October): 55–81.

Neumark, David, and William Wascher. 2000. "Minimum Wages and Employment: A Case Study of the Fast-Food Industry in New Jersey and Pennsylvania: Comment." *American Economic Review*. 90, 5 (December): 1362–1396.

Neumark, David, and William Wascher. 2011. "Does a Higher Minimum Wage Enhance the Effectiveness of the Earned Income Tax Credit?" *Industrial and Labor Relations Review*. 64 (July): 712–748.

Pohlman, H.L. 1984. *Justice Oliver Wendell Holmes & Utilitarian Jurisprudence*. Cambridge, MA: Harvard University Press.

Sabia, Joseph J., and Richard V. Burkhauser. 2010. "Minimum Wages and Poverty: Will a $9.50 Federal Minimum Wage Really Help the Working Poor?" *Southern Economic Journal*. 76, 3: 592–623.

Skousen, Mark. 2009. *The Making of Modern Economics: The Lives and Ideas of the Great Thinkers*. Armonk, NY: M.E. Sharpe.

Thurber, Maggie. 2013. "Thurbers' Thoughts." (September 25). Downloaded from http://thurbersthoughts.blogspot .com/2013/09/quotes-of-day-union-leader-samuel.html.

U.S. Congress. Joint Hearings of Committee on Education and Labor. U.S. Senate and Committee on Labor. House of Representatives. 1937. *Fair Labor Standards Act of 1937*. 75th Congress, 1st session. S.2475 and H.R. 7200. Washington, DC: Government Printing Office.

Webb, Sidney. 1912. "The Economic Theory of a Legal Minimum Wage." *Journal of Political Economy*. 20, 10 (December): 973–998.

West Coast Hotel Co. v. Parrish et al. 1936. 300 U.S. (October).

Woolner, David B. 2013. "FDR Called Minimum Wage Critics 'Hopelessly Reactionary.' He Was Right." The blog of the Roosevelt Institute. (March 19). Downloaded from http://www.nextnewdeal.net/fdr-called-minimum-wage-critics-hopelessly-reactionary-he-was-right.

Young, Angelo. 2014. "Minimum Wage Increase: Naquasia LeGrand, KFC Employee, Says Fast-Food Workers Need Better Pay, and Companies Like Yum Brands (YUM) and McDonald's (MCD) Can Afford It." *International Business Times* (February 14). Downloaded from http://www.ibtimes.com/minimum-wage-increase-naquasia-legrand-kfc-employee-says-fast-food-workers-need-better-pay-companies.

Introduction

In this chapter I present data and documents on the minimum wage, which, if nothing else, demonstrate the unsettled nature of the minimum wage as a policy issue. Data at best can be used to buttress a political argument on either side of the political debate. At the same time, it is easily manipulated. Each side uses the data that best make its case and whatever data that are used are always subject to interpretation. Which is to say that there is no such thing as dispositive data. Data are often presented as objective fact because they are based on what is observed, but because they are always subject to interpretation; it is subjective.

Data

As we mentioned in Chapter 2, much of the controversy surrounding the minimum wage has to do with measurement and definition. Data from the Bureau of Labor Statistics, for instance, in 2012 show that 3.6 million hourly paid workers in the United States had wages at or below the federal minimum wage of $7.25 an hour. This meant that they accounted for 4.7 percent of hourly paid workers. On the face of it, that does not appear to be an insignificant number. But when considered

A restaurant worker washes dishes. Many food industry jobs in the United States do not provide workers with a livable wage. (Pastoor/Dreamstime.com)

in the context of 86 million full-time workers in the private sector, that percentage is now reduced to 4.2 percent. Now within the context of the Census Bureau's report of 103,087,000 full-time workers, including those in the public sector, the percentage is now 3.5 percent. The entire labor force in 2012, which would also include part-time workers, was about 154,966,000 (based on the average over 12 months), which now means the hourly paid workers paid at the minimum wage or below was only 2.3 percent, consistent with the claims of opponents that the size of the minimum wage labor market is inconsequential. But as the next set of tables suggest, it may not be.

Consider the following chart that shows the percentage of hourly paid workers earning at or below the prevailing minimum wage to the percentage of total wage and salary workers between 1979 and 2013.

As Series 1 suggests, the percentage of total wage and salary workers does not change that much over the 34-year period. It fluctuates a bit, beginning at 59.1 percent in 1979 and winding up at 58.8 percent in 2013. Series 2, however, tells a different

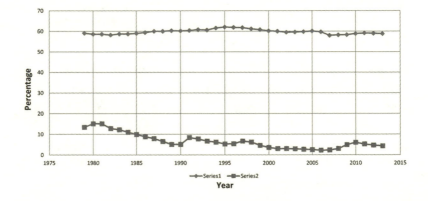

Figure 5.1   Percentage of wage workers and percentage of minimum wage workers (BLS Reports, "Characteristics of Minimum Wage Workers, 2013," Report 1048, March 2014. Data points taken from Table 10. Wage and salary workers paid hourly rates at or below the prevailing federal minimum wage by gender, 1979–2013 annual averages, p. 13).

story. The percentage of minimum wage hourly workers with slight fluctuation falls from 13.4 percent in 1979 to 4.3 percent in 2013. Interestingly enough, this percentage does rise slightly following increases in the federal minimum wage, which might suggest a couple of different things. It could be increasing following an increase because the new rate has attracted workers into the labor market, which suggests that higher minimum wages do have supply-side effects insofar as workers, particularly low-wage workers, are willing to supply their labor services following an increase. It could also be increasing because it is now a bit closer to the 50 percent of average annual hourly earnings mark, in which case more are encompassed in those averages. At the same time, the chart could be interpreted to mean that as a percentage of workers earning the minimum wage relative to total wage and salary workers, without taking into account whether they are full time or part time, has been declining. And to the extent that it has it may appear that the minimum wage in today's labor market is really inconsequential. That fewer workers are dependent on the minimum wage is seen as a positive thing.

In Table 5.1 we can see the minimum wage from 1938 until the present in both actual and 2015 inflation-adjusted dollars. Then in Table 5.2 we can see the minimum wage in 2012 by age and gender.

Table 5.1   Minimum Wage in Actual and 2015 Adjusted Dollars, 1938–2015

Year	Actual Minimum Wage	Inflation-Adjusted Minimum Wage (2015 dollars)
1938	$0.25	$4.14
1939	$0.30	$5.04
1940	$0.35	$5.84
1941	$0.35	$5.56
1942	$0.35	$5.02
1943	$0.35	$4.73
1944	$0.35	$4.65

(continued)

Table 5.1 *(continued)*

Year	Actual Minimum Wage	Inflation-Adjusted Minimum Wage (2015 dollars)
1945	$0.40	$5.19
1946	$0.40	$4.79
1947	$0.40	$4.19
1948	$0.40	$3.88
1949	$0.40	$3.93
1950	$0.75	$7.27
1951	$0.75	$6.74
1952	$0.75	$6.61
1953	$0.75	$6.56
1954	$0.75	$6.52
1955	$0.75	$6.54
1956	$1.00	$8.59
1957	$1.00	$8.32
1958	$1.00	$8.09
1959	$1.00	$8.03
1960	$1.00	$7.90
1961	$1.15	$8.99
1962	$1.15	$8.90
1963	$1.25	$9.55
1964	$1.25	$9.42
1965	$1.25	$9.27
1966	$1.25	$9.02
1967	$1.40	$9.80
1968	$1.60	$10.75
1969	$1.60	$10.19
1970	$1.60	$9.64
1971	$1.60	$9.23
1972	$1.60	$8.95
1973	$1.60	$8.42
1974	$2.00	$9.48
1975	$2.10	$9.12
1976	$2.30	$9.45
1977	$2.30	$8.87
1978	$2.65	$9.50
1979	$2.90	$9.34
1980	$3.10	$8.79
1981	$3.35	$8.61

Table 5.1 (*continued*)

Year	Actual Minimum Wage	Inflation-Adjusted Minimum Wage (2015 dollars)
1982	$3.35	$8.11
1983	$3.35	$7.86
1984	$3.35	$7.54
1985	$3.35	$7.28
1986	$3.35	$7.14
1987	$3.35	$6.89
1988	$3.35	$6.62
1989	$3.35	$6.31
1990	$3.80	$6.79
1991	$4.25	$7.29
1992	$4.25	$7.08
1993	$4.25	$6.87
1994	$4.25	$6.70
1995	$4.25	$6.52
1996	$4.60	$7.00
1997	$5.15	$7.50
1998	$5.15	$7.38
1999	$5.15	$7.22
2000	$5.15	$6.99
2001	$5.15	$6.80
2002	$5.15	$6.69
2003	$5.15	$6.54
2004	$5.15	$6.37
2005	$5.15	$6.16
2006	$5.15	$5.97
2007	$5.85	$6.59
2008	$6.55	$7.11
2009	$7.25	$7.90
2010	$7.25	$7.77
2011	$7.25	$7.53
2012	$7.25	$7.38
2013	$7.25	$7.27
2014	$7.25	$7.16
2015	$7.25	$7.25

Source: Author's calculations using the Department of Labor Calculator: http://www.bls.gov/data/inflation_calculator.htm.

Table 5.2   Minimum Wage Workers by Age and Gender for 2012

Age	Both Sexes	Men	Women
Total, 16 years and over	4.7	3.4	6.0
16 to 19 years	21.1	19.0	23.0
20 to 24 years	8.7	5.5	11.9
25 to 34 years	4.2	2.8	5.8
35 to 44 years	2.7	1.7	3.7
45 to 54 years	2.4	1.6	3.2
55 to 64 years	1.8	1.4	2.2
65 years and over	2.9	2.6	3.1

Source: Bureau of Labor Statistics, *The Economic Daily*, March 25, 2013.

On the basis of the first table we can see that when the minimum wage is adjusted for inflation it actually has lost value, especially after it reached its peak in 1968. Even following legislated increases, it appears never to recoup its former value. On the basis of this table, the largest age group of minimum wage earners would appear to be teenagers, again strengthening the argument of minimum wage critics that if there are disemployment effects owing to the minimum wage, it will be felt disproportionately by the youth labor market. But it also becomes clear from this chart that more minimum wage earners are women. Critics of the minimum wage will claim that higher percentages of women in the labor market speak to the fact that most minimum wage earners are not primary earners, but secondary earners, implying that their earnings are not essential to household or family income. Supporters of the minimum wage will most likely counter with the claim that if they are secondary earners, their income may well be essential to the family budget, and if they are not married, it speaks to the growing feminization of poverty.

As the second chart shows, between 1981 and 2012, the minimum wage as a percentage of the average annual hourly wage fell quite a bit in Series 1, and the minimum wage as

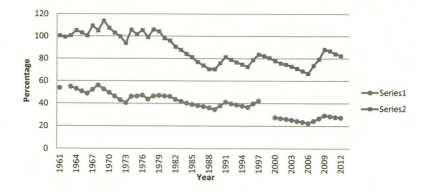

Figure 5.2 Minimum Wage as percentage of average annual hourly wage and minimum wage as percentage of poverty line (BLS Reports, "Characteristics of Minimum Wage Workers, 2013," Report 1048, March 2014. Data points taken from Table 10. Wage and salary workers paid hourly rates at or below the prevailing federal minimum wage by gender, 1979–2013 annual averages, p. 13).

a percentage of the federal poverty line also fell substantially. Again, as a percentage of the poverty line, it does appear to increase following minimum wage increases, but then it decreases following periods where the minimum wage has not been increased, thereby signifying its diminishing value and that it may be insufficient to support a family.

If the definition of the minimum wage is changed from those earning the statutory minimum wage to those earning around the minimum wage, or what we might refer to as the "effective" minimum wage population, we can see that the proportion in the effective minimum wage labor market is quite sizeable. Table 5.3 shows labor force figures from the Integrated Public Use Microdata Series Current Population Survey from 1982 to 2013. In this table, the effective minimum wage labor market is defined as those earning between the statutory minimum wage and 50 percent of average annual hourly earnings.

Table 5.3 Labor Force Figures

Year	Minimum Wage	50% of Average Annual Hourly Wage	Average Annual Hourly Wage*	Number Employed	Number of Effective Minimum Wage Earners	Percentage of Effective Minimum Wage Earners
1982	$3.35	$3.73	$7.46	54,936	1,803	3.3
1992	$4.25	$5.91	$11.82	56,284	5,522	9.8
2002	$5.15	$9.52	$19.04	81,486	12,102	14.9
2003	$5.15	$9.72	$19.44	80,034	13,840	17.2
2004	$5.15	$9.94	$19.88	78,569	13,041	16.6
2005	$5.15	$10.15	$20.30	78,062	13,546	17.4
2006	$5.15	$10.50	$21.00	78,362	13,535	17.3
2007	$5.85	$10.95	$21.90	78,846	12,484	15.8
2008	$6.55	$11.19	$22.38	78,515	11,550	14.7
2009	$7.25	$11.25	$22.50	74,988	8,469	11.3
2010	$7.25	$11.86	$23.72	73,296	9,484	12.9
2011	$7.25	$11.95	$23.90	71,486	9,186	12.9
2012	$7.25	$12.39	$24.78	71,053	10,702	15.1
2013	$7.25	$12.70	$25.40	71,646	11,718	16.4

* These wages are based on the average annual hourly wage of those in full-time work in the CPS data set.

Source: Miriam King, Steven Ruggles, J. Trent Alexander, Sarah Flood, Katie Genadek, Matthew B. Schroeder, Brandon Trampe, and Rebecca Vick. Integrated Public Use Microdata Series, Current Population Survey: Version 3.0 [Machine-readable database]. Minneapolis: University of Minnesota, 2010. Files 1982. 1992, 2002–2013.

This data is based on full-time workers and shows that the effective minimum wage population is considerably larger than the statutory minimum wage population, as shown in Table 5.1. To return to the issue of interpretation, we initially saw how the percentage of minimum wage workers as a percentage of hourly paid workers went from 4.7 percent to 2.3 percent of minimum wage workers as a percentage of the labor force. What Table 5.2 shows is that the effective minimum wage population actually grew from 3.3 percent of the labor market in 1982 to 16.4 percent in 2013, an increase of 397 percent.

Much of the criticism of minimum wage increases centers around the claim that only a very small segment of the labor market earns the minimum wage—that 2.3 percent figure discussed earlier—and that of this small segment most are either teenagers or other secondary earners. Therefore, it is maintained, the benefits of an increase in the minimum wage will be so small that it hardly justifies the cost in terms of lower employment. But as Table 5.2 makes clear, when the minimum wage labor market is redefined as the "effective" minimum wage labor market, that segment is not that small or inconsequential. Moreover, as the demographics in Table 5.4 show, most of these workers are not necessarily teenagers or secondary earners.

During this 31-year period, there was among the effective minimum wage labor market a 49.5 percent decrease in the 18- to 24-year-old cohort, a 20.7 percent increase in the 35–44 age cohort and 40.1 percent increase in the 45–54 age cohort. In other words, effective minimum wage earners were older in 2013 than they were in 1982. In 1982, the vast majority of effective minimum wage earners (75 percent) had not even completed a high school education. By 2013 only 16.7 percent of the effective minimum wage population had less than a high school education, a decrease of 77.7 percent. Meanwhile, the percentage of effective minimum wage earners with a high school diploma increased 303.7 percent from 2.7 in 1982 percent to 37.9 percent in 2013. On the surface, these changes

Table 5.4 Demographics

	1982	1992	2002	2003	2004	2005	2006	2007	2008	2009	2010	2011	2012	2013
Age														
15–17	0.2	0.2	0.4	0.2	0.3	0.3	0.3	0.3	0.3	0.2	0.2	0.2	0.1	0.2
18–24	27.3	21.9	18.2	17.4	17.8	17.6	18.8	17.1	17.3	14.7	14.1	13.3	13.0	13.8
23–34	26.6	31.0	26.6	25.7	25.8	25.8	25.4	26.3	25.8	25.3	26.9	27.0	26.4	26.5
35–44	18.4	22.3	25.5	26.4	24.9	24.6	23.6	23.7	22.4	23.0	22.1	22.7	22.6	22.2
45–54	15.0	14.7	19.0	19.7	20.1	19.8	20.0	20.0	20.3	22.3	22.0	22.3	21.9	21.1
55–64	11.2	8.0	8.5	8.9	8.9	9.8	9.6	10.1	11.2	11.5	12.2	11.8	12.6	13.1
65–74	0.9	1.6	1.5	1.3	1.6	1.7	1.9	1.9	2.1	2.1	2.0	2.1	2.4	2.4
75+	0.2	0.3	0.4	0.4	0.5	0.5	0.5	0.6	0.6	0.7	0.5	0.7	0.9	0.7
Education														
Up to 12 years	75.0	23.8	22.1	21.5	22.0	21.5	22.0	21.6	19.4	18.3	17.5	17.1	16.3	16.7
HS Diploma	2.7	44.6	42.2	41.6	40.4	41.3	40.7	40.6	40.6	39.7	40.6	41.1	39.2	37.9
Some College, No Degree	22.3	16.8	18.5	18.5	18.7	18.3	18.6	18.1	19.6	20.4	18.9	19.2	19.5	19.9
Associate Degree		4.9	7.4	7.1	7.7	7.7	7.6	8.3	8.6	9.1	9.4	9.6	10.5	10.6
BA Degree		7.8	7.9	8.9	9.0	8.9	8.9	9.1	9.4	10.3	11.1	10.1	11.7	12.0
Professional Degree		2.1	2.0	2.4	2.3	2.3	7.6	2.2	2.4	2.2	2.5	2.8	2.8	2.8
Sex														
Male	35.7	43.2	42.6	43.5	45.0	45.7	45.1	45.3	44.3	42.0	44.1	44.5	44.9	46.6
Female	64.3	56.8	57.4	56.5	55.0	54.3	54.9	54.7	55.7	58.0	55.9	55.5	55.1	53.4

Race													
White	82.5	84.4	79.6	78.6	77.7	78.7	78.2	78.5	76.7	77.3	77.0	76.5	76.1	76.9
Black	13.4	11.3	13.8	13.6	13.6	12.7	12.7	12.7	14.0	14.0	13.3	14.0	13.7	13.6
Industry														
Agriculture, Forestry, Fishing	2.7	3.1	3.2	3.0	3.6	3.4	3.8	3.5	3.5	2.7	2.9	3.3	3.5	3.5
Mining	0.3	0.4	0.3	0.3	0.3	0.3	0.3	0.3	0.3	0.4	0.3	0.3	0.3	0.3
Construction	4.2	5.3	7.2	6.9	7.6	8.1	8.5	8.5	7.4	6.6	5.7	6.0	5.4	6.5
Manufacturing	20.3	17.5	14.6	13.8	13.0	13.1	12.3	12.8	12.1	11.2	12.0	11.8	11.5	11.8
Transportation, Commu-nication & Other Utilities	3.9	3.4	4.0	3.8	3.6	3.4	3.7	3.9	3.8	4.4	4.3	4.4	4.0	4.4
Wholesale Trade	3.2	3.1	2.8	2.7	2.8	2.5	2.7	2.4	2.6	2.5	2.6	2.9	1.9	2.4
Retail Trade	20.2	24.2	22.9	23.1	23.9	23.7	24.5	23.2	24.4	24.2	24.0	23.1	23.8	23.0
Finance, Insurance & Real Estate	6.4	6.0	5.3	5.3	5.0	5.0	4.6	4.6	4.8	5.3	5.0	4.5	4.9	5.3
Business & Repair Services	5.0	6.0	7.1	7.3	7.8	7.0	6.7	7.4	7.6	7.3	7.7	7.7	8.2	8.0
Personal Services	4.9	5.6	4.9	5.4	4.8	4.5	4.6	4.8	4.5	4.2	4.7	5.1	4.8	4.7
Entertainment & Recreation	1.2	2.0	2.2	2.4	2.1	2.4	2.6	2.2	2.5	2.3	2.4	2.2	2.2	2.2
Professional & Related	24.9	20.9	22.9	23.3	23.2	24.1	23.5	23.7	23.9	26.0	25.5	25.9	26.7	25.1
Public Administration	2.8	2.4	2.5	2.6	2.4	2.5	2.4	2.8	2.5	2.8	2.8	2.7	2.7	2.8

(continued)

235

Table 5.4 *(continued)*

Occupation	1982	1992	2002	2003	2004	2005	2006	2007	2008	2009	2010	2011	2012	2013
Professional, Technical	9.7	9.2	10.7	11.7	11.4	11.6	10.9	11.4	11.4	12.2	12.0	12.4	13.1	12.9
Farmers	0.1	0.5	0.4	0.3	0.3	0.2	0.3	0.2	0.3	0.3	0.3	0.3	0.2	0.3
Managers, Officials, Proprietors	4.5	7.7	7.6	6.9	6.2	5.8	6.3	5.9	6.0	6.9	7.1	7.1	7.3	7.7
Clerical and Kindred	24.1	22.3	20.6	22.1	20.5	20.8	21.2	21.4	22.2	23.2	21.9	21.1	20.9	21.5
Sales Workers	4.5	5.2	4.8	4.9	5.3	5.0	5.1	5.0	5.0	5.0	4.7	4.5	4.2	4.5
Craftsmen	7.6	8.1	8.5	8.9	9.2	9.5	9.3	8.9	8.9	7.8	7.2	8.3	7.4	8.3
Operatives	20.1	17.7	15.6	15.6	15.2	15.3	14.8	15.2	14.4	14.2	15.6	14.1	14.3	14.1
Service Workers (private household)	0.7	0.6	0.6	2.7	2.3	2.3	2.5	2.2	2.2	2.0	2.3	2.8	2.7	1.8
Service Workers (non-private household)	21.2	20.7	22.0	20.4	21.6	21.8	21.5	21.6	21.7	21.5	22.9	22.4	23.0	21.7
Farm Laborers	1.9	1.5	1.4	1.2	1.4	1.5	1.5	1.5	1.4	1.2	1.0	1.3	1.5	1.4
Laborers	4.7	6.6	7.9	5.2	6.5	6.3	6.6	6.8	6.7	5.6	4.9	5.8	5.4	5.8

alone may tell us quite a bit about the changing nature of the U.S. economy. That only 3.3 percent of the labor market in 1982 were effective minimum wage earners and of that 3.3 percent the vast majority had not completed high school suggest that the effective minimum wage labor market—what can be referred to as the low-wage labor market—was composed of predominantly low-skilled workers.

These data tables are only part of the story involved in redefining the minimum wage debate. When the issue is conceived of in terms of wage contours, then a whole new picture emerges. Consider Table 5.5, which is based on data from the IPUMS CPS from 1962 to 2008.

Between 1962 and 2008, median wages in each contour increased in years when there was an increase in the federal minimum wage. In years when there was no increase, median wages remained unchanged for the most part. These trends alone would imply wage contour effects and that the reach of a minimum wage increase extends far beyond the limited submarket that actually earns the statutory minimum wage. Arguably there may be other factors to explain increases in median wages, especially in the upper contours, but why don't those other factors appear to be present in years when there was no increase in the minimum wages? That there were no increases in median wages during those years when there was no minimum wage increase and there were long periods when there was no minimum wage increase suggest that wage stagnation may well be attributable to the stagnation of the minimum wage. And yet, to the extent that there may be middle-class welfare benefits associated with wage policy, we aren't talking about a narrow segment of the labor market as critics claim, but of at least two-thirds of the labor market as shown in Table 5.6.

As Table 5.6 shows, a substantial percentage of the labor market during this 46-year period earns through the 10 contours. Beginning in 1964, more than 57 percent of the labor market earns through the 10 contours, and in 2008 more than

Table 5.5   Individual Income in the United States by Contour

Year	MW	1st	2nd	3rd	4th	5th	6th	7th	8th	9th	10th
1962	$1.15	$1.25	$1.59	$2.00	$2.45	$3.13	$3.85	$4.81	$5.77	$7.21	$9.62
1963	$1.25	$1.44	$1.78	$2.27	$2.74	$3.37	$4.09	$4.95	$6.73	$8.17	$10.10
1964	$1.25	$1.44	$1.78	$2.26	$2.76	$3.37	$4.09	$5.05	$6.73	$8.17	$9.61
1965	$1.25	$1.44	$1.78	$2.26	$2.79	$3.37	$4.09	$5.05	$6.73	$8.17	$9.62
1966	$1.25	$1.44	$1.78	$2.28	$2.79	$3.37	$4.09	$5.05	$6.73	$8.17	$9.76
1967	$1.40	$1.54	$1.92	$2.40	$3.08	$3.85	$4.81	$5.77	$7.21	$9.13	$12.01
1968	$1.60	$1.85	$2.36	$2.88	$3.46	$4.33	$5.43	$6.73	$8.17	$9.62	$12.72
1969	$1.60	$1.83	$2.36	$2.88	$3.46	$4.37	$5.39	$6.73	$8.17	$9.88	$13.46
1970	$1.60	$1.83	$2.31	$2.88	$3.50	$4.36	$5.39	$6.73	$8.20	$10.10	$13.03
1971	$1.60	$1.83	$2.31	$2.88	$3.51	$4.38	$5.38	$6.73	$8.22	$10.10	$13.22
1972	$1.60	$1.83	$2.31	$2.88	$3.50	$4.41	$5.38	$6.73	$8.37	$10.10	$13.46
1973	$1.60	$1.83	$2.31	$2.88	$3.49	$4.42	$5.48	$6.73	$8.37	$10.10	$13.46
1974	$2.00	$2.31	$2.88	$3.51	$4.42	$5.48	$6.73	$8.32	$10.10	$12.69	$16.83
1975	$2.10	$2.40	$2.88	$3.72	$4.64	$5.77	$7.21	$8.75	$11.06	$14.28	$17.07
1976	$2.30	$2.50	$3.17	$3.96	$4.92	$6.25	$7.69	$9.62	$12.02	$14.90	$18.61
1977	$2.30	$2.50	$3.16	$4.00	$4.94	$6.25	$7.69	$9.62	$12.02	$14.90	$19.00
1978	$2.65	$2.88	$3.75	$4.71	$5.77	$7.21	$8.99	$11.30	$14.07	$17.26	$24.04
1979	$2.90	$3.37	$4.04	$5.00	$6.25	$7.79	$9.62	$12.02	$14.90	$19.23	$24.04
1980	$3.10	$3.51	$4.42	$5.50	$6.73	$8.41	$10.34	$12.93	$16.35	$19.71	$24.04
1981	$3.35	$3.76	$4.81	$5.77	$7.21	$9.15	$11.54	$14.30	$17.55	$24.04	

1982	$3.35	$3.76	$4.81	$5.77	$7.21	$9.25	$11.54	$14.38	$17.40	$22.12	$27.40
1983	$3.35	$3.77	$4.81	$5.77	$7.21	$9.21	$11.54	$14.42	$17.50	$22.12	$26.92
1984	$3.35	$3.75	$4.81	$5.77	$7.21	$9.14	$11.54	$14.42	$17.60	$22.12	$27.40
1985	$3.35	$3.76	$4.81	$5.77	$7.21	$9.23	$11.54	$14.42	$17.60	$22.12	$27.40
1986	$3.35	$3.75	$4.81	$5.77	$7.21	$9.33	$11.54	$14.42	$17.55	$21.92	$27.16
1987	$3.35	$3.75	$4.81	$5.77	$7.26	$9.31	$11.54	$14.42	$17.79	$22.12	$27.31
1988	$3.35	$3.80	$4.81	$5.77	$7.21	$9.25	$11.54	$14.42	$17.79	$22.12	$27.40
1989	$3.35	$3.81	$4.81	$5.77	$7.21	$9.23	$11.54	$14.42	$17.72	$21.95	$26.92
1990	$3.85	$4.50	$5.64	$6.73	$8.50	$10.56	$12.98	$16.59	$20.19	$24.39	$31.25
1991	$4.25	$4.81	$5.91	$7.21	$9.43	$11.54	$14.42	$17.79	$22.60	$28.06	$35.58
1992	$4.25	$4.81	$5.86	$7.27	$9.45	$11.54	$14.42	$17.98	$22.74	$28.37	$35.60
1993	$4.25	$4.81	$5.84	$7.21	$9.38	$11.54	$14.42	$18.27	$22.66	$28.37	$34.67
1994	$4.25	$4.81	$5.85	$7.29	$9.61	$11.54	$14.42	$18.27	$22.75	$28.37	$35.58
1995	$4.25	$4.81	$5.92	$7.39	$9.49	$11.54	$14.42	$18.27	$22.98	$28.37	$35.58
1996	$4.70	$5.29	$6.73	$8.17	$10.10	$12.50	$15.87	$19.71	$24.04	$30.77	$38.46
1997	$5.15	$5.77	$7.21	$9.13	$11.54	$14.42	$17.31	$22.10	$27.40	$33.65	$40.87
1998	$5.15	$5.77	$7.21	$9.13	$11.54	$14.42	$17.40	$21.83	$27.40	$33.65	$40.87
1999	$5.15	$5.77	$7.21	$9.13	$11.54	$14.42	$17.31	$22.03	$27.40	$33.65	$41.26
2000	$5.15	$5.77	$7.21	$9.13	$11.54	$14.42	$17.40	$22.12	$27.40	$33.65	$40.87

(continued)

Table 5.5 *(continued)*

Year	MW	1st	2nd	3rd	4th	5th	6th	7th	8th	9th	10th
2001	$5.15	$5.77	$7.21	$9.13	$11.54	$14.42	$17.43	$22.12	$27.40	$33.65	$40.87
2002	$5.15	$5.77	$7.21	$9.13	$11.54	$14.42	$17.31	$22.12	$27.41	$33.65	$40.87
2003	$5.15	$5.77	$7.21	$9.13	$11.54	$14.42	$17.61	$22.12	$27.40	$33.65	$40.87
2004	$5.15	$5.77	$7.21	$9.13	$11.54	$14.42	$17.79	$22.12	$27.40	$33.65	$40.87
2005	$5.15	$5.77	$7.21	$9.13	$11.54	$14.42	$17.60	$22.12	$27.40	$33.65	$41.35
2006	$5.15	$5.77	$7.21	$9.13	$11.54	$14.42	$17.60	$22.12	$27.64	$33.65	$40.87
2007	$5.85	$6.92	$8.41	$10.00	$12.39	$15.87	$19.71	$24.04	$31.25	$38.46	$48.08
2008	$6.55	$7.21	$9.62	$11.90	$14.42	$17.79	$22.50	$27.88	$34.62	$44.23	$55.29

Source: Author's calculations based on Miriam King, Steven Ruggles, Trent Alexander, Donna Leicach, and Matthew Sobek. Integrated Public Use Microdata Series, Current Population Survey: Version 2.0. [Machine-readable database]. Minneapolis, MN: Minnesota Population Center [producer and distributor], 2004. Downloaded from cps.ipums.org/cps.

Table 5.6 Share of Labor Market Earning in Each Contour (Percentage)

Individual Years	Bottom*	1st	2nd	3rd	4th	5th	6th	7th	8th	9th	10th	All
1962	11.0	4.1	6.8	7.3	9.1	7.3	3.8	1.6	.7	.4	.1	34.0
1963	10.1	4.5	5.6	7.2	7.0	5.0	2.7	1.6	.5	.2	.1	34.5
1964	16.4	7.6	8.8	10.9	11.3	8.9	5.3	3.1	1.0	.3	.2	57.6
1965	16.2	7.3	9.0	10.7	10.8	9.5	5.8	4.0	1.3	.4	.3	59.0
1966	15.3	6.9	8.4	10.2	10.5	10.0	7.1	4.3	1.4	.6	.3	59.6
1967	16.4	8.0	8.4	10.2	12.6	8.9	7.2	2.3	1.4	.5	.3	59.7
1968	18.3	7.9	10.4	11.8	12.9	8.4	3.8	2.0	.8	.5	.4	58.8
1969	17.4	7.6	9.8	10.9	13.1	9.5	5.1	2.7	1.1	.6	.4	60.7
1970	15.8	7.1	8.8	10.2	12.7	10.3	6.7	3.7	1.7	.8	.5	62.5
1971	14.9	6.3	8.6	9.7	12.2	11.1	7.2	4.3	2.1	1.0	.8	63.2
1972	14.0	6.0	8.0	9.2	11.5	10.9	7.9	5.0	2.5	1.1	.8	62.9
1973	13.0	5.5	7.4	8.8	10.8	10.8	9.0	6.1	3.1	1.5	1.1	63.7
1974	15.5	7.2	8.3	10.2	10.6	9.6	7.3	4.2	2.1	1.1	.4	60.8
1975	14.2	6.7	7.4	9.9	10.3	10.1	7.3	4.4	2.1	.8	.4	59.6
1976	15.1	6.4	8.6	9.9	9.9	9.8	7.7	3.7	2.0	.7	.3	59.0
1977	14.6	6.3	8.3	9.4	9.3	9.6	8.6	4.5	2.5	1.0	.4	59.9
1978	15.1	6.0	9.0	9.1	9.7	9.3	7.5	3.9	1.7	.9	.7	57.8
1979	14.8	6.4	8.4	9.3	9.4	9.9	7.0	3.6	1.8	.8	.8	57.5
1980	17.2	8.0	9.2	9.0	9.1	8.7	7.5	4.4	1.7	.9	.9	59.4

(continued)

241

Table 5.6 *(continued)*

Individual Years	Bottom*	1st	2nd	3rd	4th	5th	6th	7th	8th	9th	10th	All
1981	16.2	7.6	8.6	10.0	10.0	8.8	7.1	4.0	2.0	2.0	1.8	59.9
1982	15.0	6.9	8.1	9.6	10.0	8.9	7.9	5.2	2.7	1.3	.5	61.1
1983	14.1	6.4	7.7	9.2	9.9	9.1	8.0	5.8	3.0	1.6	.7	61.1
1984	13.1	6.0	7.1	8.9	9.9	9.2	8.2	6.3	3.7	1.9	.8	61.9
1985	12.6	5.7	7.0	8.5	9.7	9.3	8.7	7.2	4.6	2.3	1.0	63.9
1986	11.9	5.4	6.5	8.3	9.8	9.3	9.0	7.8	5.2	2.7	1.2	65.3
1987	11.6	5.3	6.2	8.0	9.6	9.5	9.0	8.3	5.6	3.0	1.4	65.9
1988	10.8	5.1	6.0	7.9	9.7	9.7	9.2	8.6	6.3	3.7	1.6	67.8
1989	10.6	4.9	5.7	7.8	9.4	9.5	9.6	9.0	6.7	4.0	1.8	68.3
1990	11.3	5.4	5.9	7.8	8.7	10.2	10.3	7.8	5.3	9.1	1.6	66.2
1991	12.7	6.4	6.3	9.0	9.7	9.6	9.4	7.9	4.7	2.3	1.2	66.6
1992	12.8	6.8	6.0	8.6	9.3	9.6	9.4	8.4	4.9	2.6	1.3	66.9
1993	12.1	6.2	5.8	8.4	9.0	9.6	9.6	8.8	5.3	2.9	1.5	67.0
1994	11.4	5.8	5.6	8.3	9.1	9.4	9.4	8.8	5.5	3.3	1.7	66.9
1995	11.4	5.9	5.5	8.1	8.8	9.5	9.5	9.1	5.9	3.7	2.0	68.0
1996	13.5	6.7	6.8	8.0	8.8	9.8	10.5	7.7	5.4	3.2	1.7	62.5
1997	13.0	6.1	6.9	8.9	11.0	9.4	9.3	7.1	4.2	2.6	1.2	66.7
1998	12.5	5.8	6.7	8.6	10.3	9.5	9.5	7.4	4.5	2.8	1.5	66.7
1999	12.0	5.6	6.4	8.4	10.4	9.8	10.0	8.0	5.1	3.2	1.7	68.9

2000	11.8	5.3	6.5	8.5	10.1	9.7	10.2	8.1	5.1	3.6	1.9	69.1
2001	11.4	5.1	6.3	8.4	10.3	10.0	10.4	8.3	5.6	4.1	2.2	70.8
2002	10.3	4.5	5.7	8.0	9.7	10.0	10.7	8.8	5.9	4.4	2.7	70.4
2003	10.0	4.4	5.6	7.9	9.7	9.8	10.6	8.9	6.0	4.5	2.6	69.9
2004	9.7	4.3	5.4	7.5	9.3	9.7	10.5	9.2	6.2	4.6	2.9	69.5
2005	9.3	4.1	5.3	7.4	9.2	9.4	10.7	9.3	6.3	4.9	3.1	69.7
2006	9.1	3.9	5.2	7.4	9.1	9.0	10.7	9.5	6.6	5.1	3.3	69.9
2007	9.8	4.6	5.1	6.9	8.8	11.6	9.9	8.7	6.9	4.5	2.8	69.8
2008	12.1	5.4	6.7	7.8	9.7	10.6	9.9	7.4	6.9	4.0	2.0	70.5
Average	**13.2**	**6.0**	**7.3**	**9.0**	**10.0**	**9.5**	**8.2**	**6.1**	**3.7**	**2.2**	**1.2**	**62.8**
Decades' Average												
1960s	15.1	6.7	8.4	9.9	10.9	8.4	5.1	2.7	1.0	.4	.3	53.0
1970s	14.7	6.4	8.3	9.6	10.6	10.1	7.6	4.3	2.2	1.0	.6	60.7
1980s	13.3	6.1	7.8	9.5	9.7	9.2	8.4	6.7	4.2	2.3	1.2	63.5
1990s	12.3	6.1	8.4	8.4	9.5	9.6	9.7	8.1	5.1	3.0	1.5	66.6
2000s	10.4	9.6	5.8	7.8	9.5	10.0	10.4	8.7	6.2	4.4	2.6	70.0

* Bottom represents the first two contours together.

70 percent earn through the 10 contours. Although there is fluctuation, the share of workers earning at the bottom—the first two contours—is around 13 percent, which isn't an insignificant share of the labor market. Were the third contour to be included in what might be referred to as the low-wage labor market, then at least 20 percent of the labor market is composed of low-wage workers. This certainly accords with estimates that by any reasonable definition one quarter of the American labor market is low-wage. In 2005, the incidence of low-wage work was 25 percent in the United States; 22.1 percent in the United Kingdom; 20.8 percent in Germany; 18.2 percent in the Netherlands; 12.7 percent in France; and 8.5 percent in Denmark.[1] To the extent that the median wages in all 10 contours are rising following increases in the statutory minimum wage, over the 46-year period 62.8 percent of the labor market is seeing an increase in their wages. Between the 1960s and the 2000s, the percentage of the labor force earning through these 10 contours increased by 32.1 percent. There might be two ways to interpret this. One is that wages, in absolute terms, did creep up, as evidenced by the shrinkage in the first two contours and the increase in the eighth through tenth contours. The other is that more people earning in the top two contours may be a function of fewer people earning above those contours, which might be indicative of stagnant wages.

Another question that arises is just how the minimum wage in the United States compares to minimum wages around the world. Table 5.7 shows these comparisons.

It would appear that at least in terms of industrialized nations that the minimum wage in the United States is low relative to the other industrialized nations. In recent years, however, the federal minimum wage in the United States has also been low relative to many states that make up the United States. Because the federal minimum wage has been losing value, many states have taken the lead and either adopted their own minimum wages or increased existing ones to levels above the federal minimum. Additionally, many of these states have

Table 5.7 Minimum Wages around the World (2013 dollars)

Country	PPP* Exchange Rate ($ per hour)	USD Exchange Rate ($ per hour)
Australia	10.5	15.6
Belgium	10.1	11.9
Canada	7.8	9.9
Chile	2.9	2.3
Czech Republic	3.3	2.5
Estonia	2.8	2.4
France	10.7	12.5
Greece	4.5	4.3
Hungary	3.9	2.5
Ireland	9.0	11.5
Israel	5.3	6.4
Japan	6.7	7.7
Korea	5.3	4.4
Luxembourg	10.8	14.3
Mexico	0.8	0.6
Netherlands	9.5	11.2
New Zealand	8.7	11.2
Poland	4.8	2.9
Portugal	4.0	3.7
Slovak Republic	3.3	2.5
Slovenia	6.7	6.0
Spain	4.8	4.9
Turkey	4.4	3.0
United Kingdom	8.0	9.7
USA	7.3	7.3

* "Purchasing Power Parity": price from an economy-wide perspective.

Source: Real Minimum Wages. OECD StatExtracts. Organization for Economic Co-operation and Development. Available online at https://stats.oecd.org/Index .aspx?DataSetCode=RMW.

adopted mechanisms for automatic adjustment of their minimum wages. Table 5.8 shows what is happening in the states.

As of this writing 29 states have minimum wages that are higher than the federal minimum wage, and 16 of them have in place some type of mechanism for automatic adjustment of their minimum wages.

Table 5.8   State Minimum Wages as of January 1, 2015

State	Minimum Wage ($)
Federal (FLSA)	7.25
Alabama	None
Alaska	7.75
Arizona	7.90
Arkansas	6.25
California	9.00
Colorado	8.00
Connecticut	8.70
Delaware	7.75
Florida	7.93
Georgia	5.15
Hawaii	7.25
Idaho	7.25
Illinois	8.25
Indiana	7.25
Iowa	7.25
Kansas	7.25
Kentucky	7.25
Louisiana	None
Maine	7.50
Maryland	7.25
Massachusetts	8.00
Michigan	8.15
Minnesota	6.50–8.00
Mississippi	None
Missouri	7.50
Montana	7.90
Nebraska	7.25
Nevada	7.25–8.25
New Hampshire	7.25
New Jersey	8.25
New Mexico	7.50
New York	8.00
North Carolina	7.25
North Dakota	7.25
Ohio	7.25–7.95
Oklahoma	2.00–7.25

Table 5.8   (*continued*)

State	Minimum Wage ($)
Oregon	9.10
Pennsylvania	7.25
Rhode Island	8.00
South Carolina	None
South Dakota	7.25
Tennessee	None
Texas	7.25
Utah	7.25
Vermont	8.73
Virginia	7.25
Washington	9.32
West Virginia	7.25
Wisconsin	7.25
Wyoming	5.15
District of Columbia	9.50
Guam	7.25
Puerto Rico	5.08–7.25
U.S. Virgin Islands	4.30–7.25

Source: Minimum Wage Laws in the States–January 1, 2015. U.S. Department of Labor, Wage and Hour Division. http://www.dol.gov/whd/minwage/america.htm.

Documents

In this section, we look at excerpts from key documents.

1914 Chicago Debate League on the Minimum Wage

In January 1914 a debate took place in Chicago over the idea of the minimum wage. It was between members from the University of Chicago and the University of Michigan and Northwestern University. While there were six debaters between the three schools, they were divided into two sides: affirmative v. negative. The question being debated was: "Resolved, That the States Should Establish a Schedule of Minimum Wages for Unskilled Labor,

Constitutionally Conceded." The reason for stating "constitutionally conceded" was that in 1914 it was not firmly established that a minimum wage was not an unconstitutional violation of an individual's liberty of contract. Therefore, assuming its constitutionality wasn't in question, the issue was whether the minimum wage made good policy from an economic and social point of view. The following are excerpts from that debate:

Arguing the first affirmative was Harry Rosenberg.

When conditions such as these exist, there must be something wrong with our wage system. They are not due to lack of productivity on the part of the American people. The United States is not poverty-stricken. . . .

We of the affirmative believe that unskilled labor is earning and producing enough to maintain itself in a state of physical efficiency, but that it is being deprived of a fair return upon the product which it contributes. The wage that a labor group receives is determined by the relative bargaining strength of the employer and employee. Under present competitive conditions the bargaining strength of the employer is greater than that of the worker because (1) the employer has better knowledge of labor and market conditions than has the inexperienced and often times foreign worker; (2) the employer has greater reserve power than has the worker. If the employer does not make a contract with the worker at once, it means at most a question of a day's profits. But if the worker does not make a contract with the employer, it may be a question of livelihood with him. A man with an empty stomach and starving wife and children, is surely in an inferior bargaining condition to the rich and secure employer. (3) There is under-cutting by the workers. Driven by the stress of necessity, one worker will take a job at less than will another. As a result of these causes, the wage that the labor group finally receives is determined not by its worth but by the bargaining strength of the weakest member of the group.

That bargaining strength and not worth determines the wage that the group receives is evidenced by those cases where unskilled labor has been able to raise its wages. . . .

If the unskilled worker were able to organize, the need for the minimum wage would not be so imperative. But unskilled labor cannot organize. Here and there have appeared isolated cases of organization, but in the main it cannot organize. . . . Arguing the first negative was Willard Atkins.

The strength of radical legislation lies in its appeal to the emotions, and its dangers, we may add, lies in this same fact. It finds its support in the heart and not in the mind; in sympathy, not in cool thought. . . .

As negative speakers we challenge the minimum wage on three grounds which we believe are fundamental:

1. On account of its inherent nature the law could not be enforced.
2. Even if it could be enforced it would not help the laboring man but would add to his poverty and degradation.
3. There is an effective means of raising wages without resorting to the minimum wage. . . .

Necessity holds the whip hand, and, driven by the cries of your family, if you cannot get work at the legal rate you will take it at less. Out of work and out of food you will not refuse to work for $2 a day just to enable those who have jobs getting $2.50 to maintain their standard. . . .

The second party to the labor contract is the employer, and we now ask, will he find it in his interest to observe the law? The affirmative tell us that he is at present engaged in reducing wages to the lowest level. Thus we see by the force of their own argument that the employer will oppose the law. Manifestly, in the absence of any further argument to the effect that the minimum wage will breed men of a different character, there can be but one conclusion; the businessman will oppose the law. . . .

It simply means that law-abiding Mr. Smith must get around the minimum in order to compete on equal terms with law-evading Jones. Prof. Tufts has said: "Under competitive conditions the standard of business honesty is inevitably reduced to the minimum." Again the honorable Tom Johnson of Cleveland, the advocate of the three-cent fare and as worthy a defender of the poor as the gentlemen of the affirmative, has said in this connection: "If you cannot pass a law and legislate people into being good, it is your duty not to pass a law and create an artificial stimulus for the doing of evil." The passage of a minimum wage bill simply means that every law-abiding employer will be placed under a powerful artificial stimulus to get around the law in order to compete on equal terms with his law-evading rival. What chance has the minimum wage of enforcement under these circumstances? What possibilities for under-cutting and secret bargaining present themselves! What chance of enforcement can be promised when it is contrary to the interests of the laboring man and the employer at one and the same time? . . .

The cost of living is largely psychological. The luxury of yesterday are the necessities of today. As human beings we always want more and more. It is in our nature. Then let us give labor a minimum wage of $15, which may be enough to live on this year; but next year $20 is necessary; and the third year 25 is the indispensable minimum.

Thus we see that the minimum wage, altho a worthy philanthropic aim advocated by people who are moved by none but the best impulses, is bound to fail, because it cannot be enforced, and because it offers nothing for the condition of nine million workers seeking seven million jobs. . . .
Arguing the second affirmative was Arnold Barr.

First, let me explain what we mean by the minimum wage which we support. The question calls for the adoption by the states of schedules of minimum wages for unskilled labor. This means a law which prohibits any employer from paying, or any laborer from accepting a wage less than the minimum fixed by the law. The word "schedule" shows that this does not mean a wage uniform for all the states, nor for all the workers within the single state, but that the wage may vary as necessary to apply it to different localities and different conditions of employment. The question does not state how high or low the minimum shall be, nor upon what basis it shall be determined. The minimum which we advocate, then, is the wage which will buy enough food clothing, fuel, and shelter to keep the laborer and the average family in health and physical efficiency. We stand for the wage which will supply the physical requirements of this generation of workers and of the coming one. So the proposition to which the arguments must be directed may now be stated: "Resolved, that the States should prohibit by law the payment to any unskilled laborer of a wage less than that necessary to maintain him in physical efficiency." This statement of the proposition should make it clearly understood at the outset that this is not an attempt to revolutionize our wage system nor to attack the competitive, individualistic order of society. Obviously this proposition does not deal with general wages at all. We are concerned with only the lowest strata of wages, leaving competition just as at present, entirely free for all above that, but saying that the unskilled laborer shall not be forced by competition below this line which the state has drawn. . . .

The first point in reply is that in many cases the increase in wage will not cause a rise in prices at all, but will come directly out of the profits of the employer. Take the large number of monopolies, which employ millions of unskilled laborers. They have already fixed prices as high as the public will stand and cannot raise them any higher without losing business. . . .

In the second place, under competition, there are many employers who are making fortunes by forcing upon their laborers a wage even less than that which their competitors pay. . . .

Now the third reason why prices will not rise, is that in many cases the minimum wage law will positively reduce the cost of production. It might at first seem that employers would be so anxious for profits that they would already be producing as cheaply as possible, but a little reflection allows that this is not always the fact. We can all remember cases where an employer has established his business on a firm foundation, and has then rested on his oars for a while, allowing things to go along in the accustomed groove. Now there is a sudden rise in one item of the labor cost which will jolt him out of inaction. . . .

Two spurs will always make a horse go faster than one. The minimum wage law would be a powerful stimulus to careless employers to apply all their ingenuity to the processes of the industry, eliminating waste and increasing efficiency. The great possibilities of this tendency are well shown by the achievements of the new scientific management. . . .

The minimum wage will be a stimulus to this higher efficiency. This is our third reason why it will not increase the cost of living, but will give the laborer the real increase in wages.

Fourth, prices will not necessarily be raised, since the employer will find in many cases that he is able to pay the higher wage because of the increased productivity of the very laborer to whom he must pay it. For we advocate, as you remember, raising wages only for those who are now getting not enough to maintain themselves in physical efficiency, and in unskilled labor this physical element is a large factor in productivity. A well-fed man will pick up a larger shovelful of coal; will walk faster behind his wheelbarrow; will use fewer because stronger blows to drive each spike or rivet; will keep pace with a machine at a higher speed, than can a man under-nourished and unhealthy. . . .

. . . Industry as a whole cannot exist permanently if it denies to its workers the necessities of life. Such an industry is parasitic and undesirable.

Therefore, the minimum wage is socially as well as economically sound, when it increases and re-apportions the product of our industry to secure to every laborer, who does his share in the production, the opportunity to support himself and his family in bodily efficiency and health. . . .

Arguing the second negative was Leon Powers.

The notion of the affirmative, that all we need to do to raise people from poverty to affluence is to pass a law, is a common form of fallacy. There was a time when people thought that they could eliminate poverty merely by having more money. They passed a law providing for an increase in the quantity of paper money. They passed a law providing for an increase in the quantity of paper money. But they found they could not create any new wealth out of a printing press. . . .

Having seen that, aside from the question of enforcement, a minimum wage law is powerless to produce good results, it shall now be my purpose to show that even if it could be enforced, it would have positively harmful results.

The first and most obvious result of the enforcement of such a law will be to increase the number of unemployed. No employer will continue to employ a worker when it becomes unprofitable to do so. When a minimum wage law is passed, and it is made unlawful to pay a worker less than a certain wage, what is going to happen? Simply that those who are unable to earn the minimum wage will have to go out of employment. Take a concrete case: Here is a worker, who is able to earn $1 a day for his employer, and he receives that wage. Now a minimum wage of $1.50 is established. What is going to be the result? That worker will be discharged, for no employer will continue to employ at $1.50 a worker who can earn only one dollar.

But, you say, the employer may increase the price of the product, and thus recoup the additional amount he will need to pay out of wages. Suppose he does increase the price. An increase in the price of an article will mean a falling off in demand for that article. Then, since there will be not so much of the article consumed at this higher price, fewer men will be required to produce it, which in turn will mean unemployment. . . .

The second harmful result of the attempted enforcement of the minimum wage is that it will demoralize the efficiency of the workers themselves. There is a popular notion, all too common these days, that the world owes every man a living. This view is peculiarly prevalent among unskilled workers. Let the state place its stamp of approval on this vicious doctrine, and let wages be determined not by efficiency but by the needs of the worker; let the state say, your wage is going to be determined by what it costs you to live, not by what you earn; and the result will inevitably be disastrous. Give legal sanction to the doctrine that the world owes every man a living and it will not be in human nature to strive as hard as before. Inefficiency is as sure to result under such a socialistic scheme as efficiency does under a competitive and individualistic system of society where every man must depend on his own resources. The progress of the race has been based on struggle. Self-reliance, industry, and perseverance are the qualities which make for progress. In supporting a minimum wage that removes the pressure on individuals; that divorces wages from efficiency, that attempts to guarantee a living wage regardless of earning power, the gentlemen have assumed a burden impossible to carry. . . .

Arguing the third affirmative was Benjamin Bills.

Our concluding proposition is that the minimum wage measure is sound. Sound, because, while not insuring the workmen one penny more than they earn, it does insure them such fair share of what they do earn as will give them a fit living, a share which today their weak bargaining position denies them. . . .

The minimum wage measure is sound socially and sound economically. The public in the end pays the cost of supporting its workmen prematurely to be worn out by the conditions of living enforced by the low wage and thrown on the scrap heap, the public then supporting them in its tubercular camps, its hospital wards, its charitable institutions—fifty-two percent of them there as a result of the low-wage; or by requiring industry to pay their workmen a wage sufficient for the workmen to support themselves in their present homes.

Arguing the third negative was Ralph Swanson.

. . . We contend that the cause for low wages is due to the fact that there is an over-supply of labor. Let us refresh our minds concerning one of the fundamental laws of economics—the law of supply and demand. The law of supply and demand determines the cost of production, and determines the cost of raw material, determines the cost of production, and determines the selling price of an article. That same law determines the wages of labor. . . .

If, on the other hand, the supply of labor is great and the demand for that labor is relatively small, then we will naturally find low wages, because the competition among the laborers to secure the available jobs will force wages down.

Our first proposition then is that the law of supply and demand determines the wages of the laborer. The gentlemen of the affirmative tell us that wages are low. Granted, for the sake of argument, that wages are low, we would naturally expect to find as the cause for low wages the fact that there is an over-supply of labor. And our second proposition is that there *is* an over-supply of labor. . . .

Our next proposition is that this over-supply of laborers produces low wages. How does it produce low wages? In the first place, it results in unemployment. As my first colleague has pointed out, though a man may be getting a high daily wage, but is working only half the time, that high daily wage will result in a low weekly wage . . . the reason for the low weekly wage lies in the fact that over-supply of labor results in low wages, because it results in low wages, because it results in unemployment. . . .

Speaking again for the first affirmative was Harry Rosenberg.

We of the affirmative have based our case upon these fundamental propositions: (1) That the minimum wage is justifiable because, wages are low, and these wages result in deplorable conditions; (2) the low wages are not due to a lack of worth on the part of unskilled labor, but to lack of bargaining strength, which is due to three reasons: (a) inferior knowledge of labor and market conditions on the part of the worker, (b) lack of reserve power, (c) undercutting; (3) that the minimum wage will better the conditions of the unskilled, because it means not merely a nominal increase in wages, but a real increase as well;

(4) the minimum wage is practicable; (5) it is economically and socially sound. Now the gentlemen have admitted the first and last of these propositions, namely that wages are low and conditions are deplorable, and that the minimum wage is economically and socially sound. . . .

The gentlemen tell us that our plan will not improve the conditions of the workers because unemployment will result. If they mean unemployment for the women and the children, who ought to be home and in school, we want that kind of unemployment. . . .

Speaking again for the second affirmative was Arnold Barr.

. . . The minimum wage law, on the other hand, merely takes one part of the wage field out of the operation of these causes, and removes it entirely from the bargaining struggle. Where the rights of the state begin, namely at the point of physical efficiency, there let freedom of competition stop. . . .

Speaking again for the third negative was Ralph Swanson.

The affirmative tell us that poor bargaining power is the cause for low wages, and that poor bargaining power is due to three causes—first, poor waiting power on the part of the laborer; second inferior knowledge of labor conditions by the laborers; and third, under-cutting by the laborers themselves. We admit that poor bargaining power produces low wages, but what is the cause for poor bargaining power? In other words, are not the causes for low bargaining power the causes given by the gentlemen of the affirmative? We contend that poor bargaining power is due to an oversupply of labor. The affirmative have admitted that if we limit the oversupply and thus bring about an equilibrium between supply and demand, undercutting will be eliminated. But they still contend that the other two causes will operate to produce low wages. Let us see. If we bring about an equilibrium between supply and demand, we will give to every laborer a job. Instead of having nine million men seeking seven million jobs, we will have seven million men for seven million jobs. In other words, all the laborers will be working. . . .

Source: *The Minimum Wage: A Debate. The Constructive and Rebuttal Speeches of the Representatives of the University of Chicago.* January 17, 1914. Published by Delta Sigma Rho, University of Chicago Chapter, 1914.

Report on Economic Conditions of the South (1937)

In 1937 the National Emergency Council submitted a report to the President of the United States where it was made clear that federal intervention would be needed to address what the president believed to be the nation's number one problem, which was the underdevelopment and poverty of the South relative to the North. What follows are excerpts from that report:

The South's industrial wages, like its farm income, are the lowest in the United States. In 1937 common labor in 20 important industries got 16 cents an hour less than laborers in other sections received for the same kind of work. Moreover, less than 10 percent of the textile workers are paid more than 52.5 cents an hour, while in the rest of the Nation 25 percent rise above that level. A recent survey of the South disclosed that the average annual wage in industry was only $865 while in the remaining States it averaged $1219. . . .

The insecurity of work in southern agriculture, its changes in method, and its changes in location, make the labor problem of the South not simply an industrial labor problem. Neither the farm population nor the industrial workers can be treated separately, because both groups, as a whole, receive too little income to enable their members to accumulate the property that tends to keep people stable. Industrial labor in the South is to a great extent unskilled and therefore, subject to the competition of recurring migrations from the farm—people who have lost in the gamble of one-crop share farming. On the other hand, the industrial workers, with low wages and long hours, are constantly tempted to return to the farm for another try. . . .

. . . This backbone of southern industry ranks nationally as one of the low-wage manufacturing industries. In the South it pays even lower wages than elsewhere. According to 1937 figures, the pay for the most skilled work in this industry is about 12 cents an hour less in the South than the pay for the same work elsewhere. . . .

The average differential in rates for new labor between the South and the rest of the country in 20 of the country's important industries in 1937 amounted to 16 cents an hour. . . .

Wage differentials are reflected in lower living standards. Differences in costs of living between the southern cities and cities in the Nation as a whole are not great enough to justify the differentials in wages that exist. In 1935 a study of costs of living showed that a minimum emergency standard required a family income of $75.27 a month as an average for all cities surveyed. The average of costs in southern cities showed that $71.94 a month would furnish the minimum emergency standard. This would indicate a difference of less than 5 percent in living costs. Industrial earnings for workers are often 30 to 50 percent below national averages.

Low wages and poverty are in great measure self-perpetuating. Labor organization has made slow and difficult progress among low-paid workers, and they have had little collective bargaining power or organized influence on social legislation. Tax resources have been low because of low incomes in the communities, and they have been inadequate to provide for the type of education modern industry requires. Malnutrition has had its influence on the efficiency of workers. Low living standards have forced other members of workers' families to seek employment to make ends meet. These additions to the labor market tend further to depress wages.

Low wages have helped industry little in the South. Not only have they curtailed the purchasing power on which local industry is dependent, but they have made possible the occasional survival of inefficient concerns. The standard of wages fixed by such plants and by agriculture has lowered the levels of unskilled and semiskilled workers, even in modern and well trained and working under modern conditions, are thoroughly efficient producers, there is not enough such employment to bring the wage levels into line with the skill of the workers.

Source: National Emergency Council, *Report on Economic Conditions of the South* (Washington, D.C.: Government Printing Office, 1938).

Franklin Roosevelt's Defense of the FLSA (1938)

In his State of the Union Address in 1938, President Franklin Roosevelt defended the idea of wage legislation to help the disadvantaged and to assist in economic recovery by affording more people greater purchasing power.

We have not only seen minimum-wage and maximum-hour provisions prove their worth economically and socially under Government auspices in 1933, 1934, and 1935, but the people of this country, by an overwhelming vote, are in favor of having Congress—this Congress—put a floor below which industrial wages shall not fall, and a ceiling beyond which the hours of industrial labor shall not rise.

Here again let us analyze the opposition. A part of it is sincere in believing that an effort to raise the purchasing power of lowest paid industrial workers is not the business of the Federal Government. Others give "lip service" to the general objective, but do not like any specific measure that is proposed. In both cases it is worth our while to wonder whether some of these opponents are not at the heart opposed to any program for raising the wages of the underpaid or reducing the hours of the overworked.

Another group opposes legislation of this type on the ground that cheap labor will help their locality to acquire industries and outside capital. . . .

Another group opposes legislation of this type on the ground that cheap labor will help their locality to acquire industries and outside capital, or to retain industries which today are surviving only because of existing low wages and long hours. It has been my thought that, especially during the past 5 years, this nation has grown away from local or sectional selfishness and toward patriotism and unity. I am disappointed by some recent actions and by some recent utterances which sound like the philosophy of half a century ago.

There are many communities in the United States where the average family income is pitifully low. It is in those communities that we find the poorest educational facilities and the worst conditions of health. Why? It is not because they are satisfied to live as they do. It is because those communities have the lowest ability to pay taxes; and therefore inadequate functioning of local government. . . .

No reasonable person seeks a complete uniformity in wages in every part of the United States; nor does any reasonable person seek an immediate and drastic change from the lowest to the highest pay. We are seeking, of course, only legislation to end starvation wages and intolerable hours; more desirable wages are and should continue to be the product of collective bargaining. . . .

Wage and hour legislation, therefore, is a problem which is definitely before the Congress for action. It is an essential part of economic recovery. It has the support of an overwhelming majority of our people in every walk of life. They have expressed themselves through the ballot box.

Again I revert to the increase of national purchasing power as an underlying necessity of the day. If you increase that purchasing power for the farmers and for the industrial workers—especially those in both groups who have the least of it today—you will therefore increase the purchasing power of those professions which serve these groups, and therefore those of those professions who serve all groups. I have tried to make clear to you, and through you to the people of the United

States, that this is an urgency which must be met by complete and not by partial action. . . .

For economic and social reasons, our principal interest for the near future lies along two lines: First, the immediate desirability of increasing the wages of the lowest paid groups in all industry, and second, in thinking more in terms of the worker's total pay for a period of a whole year rather than in terms of his remuneration by the hour or the day.

Source: Franklin D. Roosevelt, "Annual Message to Congress," January 3, 1938. Online by Gerhard Peters and John T. Woolley, *The American Presidency Project.* http://www.presidency.ucsb.edu/ws/?pid=15517.

Report of the National Advisory Commission on Civil Disorders (1968)

This report, known as the Kerner Commission report after the commission's chair, Governor Otto Kerner of Illinois, was released in April 1968. In July 1967, President Lyndon Baines Johnson formed an 11-member National Advisory Commission on Civil Disorders to explain the rioting that had plagued many of America's cities each summer since 1964. The report specifically addresses issues of poverty, the low wages of blacks relative to whites, and other social conditions that need to be addressed in order to prevent the upheaval that had been plaguing America's cities. Depending on one's viewpoint, the Kerner Commission report can be viewed as representing a major next step in the broader Civil Rights movement. For many others, it was the opening salvo in the expansion of public assistance programs that would come to characterize the Johnson administration's War on Poverty and Great Society programs. Although the report does not say anything specifically about the minimum wage or even a need for one, the implications are clear enough: many of the social and economic problems plaguing these communities stem from severe poverty and that many simply do not earn enough to live above poverty. To some extent, the

*descriptions of conditions mirrors some of the arguments made ear-
lier in the Chicago Debate League by those arguing the affirmative.*

Social and economic conditions in the riot cities constituted a
clear pattern of severe disadvantage for Negroes compared with
whites, whether the Negroes lived in the area where the riot
took place or outside it. Negroes had completed fewer years of
education and fewer had attended high school. Negroes were
twice as likely to be unemployed and three times as likely to be
in unskilled and service jobs. Negroes averaged 70 percent of
the income earned by whites and were more than twice as likely
to be living in poverty. Although housing cost Negroes relatively more, they had worse housing-three times as likely to be
overcrowded and substandard. When compared to white sub-
urbs, the relative disadvantage is even more pronounced. . . .

White racism is essentially responsible for the explosive mixture which has been accumulating in our cities since the end of
World War II. Among the ingredients of this mixture are:

- Pervasive discrimination in employment, education and
  housing, which have resulted in the continuing exclusion
  of great numbers of Negroes from the benefits of economic
  progress.
- Black in-migration and white exodus, which have produced the massive and growing concentrations of impoverished Negroes in our major cities, creating a growing crisis
  of deteriorating facilities and services and unmet needs.
- The black ghettos where segregation and poverty converge
  on the young to destroy opportunity and enforce failure.
  Crime, drug addiction, dependency on welfare, and bitter-
  ness and resentment against society in general and white
  society in particular are the result. . . .

Employment is a key problem. It not only controls the
present for the Negro American but, in a most profound way,
it is creating the future as well. Yet, despite continuing economic growth and declining national unemployment rates, the

unemployment rate for Negroes in 1967 was more than double that for whites.

Equally important is the undesirable nature of many jobs open to Negroes and other minorities. Negro me are more than three times as likely to be in low paying, unskilled or service jobs. This concentration of male Negro employment at the lowest end of the occupational scale is the single most important cause of poverty among Negroes. . . .

Employment problems have drastic social impact in the ghetto. Men who are chronically unemployed or employed in the lowest status jobs are often unable or unwilling to remain with their families. The handicap imposed on children growing up without fathers in an atmosphere of poverty and deprivation is increased as mothers are forced to work to provide support. . . .

- The Maturing Economy: When the European immigrants arrived, they gained an economic foothold by providing the unskilled labor needed for industry. Unlike the immigrant, the Negro migrant found little opportunity in the city. The economy, by then matured, had little use for the unskilled labor he had to offer.

- The Disability of Race: the structure of discrimination has stringently narrowed opportunities for the Negro and restricted his prospects. European immigrants suffered from discrimination, but never so pervasively. . . .

Today, whites tend to exaggerate how well and quickly they escaped from poverty. The fact is that immigrants who came from rural backgrounds, as many Negroes do, are only now, after three generations, finally beginning to move into the middle class.

By contrast, Negroes began concentrating in the city less than two generations ago, and under much less favorable conditions. Although some Negroes have escaped poverty, few have been able to escape the urban ghetto. . . .

The Commission recommends that the federal government:

- Undertake joint efforts with cities and states to consolidate existing manpower programs to avoid fragmentation and duplication.

- Take immediate action to create 2,000,000 new jobs over the next three years—one million in the public sector and one million in the private sector-to-absorb the hard-core unemployed and materially reduce the level of underemployment for all workers, black and white. We propose 250,000 public sector and 300,000 private sector jobs in the first year.

- Provide on-the-job training by both public and private employers with reimbursement to private employers for the extra costs of training the hard-core unemployed, by contract or by tax credits.

- Provide tax and other incentives to investment in rural as well as urban poverty areas in order to offer to the rural poor an alternative to migration to urban centers.

- Take new and vigorous action to remove artificial barriers to employment and promotion, including not only racial discrimination, but in certain cases, arrest records or lack of a high school diploma. Strengthen those agencies such as the Equal Employment Opportunity Commission charged with eliminating discriminatory practices, and provide full support for Title VI of the 1964 Civil Rights Act allowing federal grant-in-aid funds to be withheld from activities which discriminate on grounds of color or race. . . .

The Commission recommends that the federal government, acting with state and local governments where necessary, reform the existing welfare system to:

- Establish uniform national standards of assistance at least as high as the annual "poverty level" of income, now set by the Social Security Administration at $3,335 per year for an urban family of four.

- Require that all states receiving federal welfare contributions participate in the Aid to Families with Dependent Children Unemployed Parents program (AFSC-UP) that permits assistance to families with both father and mother in the home, thus aiding the family while it is still intact.

- Bear a substantially greater portion of all welfare costs-at-least 90 percent of total payments.

- Increase incentives for seeking employment and job training, but remove restrictions recently enacted by the Congress that would compel mothers of young children to work.

- Provide more adequate social services through neighborhood centers and family-planning programs.

- Remove the freeze placed by the 1967 welfare amendments on the percentage of children in a state that can be covered by federal assistance.

- Eliminate residence requirements.

Source: United States, *Kerner Commission, Report of the National Advisory Commission on Civil Disorders* (Washington, D.C.: U.S. Government Printing Office, 1968).

Excerpts from the 1981 Minimum Wage Study Commission

In 1981 the Federal Minimum Wage Study Commission comprising leading economists in government and the academy released a detailed study of the effects of the minimum wage. While critics were quick to seize upon the findings that the effects of a minimum wage increase would be harmful, there was much in the report to buttress the arguments of those who supported increases in the minimum wage. What follows are excerpts specifically from the first volume of the report:

Minimum Wage Workers: Their Personal and Household Characteristics

In the second quarter of 1980, 10.6 million wage and salary workers had jobs paying the minimum wage ($3.10 per hour) or less. These workers accounted for 12.4 percent of total wage and salary employment, with half of the 10.6 million earning wages less than the mandated minimum. Noteworthy differences occur among the various subgroups of this minimum wage population.

Examination by age groups reveals that teenage and elderly workers were much more likely to earn a wage less than or equal to the minimum wage compared to workers in other age groups. Over 60 percent of 16 and 17 year-olds and one third of 18 and 19 year-olds worked at or below the minimum wage. Although 40 percent of workers were seventy and 29 percent of those aged 65–69 also earned low wages, those segments of the labor force were relatively small. . . . Almost 70 percent of all minimum wage workers were adults 20 years of age or over; 50 percent were 25 or over.

Considerable differences also exist in the composition of this minimum wage population by sex as women have historically been overrepresented at the low end of the earnings scale. Approximately 18 percent of all working women earned $3.10 an hour or less compared to 8 percent of all working men. These 6.7 million women accounted for nearly two thirds of the minimum wage population. Other factors should, however, be considered before hasty conclusions are reached. The data show that part-time workers were much more likely than full-time workers to be earning the minimum wage or less. Given that over 25 percent of all working women were part-timers compared to 11 percent of all working men, some of the preponderance of women in the low-wage group may be related to their part-time status. Nevertheless, even among full-time workers, a greater proportion of women than men work at or below the minimum wage. . . .

There were far more families maintained by single women with minimum wage workers, both in number and percent, than those headed by single men. The 1.3 million female-headed families accounted for 19 percent of all families with workers at or below the minimum; the 229,000 families headed by single men made up 3 percent. When the wages are adjusted by hours worked to determine the weighted average family wage, families headed by women made up 35 percent of all families with workers earning the minimum or less, and those maintained by men, 4 percent. Twenty-four percent of families maintained by women contained minimum wage workers while only 15 percent of those maintained by men contained minimum wage workers.

Relatively large proportions of minimum wage workers were found in all classes below $50,000 in annual income, although a greater proportion of workers from low-income than from high-income families worked at or below the minimum. In 1978, over 40 percent of all minimum wage workers came from families with annual incomes under $10,000. One fourth of all minimum wage workers were from families with incomes between $15,000 and $25,000 annually, but only 10 percent of workers from those families earned the minimum or less. Families with incomes between $25,000 and $50,000 still accounted for 12 percent of all minimum wage workers.

Spouses, mostly wives, earning the minimum wage or less made up a relatively high percentage of minimum wage workers in middle-income families and a relatively low percentage in both high- and low-income families. For example, spouses made up only 8 percent of minimum wage workers in families with less than $6,000 in annual income and 10 percent of minimum wage workers in families with more than $50,000 in annual income, but they constituted over 40 percent of minimum wage workers in families with $10,000 to $15,000 in annual income.

Household heads, mostly husbands, earning the minimum wage or less made up a relatively high percentage of minimum wage workers in low-income families and a relatively low-percentage of minimum wage workers in high-income families. In families earning less than $6,000 annually, 70 percent of the minimum wage workers were heads of households, only 22 percent of minimum wage workers in families earning between $10,000 and $15,000 annually were heads of households, and only 3 percent of minimum wage workers in families with $50,000 or more in annual income were household heads.

Teenagers made up a greater percentage of minimum wage workers in higher-income families. More than 50 percent of minimum wage workers in families with incomes greater than $15,000 were teenagers. Nearly 75 percent of all minimum wage workers in families with incomes greater than $25,000 were teenagers. In addition, 70 percent of teenagers who were minimum wage workers were found in families with income greater than $15,000; 37 percent were in families with incomes greater than $25,000.

Three fourths of all minimum wage workers were in families with incomes well above the poverty line in 1978. Only 11 percent of minimum wage workers in that year were in families with incomes below the poverty threshold, and another 6 percent were in families with incomes between one and one-and-a-half times the poverty level. The official poverty level varies depending on the size of the family unit, age and sex of the family head and whether the family head is employed in the farm or nonfarm sector. The 1978 poverty level ranged from $2,650 to $11,038, depending on these factors.

The Minimum Wage and Employment—Theory

Academic discussions of the minimum wage typically begin with the implications of standard economic theory for the effects of minimum wages on employment. Usually, the goal is to present the "predictions" of the theory, which can later be tested against the data.

Our presentation of the theory is guided by rather different motivations. First, a simple theoretical framework is useful in interpreting the evidence. Often, different conclusions about the effect of a minimum wage are due to different ways of measuring that effect. Understanding these differences requires a theory of what is being measured. Second, in some cases theoretical models have advanced faster than the available data. While existing empirical studies offer at best a weak test of such models, the theory provides an informed speculation that may be the best available guide in the absence of satisfactory data. A third reason for at least a brief discussion of the theory is to show that the theory predetermines the result of any subsequent empirical investigation is false.

The simplest theory of the employment effects of a minimum wage is that as the wage is increased employers will decide to employ fewer workers, or employ the same number of workers fewer hours per week. This "theory" follows from the fact that minimum wage laws determine the lowest wage an employer can pay but leave the employer free to decide how many workers are desirable at that wage. The theory says nothing about the size of the reduction in the number of workers or the workweek, only that it will take place.

Increasing the minimum wage reduces the employment of low-wage workers for two reasons. First, it encourages firms to use more of other inputs such as machinery or more skilled workers in place of the now more expensive workers. A worker-replacing machine which was not worth buying if the hourly wage was $3.00 might become worthwhile if that wage were set at $4.00. Second, increasing the price of labor will increase the cost of the product and lead firms to raise their prices. As these prices rise, fewer units would be purchased, fewer would be produced, and fewer workers would be needed to produce them.

Even at this simple level, the theory is useful for resolving some contradictory assertions about the minimum wage's effect. When one says that the minimum wage will reduce employment, the basis for comparison is the level of employment that would otherwise occur if everything else except the level of the minimum wage were the same. Thus the theory does not imply that, if the minimum wage is increased, employment will be lower this year than last. Rather, it predicts that, with a higher minimum wage, employment will be lower than it otherwise might be. It is not necessary that the reduced employment take the form of layoffs or discharges, though these dominate public attention in the period following a minimum wage increase. Reduced employment can be achieved simply by not hiring workers who would have been hired or not replacing those who leave voluntarily but would have been replaced had the minimum not been increased.

This insight has two implications. First, the fact that employment often rises following an increase in the minimum does not disprove the theory. The important issue is whether employment rose less than it otherwise would have. . . .

This simple theory, which applies to a labor market that approaches perfect competition, has been criticized in two ways. First, one can show that in labor markets characterized by monopsony (a small number of employers competing for workers in a given labor market) a skillfully set minimum wage may actually increase employment. If the minimum wage is set above the level that would occur in a competitive labor market, further increases in the minimum will tend to reduce employment. . . .

A second line of criticism is the argument that a minimum wage increase will "shock" employers into organizing production more efficiently. This might allow the firm to continue employing the same number of workers as it would have in the absence of or at a lower level of the minimum wage. A more recent version of this argument suggests that a minimum wage would allow employers to require greater levels of effort from the workers they do hire, thus at least partially offsetting the increase in the cost of employing low-wage labor. But even if one grants the possibility of this taking place, it is not obvious that it would happen often enough to offset the full disemployment effect of the minimum wage increase.

Thus, while the simple theory based on perfect competition suggests that the minimum wage will reduce employment, the two criticisms say that the minimum wage could increase employment, decrease it, or have no effect. Yet despite these differences, the statistical procedures used by authors whose introductory discussion is closely tied to the standard model of the minimum wage are often almost indistinguishable from those of researchers openly critical of that model's assumptions.

Nothing has been said thus far about differences among workers. Workers come in nearly infinite variety: some old, others young, some skilled, some with very few skills, and so on. Realizing that these differences are often very important to employers does not change the fundamental conclusion that an increased minimum wage is expected to reduce employment, but it leads to a much more complicated and interesting picture of the employment response. Presumably, those whose employment is most threatened by an increase in the minimum wage are those who would otherwise earn less than the new minimum—those whose wages must be increased if the employer is to remain in compliance with the law. Those who are more highly valued by employers may suffer no employment reduction; indeed, demand for their services may be increased by the minimum wage. If the price an employer must pay for a fresh-out-of school teenager with no work record and hence little evidence of reliability is increased, the employer may decide instead to hire an older worker, even though that older worker commands a wage somewhat above the new minimum. Alternatively, the employer may turn to a young worker with a more extensive work history—again, even at a somewhat higher wage.

These observations are important for interpreting estimates of the effects of the minimum wage on the employment of various groups of workers. One almost never has data on employment of a group of workers so nearly identical that all are directly affected by the minimum wage. Rather, one has data on groups classified by age or industry. Employment effects should be most pronounced among groups which have the heaviest concentration of workers who would otherwise earn less than the minimum wage. Moreover, the employment of groups with a relatively light concentration of such workers might be expected to rise in response to a minimum wage. . . .

The employment reductions from a minimum wage may be partially offset by employees working harder to justify their higher wages and the availability of jobs in the uncovered sector. But critics of the minimum wage would argue that such offsets may themselves entail considerable cost. If employees have to work harder for the higher wage, they may be less satisfied than with the lower-effort, lower wage job that the minimum wage has eliminated. Supporters of the minimum probably would reply that at least for young workers, making them work harder than they would prefer may be desirable in the long run. . . .

Effects in Employment and Unemployment of Youth

The effects of the minimum wage in employment and unemployment have been studied most extensively for youth and especially teenagers. At least two dozen studies of the effects of the minimum wage on teenage labor force status have been conducted. The focus on youth reflects concern about the higher unemployment rate of teenagers and the expectation that, as a low-wage group, a relatively larger fraction of youth would be directly affected by minimum wage legislation. . . .

The differences among the many studies on this subject make it hard to summarize them. Most focused on teenagers

16–19 years old, though a few also considered young adults aged 20–24. Many of the teenage studies analyzed 16–17 year-olds and 18–19 year-olds separately, and separate estimates by race and sex were also common. To make it easier to compare the studies, the estimated effects of the minimum wage on various teenage subgroups were expressed by Commission staff in the same way. The most convenient way to do that was to determine the effects of arbitrary 10 percent increases or decreases in the minimum wage on teenage employment and unemployment. A 10 percent increase was assumed to have the same effect as a 10 percent decrease, except in the opposite direction. Up to a point, larger changes in the minimum had linear effects, that is, employment and unemployment went up or down to the same degree as the minimum increased or decreased. For example, the effects of a 15 percent minimum increase were 1.5 times as large as those of a 10 percent increase. The effects of major changes, however, such as doubling the minimum wage or eliminating it, could not be determined with the methods used in the studies.

A review of teenage employment and unemploy-ment time-series studies completed by 1979 found that a 10 percent increase in the minimum wage would reduce teenage employment between 0.5 and 3.0 percent, with most studies finding 1.0 to 2.5 percent reductions. The latter translates into a loss of 80,000 to 200,000 jobs from a base of 8 million. . . .

Commission staff attempted to update the studies through the fourth quarter of 1979 to explore the sensitivity of the estimates to differences in the variables held constant in estimating the minimum wage effects and to analyze other more technical issues. In general, the updated estimates were quite consistently in the lower range of estimates suggested in the earlier literature. The staff estimated that a 10 percent increase in the minimum wage would reduce teenage employment about 1 percent. Other staff estimates with alternative models were quite regularly in the 0.5 to 1.5 percent range. . . .

Other Employment Effects

Studies on general employment effects of the minimum wage did not fall neatly into simple categories as did those of youth employment. Few studies directly address the effect of the minimum wage on adult employment or even estimate adult employment effects for comparison with youth estimates. Most focus on industrial groupings rather than demographic categories. For example, there have been several analyses of the effect of minimum wages on employment in low-wage manufacturing industries and on employment in industries as they become subject to minimum wage standards for the first time.

Effects on Adult Employment. As noted in the discussion of the theory of the minimum wage, one expects to be able to detect effects of the minimum wage most readily if the group studied contains a relatively large fraction of workers who would have earned less than the mandated wage in the absence of minimum wage legislation. While teenagers and, to a lesser extent young adults fit this description, adults generally do not. As a result, it is not clear whether one should expect the minimum wage to reduce adult employment and, if it does, the amount may be small compared to total adult employment that it will not be detected with precision. . . .

A Simple Differential for Teenagers. A differential minimum wage for teenagers would reduce the wages employers pay to the lowest-paid teenagers. It would not directly affect the wages of better-paid teenager or adults, or the price of other inputs such as machinery.

A lower wage for minimum-wage teenagers will have two effects. First, production costs will be lower, and firms will have an incentive to reduce prices so that they can produce and sell more of their products. This "output expansion" effect increases the use of all workers and other inputs. Its magnitude depends on minimum-wage teenagers' share of production costs and consumers' response to the lower price charged by producers. A reasonable estimate of the effect is that a 15 percent youth differential would increase demand for all inputs by about one tenth of one percent. The second effect of a youth differential is to encourage firms to substitute minimum-wage teenagers in place of other production inputs such as higher-wage teenagers, adults, or equipment. The prospect of such substitution, particularly for minimum-wage adults, is reasonable for much of the controversy surrounding the youth differential. . . .

Industry Differences and the Inflation Effects

The Commission found that the effect of a 10 percent sustained annual rise in the minimum wage over its historical level from 1974 to the second quarter of 1979 would have increased wages 0.8 percent and consumer prices somewhat less than 0.3 percent. This effect is small, considering that the actual average annual rate of inflation during the same period was 9 percent if wages and 9.3 percent if consumer prices.

The actual 1974 and 1977 FLSA-amended minimum wage increases raised wages 0.6 percent and consumer prices 0.2 percent from 1974 through the second quarter of 1979. Without these increases, the average annual rate of inflation would have been 8.4 percent in wages and 9.1 percent in consumer prices during that period. . . .

Poverty Status

One purpose of the FLSA and its amendments is to maintain a real wage floor to insure a reasonable standard of living in the face of inflation. Because of the present system of setting increases in the nominal minimum wage several years in advance, it is not surprising to see the minimum eroded when inflation is rampant. The minimum wage was $2.65 in 1978, but in 1968 dollars it was worth only $1.42, actually below the 1968 minimum of $1.60. . . .

Source: *Report of the Minimum Wage Study Commission* (Washington, D.C.: The Commission, 1981).

President Barack Obama's Remarks
Advocating for a Minimum Wage

President Obama advocated for a higher minimum wage on several occasions, first in his State of the Union Address in 2013, again in his State of the Union Address in 2014, and then again in 2015.

From 2013 State of the Union Address

We know our economy is stronger when we reward an honest day's work with honest wages. But today, a full-time worker making the minimum wage earns $14,500 a year. Even with the tax relief we've put in place, a family with two kids that earns the minimum wage still lives below the poverty line. That's wrong. That's why, since the last time this Congress raised the minimum wage, nineteen states have chosen to bump theirs even higher.

Tonight, let's declare that in the wealthiest nation on Earth, no one who works full time should have to live in poverty, and raise the federal minimum wage to $9.00 an hour. This single step would raise the incomes of millions of working families. It could mean the difference between groceries or the food bank; rent or eviction; scraping by or finally getting ahead. For businesses across the country, it would mean customers with more money in their pockets. In fact, working folks shouldn't have to wait year after year for the minimum wage to go up while CEO pay has never been higher. So here's an idea that Governor Romney and I actually agreed on last year: let's tie the minimum wage to the cost of living, so that it finally becomes a wage you can live on.

Source: Barack Obama, *State of the Union. February 12, 2013.* Washington, D.C.: The White House.

From 2014 State of the Union Address

. . . Today, the federal minimum wage is worth about twenty percent less than it was when Ronald Reagan first stood here. Tom Harkin and George Miller have a bill to fix that by lifting the minimum wage to $10.10. This will help families. It will also give businesses customers with more money to spend. It doesn't involve any new bureaucratic program. So join the rest of the country. Say yes. Give America a raise.

Source: Barack Obama, *State of the Union. January 28, 2014.* Washington, D.C.: The White House.

From 2015 State of the Union Address

Today, thanks to a growing economy, the recovery is touching more and more lives. Wages are finally starting to rise again. We know that more small business owners plan to raise their employees' pay than at any time since 2007. But here's the thing. Those of us here tonight, we need to set our sights higher than just making sure government doesn't screw things up; that government doesn't halt the progress we're making. We need to do more than just do no harm. Tonight, together, let's do more to restore the link between hard work and growing opportunity for every American. . . .

Of course, nothing helps families make ends meet like higher wages. That's why this Congress still needs to pass a law that makes sure a woman is paid the same as a man for doing the same work. It's 2015. It's time. We still need to make sure employees get the overtime they've earned. And to everyone in this Congress who still refuses to raise the minimum wage, I say this: If you truly believe you could work full-time and support a family on less than $15,000 a year, try it. If not, vote to give millions of the hardest-working people in America a raise.

Now these ideas won't make everybody rich, won't relieve every hardship. That's not the job of government. To give working families a fair shot, we still need more employers to see beyond next quarter's earnings and recognize that investing in their workforce is in their company's long-term interest. We still need laws that strengthen rather than weaken unions, and give American workers a voice.

But you know, things like childcare and sick leave and equal pay, things like lower mortgage premiums and a higher minimum wage—these ideas will make a meaningful difference in the lives of millions of families. That's a fact. And that's what all of us, Republicans and Democrats alike, were sent here to do.

Source: Barack Obama, *State of the Union. January 20, 2015.* Washington, D.C.: The White House.

Excerpts from the 2014 Congressional Budget Office Report on the Minimum Wage

In 2014, the Congressional Budget Office released "The Effects of a Minimum Wage Increase on Employment and Family Income." The following are excerpts from the report.

Once fully implemented in the second half of 2016, the $10.10 option would reduce total employment by about 500,000 workers, or 0.3 percent. CBO projects. As with any such estimates, however, the actual losses could be smaller or larger; in CBO's assessment, there is about a two-thirds chance that the effect would be in the range between a very slight reduction in employment and a reduction in employment of 1.0 million workers.

Many more low-wage workers would see an increase in their earnings. Of those workers who will earn up to $10.10 under current law, most—about 16.5 million, according to CBO's estimates—would have higher earnings during an average week in the second half of 2016 if the $10.10 option was implemented. Some of the people earning slightly more than $10.10 would also have higher earnings under that option, for reasons discussed below. Further, a few higher-wage workers would owe their jobs and increased earnings to the heightened demand for goods and services that would result from the minimum wage increase. . . .

In addition to affecting employment and family income, increasing the federal minimum wage would affect the federal budget directly by increasing the wages that the federal government paid to a small number of hourly employees and indirectly by boosting the prices of some goods and services purchased by the government. . . .

Federal spending and taxes would also be indirectly affected by the increases in real income for some people and the reduction in real income for others. As a group, workers with increased earnings would pay more in taxes and receive less in federal benefits of certain types than they would have otherwise. However, people who become jobless because of the minimum wage increase, business owners, and consumers facing higher prices would see a reduction in real income and would collectively pay less in taxes and receive more in federal benefits than they would have otherwise. CBO concludes that the net effect on the federal budget of raising the minimum wage would probably be a small increase in budget deficits thereafter. It is unclear whether the effect for the coming decade as a whole would be a small increase or a small decrease in budget deficits. . . .

In general, increases in the minimum wage probably reduce employment for some low-wage workers. At the same time, however, they increase family income for many more low-wage workers. . . .

According to conventional economic analysis, increasing the minimum wage reduces employment in two ways. First, higher wages increase the cost to employers of producing goods and services. The employers pass some of those increased costs onto consumers in the form of higher prices, and those higher prices, in turn, lead the consumers to purchase fewer of the goods and services. The employers consequently produce fewer goods and services, so they hire fewer workers. This is known as scale effect, and it reduces employment among both low-wage workers and higher-wage workers.

Second, a minimum-wage increase raises the cost of low-wage workers relative to other inputs that employers use to produce goods and services, such as machines, technology, and more productive higher-wage workers. Some employers respond by reducing their use of low-wage workers and shifting toward those other inputs. That is known as a substitution effect, and it reduces employment among low-wage workers but increases it among higher-wage workers.

However, conventional economic analysis might not apply in certain circumstances. For example, when a firm is hiring more workers and needs to boost pay for existing workers doing the same work—to match what it needs to pay to recruit the new workers—hiring a new worker costs the company not only that new worker's wages but also the additional wages paid to retain other workers. Under those circumstances, which arise more often when finding a new job is time consuming and costly for workers, increasing the minimum wage means that businesses have to pay the existing workers more, whether or not a new employee was hired; as a result, it lowers the additional cost of hiring a new employee, leading to increased employment. There is a wide range of views among economists about the merits of the conventional analysis and of this alternative. . . .

An increase in the minimum wage also affects the employment of low-wage workers in the short term through changes in the economywide demand for goods and services. A higher minimum wage shifts income from higher-wage consumers and business owners to low-wage workers. Because those low-wage workers tend to spend a larger fraction of their earnings, some firms see increased demand for their goods and services, boosting the employment of low-wage workers and higher-wage workers alike. That effect is larger when the economy is weaker, and it is larger in regions of the country where the economy is weaker. . . .

The large majority would have higher wages and family income, but a much smaller group would be jobless and have much lower family income. Once the other changes in income would be below six times the poverty threshold under current law would see a small increase in income, on net, and families whose income would be higher under current law would see reductions in income, on net. In addition, in either case, higher-wage workers would see a small increase in the number of jobs.

Increases in the minimum wage would raise the wages not only for many workers who would otherwise have earned less than the new minimum but also for some workers who would otherwise have earned slightly more than the new minimum, as discussed above. CBO's analysis focused on workers who are projected to earn less than $11.50 per hour in 2016 under current law (who, in this report, are generally referred to as low-wage workers). People with certain characteristics are more likely to be in that group and are therefore more likely to be affected by increases in the minimum wage like those that CBO examined. . . .

According to CBO's central estimate, implementing the $10.10 option would reduce employment by roughly 500,000 workers in the second half of 2016, relative to what would happen under current law. That decrease would be the net result of two effects: a slightly larger decrease in jobs for low-wage workers (because of their higher cost) and an increase of a few tens of thousands of jobs for other workers (because of greater demand for goods and services). By CBO's estimate about 1 ½ percent of the 33 million workers who otherwise would have earned less than $11.50 per hour would be jobless—either less than $11.50 per hour would be jobless—either because they lost a job or because they could not find a job—as a result of the increase in the minimum wage. . . .

Source: Congressional Budget Office, *"The Effects of a Minimum Wage Increase on Employment and Family Income."* Pub. No. 4856 (Washington, D.C.: Congressional Budget Office, 2014).

Note

1. Solow, Robert. 2008. "Introduction: The United Kingdom Story." In Candice Lloyd, Geoff Mason, and Ken Mayhew, eds. *Low-Wage Work in the United Kingdom*. New York: Russell Sage Foundation.

Introduction

The minimum wage has been a topic of discussion and intense economic and political debate for more than a hundred years now. Economically, the debate has hinged on whether the benefits of minimum wage increases outweigh the costs. As we have seen, this has not at all been clear-cut. Aside from the question of employment effects and welfare effects for low-wage workers as well as the middle class overall, there is also the question of how the issue of the minimum wage impinges on the question of income inequality. Politically, the minimum wage is a matter of whose interests are affected by increases in the minimum wage. This chapter provides an annotated bibliography of a sample of the books, reports, articles, and Internet sources that deal with the topic of the minimum wage.

Books

Appelbaum, Eileen, Annette Bernhardt, and Richard J. Murname, eds. 2003. *Low-Wage America: How Employers Are Reshaping Opportunity in the Workplace.* New York: Russell Sage Foundation.

   This is a collection of essays addressing the nature of the low-wage labor market in the growing global economy.

Shayna Flores, 18, serves up an employment application in front of Wahoo Fish Taco restaurant in Honolulu on March 18, 2006. Flores, a full-time employee at the restaurant, is paid above the minimum wage. (AP Photo/Marco Garcia)

Essays range from the inability of low-wage workers to sufficiently support themselves to dwindling opportunities for those lacking in skills who have an education no higher than a high school diploma. It also addresses itself to how employers make choices with regard to hiring in the new global economy, in which there is less regulation but more advanced information technology. Collectively it is a study of how there are fewer opportunities available for low-wage and low-skilled workers, and how the larger global economy has effectively reshaped the landscape of the American labor market.

Bartels, Larry M. 2008. *Unequal Democracy: The Political Economy of the New Gilded Age*. Princeton, NJ: Princeton University Press.

This book is about how increasing inequality is a function not only of economic forces but also of the political choices that have also been made in a political system dominated increasingly by partisan ideology and the interests of the wealthy. The author discusses several key policy shifts that have contributed to rising inequality, including the massive Bush tax cuts in 2001 and 2003 and the erosion of the minimum wage. On the minimum wage, he shows how the minimum wage was allowed to stagnate and erode in value because members of Congress tended to be more responsive to the needs and interests of affluent voters than non-affluent ones. He specifically looks at the last minimum wage increase that was enacted in 2007 and how members of Congress voted on it. When put into broad historical perspective, the last minimum wage increase does not appear to have advanced the economic status of the working poor. He estimated that even after the full increase would go into effect during the summer of 2009, the real value of the minimum wage would still be less than it was 50 years earlier. For him, the rise and fall of the minimum wage over the last 70 years is one of the most remarkable aspects of the political economy of inequality. Partisan politics played a key role as the real value of the minimum wage rose significantly under the Democrats and fell significantly under the Republicans. When looking at the voting patterns on the minimum wage, senators were found to have attached no weight at all to the views of constituents in the bottom of the income distribution, and the views of those in the middle class were only slightly more influential. But senators were most responsive to the opinions of affluent constituents. Republicans were about twice as responsive as Democrats to the views of affluent constituents, and Democrats and Republicans were about equally responsive to the views of middle-income constituents. But there was no evidence of any responsiveness to the views of constituents in the bottom third of the distribution.

Belman, Dale and Paul J. Wolfson. 2014. *What Does the Minimum Wage Do?* Kalamazoo, MI: Upjohn Institute for Employment Research.

This book is intended to be an all-encompassing study of the effects of the minimum wage. The authors undertake a meta-analysis of more than 200 scholarly publications, mostly since 2000, on the effects of the minimum wage. Based on this meta-analysis, they conclude that moderate increases in the minimum wage, which have been characteristic of the United States, have had the intended effect of the minimum wage's original supporters: increasing the earnings of those at the bottom of the income distribution and reducing wage inequality. But they also find that negative effects on employment have been too small to be detectable in the meta-analysis, and that these effects are so modest that they could not have had meaningful public policy consequences in the dynamically changing labor market. Although evidence of positive spillover effects on the wages of those earning slightly more than the new minimum wage is mixed, it does generally support their existence, especially for women. Moreover, the minimum wage ought to be seen as one set of policy tools aimed at improving the standard of living of the less well-off, and that moderate increases in the minimum wage would likely assist low-income individuals and families with acceptable costs to the nation.

Card, David, and Alan B. Krueger. 1995. *Myth and Measurement: The New Economics of the Minimum Wage*. Princeton, NJ: Princeton University Press.

This book has become somewhat of a classic in the minimum wage literature, especially in what can be regarded as the new political economy of the minimum wage. Based on a variety of data, the authors demonstrate that minimum wage increases don't always have the adverse employment consequences predicted by the standard model. Several chapters cover studies they conducted earlier on the effects of minimum wage increases in the fast-food industry, first in California and then in New Jersey. Other chapters, however, look at some of the international evidence on the minimum wage, and how the minimum wage affects family earnings and poverty. But they also address the question of how much employers and other shareholders lose from increases in the minimum wage. Although their evidence finds no adverse employment effects from increases in the minimum wage, they do acknowledge the concept of a tipping point—a point above which we might see adverse effects. Ultimately the book concludes with a technical discussion of measurement and just what is being measured and how it is being measured. Often the findings of correlation in the data hinge on just where a researcher sets the statistical parameters for ensuring that their findings have statistical significance.

But this ultimately affects the findings, which in the end is really a matter of interpretation.

Congressional Budget Office. 2014. "The Effects of a Minimum Wage Increase on Employment and Family Income." Congress of the United States. (February). Downloaded from http://www.cbo.gov/publication/44995.
This is an official report of the Congressional Budget Office discussing the effects of a minimum wage increase on employment and family income. The report addresses itself to what the effect of a minimum wage increase would be at two levels: first, an increase to $9 an hour and, second, an increase to $10.10 an hour, both of which were proposed by President Obama in two separate State of the Union addresses. While the report notes that at both levels overall employment might be less, although less at the lower level, it still concludes that on balance, when fully implemented, the benefits to an increase outweigh the costs. Millions of low-wage workers will see their incomes rise, and this will enable them to spend more in the economy, which will have macroeconomic benefits to the overall economy in the long term. This is in addition to that it will be a tremendous boom to those who are currently in poverty. Even on the question of employment consequences, it is not clear from the report whether they will be due to the substitution of technology or laying off workers or simply not creating more jobs for low-wage workers in the future. Although the report concludes that on the whole an increase in the minimum wage is beneficial to both low-wage workers and the larger economy, there is to some extent something for everybody in this report. Both proponents and critics are able to take away something from this report that buttresses their respective positions. In this regard it is a report that presents well-rounded discussions of the costs and benefits so that policymakers can ultimately make informed decisions.

Cunningham, Wendy V. 2007. *Minimum Wages and Social Policy: Lessons from Developing Countries*. Washington: The World Bank.
> This book specifically addresses itself to the viability of the minimum wage as a policy tool for decreasing poverty and redressing social inequities in developing countries. For the author the minimum wage is a matter of social justice and that in certain developing countries, though not all, the minimum wage can be an effective tool for reducing poverty and unequal household income in developing countries. She looks at data from Latin America and the Caribbean, and the impact of the minimum wage on income, employment, poverty, income distribution, and government budgets in those economies with both large informal sectors and predominantly unskilled workers. At the same time, the effects of the minimum wage are very much contingent on the level at which it is sent. A minimum wage set low will lead to an increase in income benefits for low-income workers with little job loss. But a minimum wage set high will actually increase the income benefits of workers who are better off, with losses among low-wage workers, which can substantially increase poverty.

Ehrenreich, Barbara. 2001. *Nickel and Dimed: On (Not) Getting By in America*. New York: Owl Books.
> This book is the author's account of her experiences living as a low-wage worker, and the challenges and humiliations she was confronted with. The book very much puts a human face on people who are forced to subsist on minimum wages and would be affected by increases, who otherwise would remain nameless in the data.

Flinn, Chester J. 2010. *The Minimum Wage and Labor Market Outcomes*. Cambridge, MA: MIT Press.
> This book is a very technical discussion of how the minimum wage affects the labor market. The author argues that

when it comes to assessing the minimum wage, what is needed is a behavioral framework for guiding empirical work and interpreting results. He specifically develops a job search and wage bargaining model that is capable of generating labor market outcomes that are consistent with observed wage and unemployment duration distributions, and which can also account for changes in the unemployment rate following minimum wage increases.

Glickman, Lawrence B. 1997. *A Living Wage: American Workers and the Making of Consumer Society*. Ithaca, NY; London: Cornell University Press.

This book provides a broad historical overview of how the early American labor movement sought to create dignity in work for primarily industrial workers by fighting for livable wages. What began with unions also continued with early efforts to enact minimum wages, even though unions were not initially supportive of the minimum wage. Among the key arguments made for a living wage was that aside from the greater dignity it would afford workers, it would also enable them to be consumers, which in turn would drive the economy. A consumer society in fact required that workers be paid livable wages.

Kessler-Harris, Alice. 1988. *A Woman's Wage: Historical Meanings and Social Consequences*. Lexington: University Press of Kentucky.

This book argues that the early minimum wage laws were steeped in a world view that maintained that women needed special protection, and that paying them more livable wages would enable them to better protect their morals, and that this protection was in the larger interests of society. The author also maintains that paying a women a minimum wage was also about paying a livable family wage. The idea was that if employers had to pay women a minimum wage, employers would prefer to pay their husbands more, in which case the women would then be able to stay at home and care for their children. It was in this regard that a minimum wage intended to be a living wage would in fact become a family wage.

Kosters, Marvin H. ed. 1996. *The Effects of the Minimum Wage on Employment*. Washington: AEI Press.

This book is a compilation of essays by different authors about the effects of the minimum wage on employment. Based on the assumptions in the standard model, the overall consensus among the book's contributors is that minimum wage increases lead to lower employment.

Lehrer. Susan. 1987. *Origins of Protective Labor Legislation for Women, 1905–1925*. Albany: State University of New York Press.

This book provides an historical overview of how early minimum wage laws were really efforts to enact protective legislation specifically for women. Such legislation was sought because it was viewed as being essential to protecting their morals. At a time when prostitution was still legal, a higher wage for women might preclude the need to resort to that, or so it was thought. But because women were denied liberty of contract, they needed special legislation to protect them from exploitation. At the same time, social reformers did not see such protection as being antithetical to the idea that a women's place primarily was at home. If a higher wage for women would result in firms choosing to pay higher wages to their husbands so that they could stay at home with the children, then that too was considered to be a social good.

Levin-Waldman, Oren M. 2001. *The Case of the Minimum Wage: Competing Policy Models*. Albany: State University of New York Press.

This book traces the historical evolution of the minimum wage and discusses how models are used by different interests to achieve their particular aims. The author argues that the minimum wage was initially conceived of as a broader labor market issue intended to achieve greater productivity and labor market stability. As a policy issue, however, the minimum wage has always required, as do all policy issues, a political constituency to support it, and that constituency was always organized labor. When organized labor supported the minimum wage, it tended to be increased. But as organized labor declined in membership, there was no longer a constituency to support it and the result was a long period of minimum wage stagnation. As organized labor declined as a political force, the nature of the debate metamorphosed into a narrowly focused and highly technical discussion concerned with specific effects due to specific increases in the minimum wage, such as relieving either poverty or the so-called adverse effects of youth unemployment. The result has been for the minimum wage to become an intensely political issue.

Levin-Waldman, Oren M. 2011. *Wage Policy, Income Distribution, and Democratic Theory*. London; New York: Routledge.
This book addresses the larger philosophical question of whether the idea of a wage policy, whether in the form of a minimum wage, living wage, or stronger labor unions, is in keeping with democratic theory. After juxtaposing the policy literature with that on democratic theory, the book concludes that a policy that enables individuals to be self-sufficient and autonomous—to develop their capabilities—so that they can more ably participate in democratic society is very much in keeping with democratic theory. This book also introduces the concept of wage contours and shows on the basis of 46 years of data from the Current Population Survey that there are indeed middle-class benefits from the minimum wage. In years when the statutory minimum wage increased, median wages throughout the distribution affecting up to 70 percent of the labor force also increased. In years when the statutory minimum wage remained the same, median

wages remained flat. The book then concludes that wage policy is ultimately about shoring up the middle class.

McCarty, Nolan, Keith T. Poole, and Howard Rosenthal 2008. *Polarized America: The Dance of Ideology and Unequal Riches.* Cambridge, MA: MIT Press.

This is a book about the increasing political polarization of America and how along with that polarization have come some fundamental social and economic changes, most notably the rise in income inequality. The authors argue that economic inequality can feed directly into political polarization in that those at the top of the income distribution are able to devote more time and resources into supporting a political party strongly opposed to redistribution, whereas those at the bottom would respond in the opposite way. When it comes to the minimum wage, they note that intense opponents of the minimum wage have worked tirelessly and effectively to prevent it from being increased to prior levels or to be pegged to inflation. Minimum wage laws have always engendered liberal support and conservative opposition. Historically, minimum wage increases and expansive coverage generated a fair amount of bipartisan support. As polarization rose in the 1970s, bipartisanship disappeared. As a consequence of increasing Republican opposition in a period of polarization, there has been a dramatic decline in the real value of the minimum wage. Moreover, as polarization increased through the last quarter of the twentieth century, the direction of public policy overall has been less in the direction of redistribution.

Nordlund, Willis J. 1997. *The Quest for a Living Wage: The History of the Federal Minimum Wage.* Westport, CT: Greenwood Press.

This book provides an in-depth history of the minimum wage program in the United States and how the minimum wage was really part of a larger quest to achieve a living wage, as defined as being sufficient to support oneself and one's family.

Piketty, Thomas. 2014. *Capital in the Twenty-First Century.* Cambridge; London: Belknap/Harvard University Press.

This book is not directly about the minimum wage but is a discussion about the growth of income inequality in 20 different countries, including the United States. The author analyzes different data sets ranging as far back as the eighteenth century in an effort to uncover key economic and social patterns. He argues that the main driver of inequality, which is that the rate of return on capital exceeds the rate of economic growth, now threatens to stir discontent and undermine democratic values. But when he discusses the minimum wage in both the United States and France, he notes that France enacted a national minimum in an effort to reduce wage inequality, and that when the minimum wage more or less kept up through the 1960s into the 1970s, income inequality tended to be less. Although income inequality has its roots in several different sources, the stagnation of the minimum wage in the United States has been a contributing factor to the widening gap between the top and the bottom of the distribution.

Spriggs, William E., and Bruce E. Klein. 1994. *Raising the Floor: The Effects of the Minimum Wage on Low-Wage Workers.* Washington: Economic Policy Institute.

This book looks at the impact of increasing the minimum wage on low-wage workers, not just those who receive minimum wage increases, but those low-wage workers earning above them. The authors observed that the minimum wage's greatest import is its function as a reference point for wages around it. Here they were applying the concept of wage contours first developed by John Dunlop in the 1950s. They found that despite changes in the statutory minimum wage, firms merely maintained their internal wage structures. Increases may have resulted in employment consequences in some cases, but the effects were not found to be significant. Rather, firms simply viewed the minimum wage as a reference point for what starting wages should be.

Waltman, Jerold L. 2008. *Minimum Wage Policy in Great Britain and the United States*. New York: Algora Publishing.

This book traces the history of minimum wage legislation in the United States and Britain. The author looks at the operation of current minimum wage legislation, as well as the politics surrounding the minimum wage in both the United States and Britain. The key question is where we are now and how we arrived here. In Britain, he chronicles those events that led to the enactment and subsequent evolution of the National Minimum Wage. In the United States, he discusses what could be described as the stagnant federal minimum wage, and the efforts of various states and localities to pick up the slack.

Waltman, Jerold. 2000. *The Politics of the Minimum Wage*. Urbana and Chicago: University of Illinois Press.

This book traces the history of the minimum wage in terms of the politics of the minimum wage. The author seeks to expose the various contradictions inherent to the program. Among those contradictions is that despite the various economic models suggesting adverse economic effects, the minimum wage enjoys broad-based political support. Therefore, as an alternative to the economic arguments that tend to dominate discussions of the minimum wage, the author argues that the discussion needs to be recast in terms of the political economy of citizenship. With this perspective, the focus would then be on the communal value of work, the needs of citizens to have a stake in the community, and the effects of economic inequality on the bonds of common citizenship.

Welch, Finis. 1978. *Minimum Wages: Issues and Evidence*. Washington: American Enterprise Institute for Public Policy Research.

> This is one of the earlier books on the minimum that explores all the issues associated with the minimum wage within the context of the standard model on the minimum wage. Within that framework of analysis, the author shows that the effects of minimum wage increases are harmful to low-wage workers because they lead to lower employment.

White, Stuart. 2003. *The Civic Minimum: On the Rights and Obligations of Economic Citizenship*. Oxford; New York: Oxford University Press.

> This book makes a broader philosophical argument about the moral obligation of society to make sure that everybody who works earns an income sufficient to support oneself and one's family. But the author's idea of a minimum income far exceeds what we customarily associate with the minimum wage in the United States or even more generous countries for that matter. This is less an economic argument and more of a philosophical and moral argument. Individuals need a certain guaranteed income to function as autonomous citizens, and society is obligated to ensure that minimum is met if it is to indeed be considered a just society.

Articles

Allegretto, Sylvia, Arindrajit Dube, and Michael Reich. 2011. "Do Minimum Wages Really Reduce Teen Employment? Accounting for Heterogeneity and Selectivity in State Panel Data." *Industrial Relations*. 50, 2 (April): 205–240.

> This article argues that when controlling for heterogeneity and selectivity in state panel data, the minimum wage does not appear to have the adverse employment consequences predicted by the standard model. The authors conclude

that there is no reason to believe that an increase in the minimum wage leads to reductions in teen employment.

Brown, Charles, Curtis Gilroy, and Andrew Kohen. 1982. "The Effect of the Minimum Wage on Employment and Unemployment." *Journal of Economic Literature.* 20 (June): 487–528.

This article surveys the literature on the minimum wage up to the time it was published. The authors certainly take note of the teen disemployment effect, but they also note that the effects of the minimum wage are by no means uniform. The minimum wage affects different groups differently, and whatever effects have been observed among teenagers, those effects have been much less among adults.

Burkhauser, Richard V. 2014. "Why Minimum Wage Increases Are a Poor Way to Help the Working Poor." *IZA Policy Paper No. 86.* (June). Downloaded from http://ftp.iza.org/pp86.pdf.

This article argues that the minimum wage actually hurts the poor more than it helps them. The author argues that the minimum wage is really an ineffective means of assisting the poor because most of those who earn the minimum wage are not poor. Most minimum wage earners are not full time. A more effective means of helping the poor would be to boost their earnings through the earned income tax credit (EITC).

Card, David, Thomas Lemieux, and W. Craig Riddell. 2008. "Unions and Wage Inequality" in James T. Bennett and Bruce E. Kaufman, eds. *What Do Unions Do?: A Twenty-Year Perspective.* New Brunswick, NJ: Transaction Publishers.

This article looks at the impact of declining institutions on wage inequality in the United States, the United Kingdom, and Canada. The authors find that declining unionism contributed to a steep increase in wage inequality in both the United States and the United Kingdom during the 1980s. Moreover, wage inequality would have declined had union wage impacts remained at their 1984 levels.

In other words, had there not been a decline in unions, inequality would have been less. In Canada, however, the rise in the real minimum wage may have actually offset the pressure toward increased inequality associated with the decline in union strength during the 1980s and late 1990s, while in the United States it was approximately constant over the same period.

Currie, Janet, and Bruce C. Fallick. 1996. "The Minimum Wage and the Employment of Youth." *Journal of Human Resources*. 31, 2: 404–428.

This article looks at data from the National Longitudinal Survey of Youth (NLSY) to see what the impacts of minimum wage increases were in 1979 and 1980. The authors specifically sought to measure the effects by identifying a group of workers that would most likely be directly affected by the minimum wage and then compare their employment to the employment of a group of workers who were least likely to be affected. They found that affected workers were found to be 3 percent less likely to be employed a year later. At the same time, no evidence was found that minimum wage increases affected the wages of those workers who remained employed a year later.

DiNardo, John, and Thomas Lemieux. 1997. "Diverging Male Wage Inequality in the United States and Canada, 1981–1988: Do Institutions Explain the Difference?" *Industrial and Labor Relations Review*. 50, 4 (July): 629–650.

This article examines the impact of labor market institutions like unions and the minimum wage on wage inequality in both the United States and Canada. The authors find that in Canada where labor market institutions have been stronger wage inequality among men has been less compared to the United States, where labor market institutions have been weaker. Stronger institutions, then, could be expected to reduce wage inequality.

Drazen, Allan. 1986. "Optimal Minimum Wage Legislation." *The Economic Journal.* 96 (September): 774–784.

This article argues that a minimum wage can be Pareto-optimal, if we consider a labor market in which the quality of labor is sensitive to the wage increases. There are two markets: a primary one with higher wages and a secondary one with lower wages. Individuals enter the primary labor market if their expected income is higher than the forgone (and lower) income in the alternative or secondary market. It is also assumed that a worker's productivity in the primary market is an increasing function of his forgone income. These two assumptions together imply a positive relation between an individual's acceptance wage and his or her productivity. Therefore, there is a role for minimum wage legislation because firms would prefer to pay higher wages if they knew that labor quality would improve to reflect the higher wage level. And they would also prefer to pay above market-clearing wages if they knew that other firms were behaving the same way. By fixing wages above the market-clearing level, government can achieve a preferred equilibrium, which private competitive behavior cannot. In other words, left to their own devices, employers will not pay higher wages to achieve greater efficiency, because in the uncertainty that others will do the same, they are forced to lower their wages in order to remain competitive.

Dube, Arindrajit T., Suresh Naidu, and Michael Reich. 2007. "The Economic Effects of a Citywide Minimum Wage." *Industrial and Labor Relations Review.* 60, 4 (July): 522–523.

This article examines the effects of a minimum wage law that was enacted by a public ballot measure for the city of San Francisco in 2003. Looking at primarily the restaurant industry the authors find that the benefits outweigh the costs. Although the city wage floor did significantly raise the wages of those at affected restaurants and compressed the wage distribution among restaurant workers, as well as increased the average wages of fast-food workers twice as much as those at sit-down restaurants, there was no increase in business closure or employment loss detected.

Dunlop, John T. 1957. "The Task of Contemporary Wage Theory." In George W. Taylor and Frank C. Pierson, ed., *New Concepts in Wage Determination*. New York: McGraw-Hill Book Co.
    This article introduces the concept of the wage contour to explain how a firm's internal wage structure might be as much affected by external forces as internal ones. Wage contours were to be defined as a group of workers with similar characteristics working in similar industries and earning similar wages. And for each group there would be a group of rates surrounding a key rate, and these group rates would be affected by changes in the key rate. Within an industry, the key rate would essentially be defined as any rate serving as the reference point for that industry. Since key rates were specific to industries, they could also vary from industry to industry. The implication for the minimum wage was that it too could serve as the key rate for the larger low-wage labor market.

Fortin, Nicole M., and Thomas Lemieux. 1997. "Institutional Changes and Rising Wage Inequality: Is There a Linkage?" *Journal of Economic Perspectives*. 11, 2 (Spring): 75–96.
    This article explores the relationship between changing labor market institutions like labor unions and minimum wages and increasing wage inequality. The authors show that there is a relationship between the decline of these institutions and the rise in wage inequality.

Hayes, Michael T. 2007. "Policy Characteristics, Patterns of Politics, and the Minimum Wage: toward a Typology of Redistributive Policies." *The Policy Studies Journal*. 35, 3 (August): 465–480.
    This article seeks to situate minimum wage politics within the context of Theodore Lowi's famous definition of three

types of politics: regulatory, redistributive, and distributive. The author argues that the minimum wage exhibits features of both regulatory and redistributive policies. Redistributive policies tend to be intensely conflictual with opposition guaranteed precisely because losers from these policies are clearly identified. Here the author defines the minimum wage as essentially redistributive because it concentrates the costs on business, and, as a consequence, intense opposition is generated from business groups. As an example, when the Republican-controlled Congress passed the 1996 minimum wage increase, it did so only because it contained tax breaks for business. These tax breaks, which offset costs to business, effectively resulted in the minimum wage not really redistributing income from employers to low-wage workers, but from all taxpayers to low-wage workers.

Leamer, Edward E. 1999. "Effort, Wages, and the International Division of Labor." *Journal of Political Economy*. 107, 6, 1: 1127–1162.

This article argues that a minimum wage does not necessarily cause unemployment; instead, it forces effort in low-wage and low-effort contracts up enough to support the higher wage. In exchange for higher wages, employers are getting greater effort. The goal is not to equalize, but to ultimately push up wages through productivity gains. If capital is then interpreted as human capital, and if workers themselves invest in their own education, the message of the model is that those who choose education are also choosing higher effort. Meanwhile, if employers invest in their workers' human capital, they too are choosing higher effort. In other words, if the labor contract is multidimensional, a minimum wage law that sets a floor for one aspect of the contract will most likely be met with adjustments to other aspects of the contract. And if effort is variable, then a minimum wage could generate enough extra work effort to compensate for the increased wage level, thus ensuring that everybody is happy.

Lee, David S. 1997. "Wage Inequality in the United States during the 1980s: Rising or Falling Minimum Wage." *Quarterly Journal of Economics*. 114, 3: 997–1023.

This article is one of a series of articles that demonstrates that during the 1980s as the minimum wage stagnated wage inequality increased.

Lemieux, Thomas. 1998. "Estimating the Effects of Unions on Wage Inequality in a Panel Data Model with Comparative Advantage and Nonrandom Selection." *Journal of Labor Economics*. 16, 2: 261–291.

This article estimates the effect of unions on wage inequality. The author argues that the decline in unions has been a contributing factor to the rise in wage inequality.

Levin-Waldman, Oren M, 2004. "Policy Orthodoxies, the Minimum Wage, and the Challenge of Social Science" *Journal of Economic Issues*. 38, 1 (March): 139–154.

This article raises the question of what happens when new empirical findings grounded in social science methodology challenges supposedly scientific models also grounded in the same social sciences. The author argues that the result is to create sufficient ambiguity so as to allow for policy experimentation. Since the data on the effects of the minimum wage are ambiguous at best, policymakers are free to experiment with policies generally and the minimum wage particularly that could serve the public interest.

Levin-Waldman, Oren M. 2012. "Wage Policy as an Essential Ingredient in Job Creation." *Challenge* 55, 6 (November–December): 26–52.

This article argues that to the extent that a wage policy, whether it is in the form of stronger unions or a minimum wage, boosts wages of the middle class through wage contour effects, it can serve as a foundation for job creation. By boosting wages throughout the distribution, workers attain greater purchasing power, which in turn enables them to demand more goods and services in the aggregate. It is aggregate demand for goods and services that drive the economy, and as such a wage policy can serve as a foundation for job creation, especially when used in tandem with monetary and fiscal policy.

Levin-Waldman, Oren M. 2014. "The Conservative Case for the Minimum Wage." *Challenge* 57, 1 (January–February): 19–40.

This article argues that not only does the minimum wage have a broader influence over other wages but also that arguments in favor of the minimum wage could be grounded in conservative political ideology. Conservatives should favor higher minimum wages to the extent that it enables more people to be self-sufficient and less reliant on public assistance. As more people support themselves and become more autonomous, government might also have a basis for reducing expenditures for public social provision precisely because higher wages mean that there will be less of a need for them.

Levin-Waldman, Oren M. 2014. "Who Earns Minimum Wage in New York?" *Regional Labor Review* 16 (Spring/Summer): 20–30.

This article presents a demographic profile of the minimum wage labor market in the New York City metro area relative to New York State and the rest of the United States using data from the March Supplement of the 2012 Current Population Survey. In this article the author specifically looks at the "effective minimum" wage population, which is defined as those earning between the statutory minimum wage and 50 percent of average annual hourly earnings. What this study demonstrates is that contrary to the claims of minimum wage critics, the effective minimum wage labor market is not primarily teenagers. Moreover, some of the industry and occupational composition of effective minimum wage earners in the New York City metro area differs from the rest of the nation in ways that one would not necessarily expect. For example, there are more effective minimum wage earners in production occupations and fewer in sales and related occupations in the New York metro area than in both the United States as a whole and New York State. Still, those with less than a 12th-grade education and working in food preparation and serving related occupations are most likely to be effective minimum wage earners. While the author argues that improving inner city schools and access to GED and other type training programs would certainly help move low-wage workers into the middle class, a strong argument can be made that they can be brought into the middle class by raising the minimum wage because it will enable them to demand more goods and services in the aggregate.

Levin-Waldman, Oren M. 2015. "Why the Minimum Wage Orthodoxy Reigns Supreme." *Challenge* 58, 1 (January–February): 29–50.

> This article explores the reasons for why despite all the empirical evidence demonstrating that increases in the minimum wage will not lead to adverse employment effect; the minimum wage orthodoxy contained in the standard model still holds sway. The author argues that the minimum wage orthodoxy reigns supreme not because of its economic merits but because of how the issue ultimately affects different interests.

Neumark, David, J. M. Ian Salas, and William Wascher. 2014. "Revisiting the Minimum Wage—Employment Debate: Throwing Out the Baby with the Bathwater?" *Industrial and Labor Relations Review.* 67 (Supplement): 608–648.

> In response to those economists arguing that much of the problem with data on the minimum wage concerns

measurement and taking into account heterogeneity, this article tests the untested assumptions about the construction of better control groups. The authors argue even when using methods that let the data identify the appropriate control groups, there is still evidence of disemployment effects, particularly for teens. In other words, the minimum wage still posed a trade-off of higher wages for some against some job losses for others.

Neumark, David, Mark Schweitzer, and William Wascher. 2004. "Minimum Wage Effects throughout the Distribution." *The Journal of Human Resources.* 39, 2: 425–450.

This article actually explores the issue of wage contours and the impact of minimum wage increases on those not earning the minimum wage, but in ranges above the minimum wage. Although the authors acknowledge there to be wage contour effects, particularly for those earning immediately above the minimum wage, they nonetheless conclude the minimum wage to have negative effects for those throughout the distribution, because low-wage workers were bound to be hurt through a reduction in hours. Employers will compensate for higher wages by reducing their workers' hours.

Partridge, Mark D., and Janice S. Partridge. 1999. "Do Minimum Wage Hikes Raise U.S. Long Term Unemployment? Evidence Using State Minimum Wage Rates." *Regional Studies* 33, 8 (1999): 713–726.

This article looks at the relationship between the minimum wage and long-term unemployment. The authors argue that the minimum wage is positively related to long-term unemployment rates. This is because, according to the standard model, a minimum wage prevents workers from lowering their wage demands and employers will demand less labor. If low-skilled workers with a low value of marginal product cannot take a job below the minimum wage, the probability of them being offered a job at all will only diminish and the duration of their unemployment will increase.

Reich, Michael. 2010. "Minimum Wages in the United States: Politics, Economics, and Econometrics." In Clair Brown, Barry Eichengreen, and Michael Reich, eds. *Labor in the Era of Globalization*. Cambridge and New York: Cambridge University Press.

This article looks at the minimum wage in the United States within the context of less than perfect data. The author argues that the problem with much of the data suggesting large negative effects due to minimum wage increases only show these large negative effects to be among teenagers. Moreover, there is a tendency to look at trends both prior to an increase and following one. But it is incorrect to attribute a post–minimum wage trend to minimum wage policy, because the negative post-minimum trend could be due to other factors, especially when there is often a good six-month lag time between the enactment of an increase and the implementation of that increase. Therefore, when the minimum wage is placed in its larger context, between 1955 and 1996 when the minimum wage was increased 16 times, these increases were also more likely to occur in times of relatively strong employment growth. At the same time, these increases have also been occurring in the context of more and more states raising their minimum wages above the federal level, beginning in the late 1980s. The author argues that rather than assume, as the standard model does, that a reason for not observing employment effects is due to a minimum wage below a market-clearing wage, it may be that higher wage floors can significantly reduce employers' recruitment and retention costs. Low-wage employers typically experience above-average turnover and job vacancy rates. Contrary to the argument that minimum wages kill jobs, they kill vacancies, which is to say that minimum wage increases do not necessarily lead to disemployment because workers were fired; rather, they decrease the number of jobs created in the future for low-wage workers.

Sabia, Joseph J., and Richard V. Burkhauser. 2010. "Minimum Wages and Poverty: Will a $9.50 Federal Minimum Wage Really Help the Working Poor?" *Southern Economic Journal.* 76, 3: 592–623.

This article argues on the basis of data from the Current Population Survey (CPS) that federal and state minimum wages increases between 2003 and 2007 had no effect on poverty. They estimated that those workers who would directly benefit from an increase in the minimum wage were already earning between $7.25 and $9.49 an hour while the minimum wage was still $5.85 an hour. While 17.7 percent of all workers earning between $5.70 and $9.49 an hour stood to benefit from an increase in the minimum wage, 80.3 percent of all workers were earning a wage of $9.50 or more. Therefore, the proposal in 2010 to raise the minimum wage to $9.50 an hour would not have been well targeted toward poor workers, and that it would been even less target-efficient than the increase that took effect in 2009.

Shapiro, Carl, and Joseph Stiglitz. 1984. "Equilibrium Unemployment as a Worker Discipline Device." *American Economic Review.* 74, 3 (June): 433–444.

This article argues the efficiency wage effects of the minimum wage from the perspective of the standard model, or what is commonly referred to as the neoclassical model. Workers paid a higher wage will become more productive and, hence, more efficient. The higher wage is regarded as an anti-shirking wage because employees understand that by shirking they may lose their jobs, which in turn will force them into a lower-paying wage market. Consequently, higher-paid workers seek to avoid shirking. Meanwhile, the employer realizes some cost savings because they are able to reduce their monitoring of employees, who are now working harder to maintain their better paying jobs.

Stigler, George. 1946. "The Economics of Minimum Wage Legislation." *American Economic Review*. 36 (June): 358–365.

This article has become a staple, if not a classic, of the minimum wage literature. It lays out the standard model's prediction of what can be expected to occur when there are increases in the minimum wage. The author argues that the minimum wage will result in one of two things: either workers will lose their jobs or productivity will increase.

Volscho, Thomas W. Jr. 2005 "Minimum Wages and Income Inequality in the American States, 1960–2000." *Research in Social Stratification and Mobility*. 23: 347–373.

This article looks at those states where there is a minimum wage and the extent to which state minimum wages reduce income inequality. The author finds that in those states where minimum wages have been higher than the federal minimum wage, income inequality in those states has been lower. Looking at state minimum wages from 1960 to 2000, he estimates that each $0.81 increase in the minimum wage results in a 35.5 percent reduction in the Gini coefficient.

Webb, Sidney. 1912. "The Economic Theory of a Legal Minimum Wage." *The Journal of Political Economy*. 20, 10 (December): 973–998.

This article makes an efficiency argument for the minimum wage, which has come to be known among heterodox economists as the "Webb" effect. The author argues that workers who are paid higher wages are better able to maintain themselves, and hence they will be able to work more effectively and efficiently. Because they are paid better, their morale improves and they feel better about their jobs, and because they feel better about their jobs, they put more effort into their work. As a result, their productivity increases and so too does overall efficiency.

Zatz, Noah D. 2009. "The Minimum Wage as a Civil Rights Protection: An Alternative to Antipoverty Arguments?" *The University of Chicago Legal Forum.* Downloaded from: http://www .lexisnexis.com/ex-proxy.brooklyn.cuny.edu:2048/Inacui2api/ delivery/PrintDoc.

This article explores a civil rights argument as an alternative to the anti-poverty arguments typically made by supporters of the minimum wage. The author suggests that for employers to pay below a certain threshold is akin to stealing from their workers and depriving them of their civil rights. The argument rests on the assumption that workers' labor constitutes, or it should, a property right in the same way that traditional forms of capital constitute property rights.

Internet

AFL-CIO > Home > Issues > Jobs and Economy > Wages and Income > Minimum Wage. http://www.aflcio.org/Issues/Jobs-and-Economy/Wages-and-Income/Minimum-Wage.

This is information from the AFL-CIO's website on the minimum wage. It begins with a short history of the program, and a chart showing the real value of the minimum wage between 1968 and 2012 in 2012 dollars. It also notes the current legislation introduced by Senator Tom Harkin of Iowa and Rep. George Miller of California to raise the minimum wage to $10.10 an hour and provides information on how many Americans support increases in the minimum wage and how much additional consumer spending will be generated as a result of increasing it. It then lists links to several resources on the minimum wage.

Babones, Salvatore. 2012. "The Minimum Wage Is Stuck at $7.25: It Should Be $21.16—or Higher." Inequality.org; "A Project of the Institute for Policy Studies." http://inequality.org/minimum-wage/. (July 24).

The author notes that the minimum wage reached its historic high in 1968 when it was raised from $1.40 an hour to $1.60 an hour. Adjusted for inflation, that would have come up $10.55 an hour in 2012 dollars. But had the minimum wage been benchmarked with personal income growth, and had it kept pace with personal income growth, the minimum wage in 2012 would have actually been $21.16 an hour. Or, as the author puts it, had the U.S. income distribution and standard of decency remained exactly at its 1968 level, the minimum wage in 2012 would have been $21.16 in 2012 dollars. But for the author, a minimum wage of $21.16 an hour still would not represent progress; that would require an even higher minimum wage. It isn't that a minimum wage that high isn't economically and socially realistic: rather, it is politically inconceivable. Society, the author concludes, simply does not want a minimum wage that high, and that is the only reason we cannot have it.

DePillis, Lydia. 2015. "What If Walmart Raised Its Minimum Wage to $70,000 a Year?" *The Washington Post*. http://www.washingtonpost.com/blogs/wonkblog/wp/2015/04/22/thought-experiment-what-if-walmart-raised-its-minimum-wage-to-70000-a-year/ (April 22).

This is an interesting article about the CEO of a small Seattle-based company called Gravity Payments who decided to boost the annual salary of his 120 employees to $70,000, which would be paid for by reducing his $1 million compensation to the same $70,000. At the same time, he directed that most of the firm's profits go back into the staff. He chose the $70,000 figure on the grounds that it is the level at which money is presumed to buy the most happiness, while at the same time making for a productive workforce. The CEO also wanted to demonstrate what is possible if workers can actually share the gains of their labor. Still the author acknowledges that while this may be feasible in some small companies, it may not be feasible in companies with larger workforces. In the case of Walmart, it might leave the company unable to cover all of its expenses. And yet, the larger point is that there is still room to maneuver. In other words, Walmart could make all of its workers full time and pay them a minimum wage of $15 an hour, costing the company $5.2 billion a year and still be left with a hefty profit.

Economic Policy Institute. 2014. "Over 600 Economists Sign Letter in Support of $10.10 Minimum Wage: Economist Statement on the Federal Minimum Wage." http://www.epi .org/minimum-wage-statement/ (January 14).

This is a petition that was signed by more than 600 economists, including those who subscribe to the standard model of the minimum wage and several Nobel laureates, which was sent to President Obama and congressional leaders from both political parties calling for an increase in the minimum wage to $10.10 an hour. The letter notes that close to 17 million workers would directly benefit from the increase and that an additional 11 million workers earning above the new minimum would also derive benefit. It calls attention to new research findings suggesting no, or little, adverse employment effects, and suggests that a higher wage could even have stimulative effects for the economy as a whole.

Garcia, Eric. 2015. "Who Are the Minimum-Wage Workers of America?" *National Journal.* http://www.nationaljournal .com/economy/who-are-the-minimum-wage-workers-of- america-20150428 (April 28).

This article presents a profile of just who are the workers earning the minimum wage today. Many of them are young men and women and are likely to be employed in certain sectors of the economy. These workers also tend to have lower levels of educational attainment, many of whom have less than a high school education. This article also notes that according to the Bureau of Labor Statistics many of the states with the highest percentage of workers earning the minimum hourly wage rate resided in the American South, including Arkansas, Louisiana, Mississippi, and Tennessee. The article appears to suggest that where people live may be a determinant of earning the federal minimum wage. On one level, the article may be seen as attempting to put a human face on low-wage America. But on another level, it is suggestive that determinants of who earns the minimum wage may in the end be more about politics than economics.

Institute for Cultural Communicators. 2015. "Minimum Wage and Poverty: Guide to Research Resources." http://iccinc.org/files/tour2014/PF_ResourcesPreview.2014July21.pdf.

This is a resource guide that was compiled by Ka-Neng Au, a reference librarian at Rutgers University. It provides students and others a guide to understanding the ICC Resolution on the minimum wage: "Resolved that raising minimum wage rates reduces poverty in the United States." The resources are primarily links to agencies like the Department of Labor Wages and Hours Division, the MIT calculator on the living wage, and various studies that support the resolution.

International Labor Organization—Information Resources—Research Guides—Minimum Wages. http://www.ilo.org/inform/online-information-resources/research-guides/minimum-wages/lang—en/index.htm.

This site presents information from the International Labor Organization on the minimum wage worldwide. It also contains links to ILO publications—studies and reports—on the minimum wage.

Kearney, Melissa, and Benjamin H. Harris. 2014. "The 'Ripple Effects' of a Minimum Wage Increase on American Workers." The Hamilton Project. http://www.hamiltonproject.org/papers/ the_ripple_effect_of_the_minimum_wage_on_american_ workers/.

This article put out by the Hamilton Project of the Brookings Institution argues that the benefits of the minimum wage are much broader than those low-wage workers whose pay will be raised to the level of a new minimum wage. In talking about ripple effects, the authors appear to be making reference to wage contour effects. Because those earning above the new minimum wage will also get pay increases, and so too will those earning above them and so on, the minimum wage can provide a stimulus to the economy that extends beyond those low-wage workers paid at or below the current minimum wage. In this article the authors find that up to 35 million workers would receive a wage increase, which accounts for 29.4 percent of the workforce. Their conclusion is that the nature of the current minimum wage focuses too narrowly on those workers earning exactly the minimum wage, and in so doing overlooks a much larger number of low-wage workers who would also get wage increases through the ripple effects.

Massachusetts Institute of Technology. Poverty in American Living Calculator. http://livingwage.mit.edu/.

This site provides a living wage calculator to estimate the cost of living in a given community or region. The calculator lists typical expenses, the living wage and typical wages for a selected region. What the calculator makes clear is that while the minimum wage establishes a minimum earnings threshold under which society will not allow families to fall below, it has nonetheless failed to approximate families' basic expenses in 2013. The result is that many families are forced to seek either public assistance or multiple jobs in order to pay for food, clothing, shelter, and medical care for themselves and their families.

Meer, Jonathan, and Jeremy West. 2015. "Effects of the Minimum Wage on Employment Dynamics." http://econweb.tamu .edu/jmeer/Meer_West_Minimum_Wage.pdf. (January).

This article argues that although the evidence isn't there that an increase in the minimum wage will lead to an immediate and dramatic decrease in employment, it will nonetheless impact employment over time. The authors argue that the principal consequence will be a slowdown in economic growth, which will lead to lower employment over time because fewer jobs will be created. The authors use three separate panels of administrative employment and find that the rate of job growth is reduced over several years. Moreover, the effects are more pronounced for younger workers and those in industries employing a higher proportion of low-wage workers. This article could be viewed as significant because it is qualifying what it means to talk about reduced employment by distinguishing between the disemployment effect—those who are laid off following an increase—and lower employment because fewer jobs are created.

National Conference of State Legislatures. 2015. "State Minimum Wages/2015 Minimum Wages by State." http://www .ncsl.org/research/labor-and-employment/state-minimum-wage-chart.aspx (February 24).

This is a source of information for those who want to know what the minimum wage is in various states. It provides a table with each state's minimum wage as of February 24, 2015, which in some cases is none, future enacted increases, and indexed automatic annual adjustments. For those states that adopted indexation mechanisms, it indicates whether they came about through legislation, ballot initiative, or constitutional amendment. It also provides links to a minimum wage legislation database for 2014 and 2015.

National Women's Law Center. 2015. Home > Our Issues > Employment > Women and the Minimum Wage, State by State. http://www.nwlc.org/resource/women-and-minimum-wage-state-state (January 5).

This site provides a state-by-state analysis of women who are earning the minimum wage. Two-thirds of minimum wage workers nationwide are women and at least half of minimum wage workers in each state are women. Although 29 states and the District of Columbia have minimum wages higher than the federal minimum wage of $7.25 an hour, in every state the minimum wage leaves a full-time workers with two children below the official federal poverty line. This site has a link to aggregate data nationwide.

Neumark, David. 2014. "Who Really Gets the Minimum Wage." *The Wall Street Journal*. http://www.wsj.com/articles/who-really-gets-the-minimum-wage-1404683348. (July 6).

This is an op-ed piece that argues that the minimum wage is not really targeted well. The author argues that were the minimum wage to be raised to as $10.10 an hour as proposed by President Obama, only 18 percent of the benefits would go to poor families, while 29 percent would go to families whose incomes are three times the poverty level. Still, the author acknowledges that while most of the evidence points to job losses, it does not point to widespread declines in employment. Rather, consistent with the Congressional Budget Office report of 2014, many more low-wage workers will get a raise than lose their jobs. Nevertheless, the argument is about low-wage workers, not low-income families. On the contrary, the minimum wage is ineffective in helping poor families because such a small share of the benefit actually flows to them. For the author, low-wage workers and low-income families are not the same thing. Rather, many higher-income families have low-wage workers, and some poor families have some workers who earn higher wages but cannot get enough hours. And then there are poor families with no workers, in which case the minimum wage is of no use to them. Although a higher minimum wage can reduce poverty if the wage gains in poor families outweigh job losses caused by the increase, most evidence suggests that minimum wage increases don't reduce poverty. Therefore, a better alternative for reducing poverty would be the earned income tax credit.

Pew Research Center. 2014. "Most See Inequality Growing, But Partisans Differ over Solutions." (January 23). http://www .people-press.org/2014/01/23/most-see-inequality-growing-but-partisans-differ-over-solutions/.
This is a short piece that summarizes Americans' attitudes toward rising income inequality and whether the wealthy should be taxed more as a means of addressing the issue. Sixty-five percent of Americans (out of a survey of 1,504 adults) believe that the gap between the rich and poor has widened, and 54 percent believe that the wealthy should be taxed more to expand aid to the poor. Meanwhile, 73 percent of the public favored raising the federal minimum wage to $10.10 an hour. Still there was considerable partisan division on these issues, with 65 percent of Republicans opposing minimum wage increases. Although just a survey of public opinion on the issue, it is important because it highlights a divide between policymakers who often reflect the interests of the business community buttressed by the standard model on the minimum wage and the public that often tends to favor increases in the minimum wage.

Raise the Minimum Wage.com. http://www.raisetheminimum wage.org/.
This site is a project of the National Employment Law Project. It is intended as a resource for those interested in knowing more about the minimum wage, and especially

public officials at the local level interested in enacting one. Among the available resources are fact sheets, minimum wages in "your community," minimum wage laws and proposals in major U.S. cities, research, polling, questions and answers, reasons for why the minimum wage should be raised, other minimum wage partners, and testimony. It also contains a blog, a media center, and information about campaigns in progress for minimum wages, whether it be increases or new legislation. Among the first pieces of information provided is a statistic showing that 75 percent of Americans support an increase in the minimum wage to $12.50 an hour.

Time for a Raise. 2013. http://www.timeforaraise.org/benefits-of-raising-the-minimum-wage/.
This appears to be the website of an advocacy group supporting higher minimum wages. It provides interesting figures on the state of the minimum wage and who earns it. In 2011, for example, 3.8 million people were paid at or below the minimum wage, and had the minimum wage been raised to $8.50 an hour then, about $9.5 billion in additional spending would have been injected into the economy. And were the minimum wage raised to $10 an hour, which would still be below its 1968 value, an additional $60 billion in additional spending would have been injected into the economy. This website makes clear that more than a matter of assisting the poor, raising the minimum wage is about stimulating the economy and providing benefits to small businesses that were hit hardest during the Great Recession.

U.S. Department of Labor. Wage and Hours Division. 2014. "Final Rule: Executive Order 13658, Establishing a Minimum Wage for Contractors." (February 12). http://www.dol.gov/whd/flsa/eo13658/index.htm.
This is the Executive Order that President Obama issued in February 2014 directing that all businesses that contract

with the federal government to perform various services pay their workers a minimum wage of $10.10 an hour as a condition of those contracts. Because the minimum wage requires an act of the U.S. Congress, this order applied only to contractors and as such was limited in scope. The president could issue the order under Executive Branch's contract authority. Still, these contractors would only have to pay the ordered minimum wage to those employees working on the government contracts.

U.S. Department of Labor. Summary of the Major Laws of the Department of Labor. http://www.dol.gov/opa/aboutdol/lawsprog.htm.

This site from the U.S. Labor Department provides information on all the major pieces of labor legislation affecting the workers and their workplaces. On the very first page of the site is a link to the Wages & Hours Division, which administers the Fair Labor Standards Act (FLSA) with a link to that as well. On the FLSA link, one can find information about the law, who is covered, the history of the law, its 75th-anniversary celebration, employee rights, as well as FLSA posters, bulletins, and presentations in several different languages.

Wihbey, John. 2014. "Effects of Raising the Minimum Wage: Research and Key Lessons." Journalist's Resource, Harvard Kennedy School, Shorenstein Center on Media, Politics and Public Policy. (February 20). http://journalistsresource.org/studies/economics/jobs/the-effects-of-raising-the-minimum-wage#.

This short article presents an overview of issues and lessons from the minimum wage. It contains links to key reports put out by government agencies like the Congressional Budget Office and studies done by various economists. It also contains links to organizations like the Center for American Progress that supports minimum wage increases and the National Bureau for Employment Research that still hews to the standard model. This piece is intended mainly as a resource guide for journalists seeking to navigate this issue, but can certainly be used as a point of departure for anybody interested in studying the issues.

Wilson, Mark. 2012. "The Negative Effects of Minimum Wage Laws." Cato Institute/Downsizing the Federal Government. http://www.downsizinggovernment.org/labor/negative-effects-minimum-wage-laws (September).

This article is more of a position paper put out by the Cato Institute, a libertarian think tank devoted to free unfettered markets that allow for individuals to pursue their liberties unfettered by government interference of any kind. At the outset, the author makes it clear that minimum wages stifle job opportunities for low-skilled workers, youth, and minorities. Because there is no such thing as a free lunch, employers will compensate for higher wages by reducing hours, reducing hiring, reducing benefits, or simply raising their prices. The author reviews the history of the minimum wage, the various economic models, statistics on who is paid the minimum wage, and the effects of the minimum wage on employment. The author concludes that low wages are usually paid to entry-level workers who do not earn these wages for extended periods of time. The author cites studies that claim that nearly two-thirds of minimum wage workers move above that wage within a year. Therefore a minimum wage is not needed. Moreover, in tough economic times when workers will produce less value than the wage that employers are forced to pay, employers simply will not hire workers whose value is less than the new minimum wage. Policymakers, then, should pursue policies that generate faster growth to benefit all workers rather than those, like the minimum wage, that create winners and losers.

Introduction

The minimum wage has been in existence in one form or another since the late 1800s. It has long been, and continues to be, a controversial issue. This chapter presents a brief chronology of the some of the milestones in the history and evolution of the minimum wage. Although coverage has greatly expanded, the minimum wage in the United States remains little more than a wage floor. In several other developed countries, it has become more encompassing.

1894   New Zealand passes the first national minimum wage through its Industrial Conciliation and Arbitration Act. It was the world's first system of a compulsory arbitration. It gave legal recognition to unions and allowed for them to take labor disputes to the conciliation board, which was made up of both employers and workers. An unsatisfactory decision on either side could then be appealed to the Arbitration Court, which was made up of one Supreme Court judge and two assessors. Employers' associations elected one assessor, while unions elected the other. This law became the foundation for determining minimum wage rates and settling labor disputes.

Democratic presidential candidate Sen. Bernie Sanders (I-Vt.) speaks during a rally on Capitol Hill in Washington, D.C., on July 22, 2015. Sanders pushed to raise the minimum wage to $15 an hour. (AP Photo/ Andrew Harnik)

1896   Victoria, Australia, amends its Factories Act to create wage boards. This was actually the last of a series of nineteenth-century legislation intended to establish minimum standards for wages and working conditions, particularly in the Melbourne district. It gave legitimacy to state intervention in the workplace in order to reconcile the conflicting rights of labor and capital. It also sought to limit the employment opportunities of women, children, and Chinese immigrants.

1905   The U.S. Supreme Court decides *Lochner v. New York,* which affirmed the "liberty of contract" doctrine. This doctrine would overshadow all attempts to pass legislation regulating hours and wages in the United States until the late 1930s. In *Lochner,* the Supreme Court held that a New York State statute limiting a baker's hours to 10 hours a day and 60 hours a week violated a baker's liberty of contract—the right to work more hours if desired. The Court rejected the application of an earlier case, *Holden v. Hardy,* that a worker's hours could be regulated in order to protect the workers' health and welfare. In *Lochner* the Court maintained that there was nothing in what a baker did that presented a health risk. The precedent from this case was critical because if a state was effectively prohibited from imposing a maximum hours law because it violated workers' liberty of contract, it would effectively be prohibited from imposing a minimum wage floor for the same reason.

1908   The U.S. Supreme Court upholds *Mueller v. Oregon,* which qualified the liberty of contract doctrine coming from *Lochner v. New York.* In this case the Court said that the state of Oregon could limit the hours of women working in laundries to 10 hours a day and 60 hours a week because their liberty of contract needed to be protected. Women needed special protection because they had the essential function of caring for the next generation as mothers. Therefore, to limit their liberty of contract was deemed to be in the larger public interest and was covered by the state police power of protecting health welfare and morals. This case was important because it established the principle of protective labor legislation for women and effectively suggested that states would be free to now establish maximum hours and minimum wage legislation, at least for women.

1909 Great Britain passes the Trades Boards Act, which became the basis for minimum wages in Britain. The law was intended to wipe out sweating where workers paid by manufacturers were not paid wages but for the pieces they produced. The idea was to create the first steps toward a universal minimum wage in Britain.

1912 Massachusetts passes the first minimum wage in the United States. The law covered only women and children and allowed for a commission to determine where the wage would actually be set. Although it called for weak penalties for violators, the commonwealth's 1912 report of the Commission on Minimum Wage Boards still made it clear that whenever wages "are less than the cost of living and the reasonable provision for maintaining the worker in health, the industry employing her is in receipt of the working energy of a human being at less than its cost, and to that extent is parasitic." As weak as the law was, it introduced the concept of parasitic industries and, in the spirit of incrementalism, created the foundations for what would ultimately evolve into a more encompassing wage floor. At the same time, it appeared to be navigating the difficult terrain between *Lochner* and *Mueller*.

1912 Sidney Webb publishes "The Economic Theory of a Legal Minimum Wage" in the *Journal of Political Economy*. Speaking from the school of institutional economics, Webb argued that a higher minimum wage would enable workers to better maintain themselves. They would feel better about their work and consequently their productivity would increase, which in turn would add to the efficiency of their employers. Webb was making an efficiency argument for the minimum wage, which has come to be known as the Webb effect. He also argued that a higher minimum wage would create an incentive for employers who did not consider their employees to be worth a higher wage to invest in their training so that their productivity would increase to justify a higher wage.

1918 The U.S. Congress enacts the first federal minimum wage law specifically for the District of Columbia, which was to apply only to women under the model of protective legislation for women. While reformers made the essentialist arguments for it coming out of *Mueller,* they in this case offered some pragmatic ones as well. They noted that women were among the lowest-paid workers and were thus in desperate circumstances. Moreover, because women weren't unionized, a legislated minimum was therefore necessary.

1923 The U.S. Supreme Court decides *Adkins v Children's Hospital,* which said that the 1918 federal minimum wage law for the District of Columbia was unconstitutional because women were no longer entitled to protective legislation that would interfere with their liberty of contract. The Court said that they no longer needed special protection because the constitutional amendment of 1920 that granted them the right to vote effectively eliminated the biological difference between men and women asserted by the Court in *Mueller.* Now they enjoyed the same liberty of contract as men, and it would be more difficult to pass laws mandating minimum wages.

1933 Congress passes the National Industrial Recovery Act (NIRA). The legislation was designed to maintain price and market stability by adopting industry codes to safeguard against unfair competition. The codes contained provisions on hours, wages, unions, and collective bargaining. By establishing codes for minimum wage rates for specific industries, which would also vary from industry to industry, the legislation was creating a precedent for general minimum wage legislation. Moreover, it was making a statement about the importance of a minimum wage floor for the general health of the economy on the assumption that aggregate demand for goods and services cannot be maintained if workers don't have wages sufficient to maintain purchasing power.

1936 The Supreme Court decides *Morehouse Warden v. Tipaldo.* This was an important case because it demonstrated that as late as 1936, the influence of *Lochner* was still quite strong.

At issue was a 1933 law in New York State that authorized the state's labor commissioner to fix wages for women. New York State attempted to argue that given the depths of the Great Depression, a state minimum wage constituted emergency legislation that would override the prevailing liberty of contract doctrine. The Court, however, did not view a minimum wage to be a matter of emergency legislation and therefore held the measure to be an unconstitutional abridgement of a women's liberty of contract. Moreover, the Court maintained that men were just as susceptible to exploitation.

1937   The National Emergency Council submits a report to President Franklin Roosevelt titled *Report on Economic Conditions of the South*. This report detailed how the economy of the South lagged behind the economy of the North in a wide variety of measures, most notably education, industry, and wage structure. The findings of this report helped bolster the argument that a uniform minimum wage would not only reduce industrial strife by giving workers more bargaining power and enable them to demand more goods and services because of greater purchasing power, but it would also be a key ingredient in the economic development of the South.

1937   The U.S. Supreme Court decides *West Coast Hotel Co. v. Parrish*. This case involved the constitutionality of a Washington State minimum wage law that had been on the books since 1913. In this case the state of Washington argued that a minimum wage was necessary to preclude possible wage disputes that could disrupt normal business activity, which in turn could inconvenience all concerned. Coming a month after the Supreme Court's failed court-packing plan, the Supreme Court now overturned its prior decisions and upheld the constitutionality of the Washington state statute. Now the Court made it clear that the law did not really compel an employer to pay anything; rather, it merely created a minimum floor. The Court was now prepared to recognize that a minimum wage could be a matter of emergency legislation, especially during a depression. Moreover, the Court appeared to recognize that the standard for state regulation of public health and welfare now went beyond those matters that merely caused physical harm; they now included economic harm. This case was critical because the path was now clear for government, whether at the federal or state level, to pass a minimum wage law on the basis of a compelling public interest.

1938   In his State of the Union Address President Franklin Roosevelt defends the idea of wage legislation. He argues that it will assist the disadvantaged and assist in the economic recovery of the nation by affording more people purchasing power. When the purchasing power of those groups who are disadvantaged are increased, so too is the purchasing power of those in professions that serve them. Roosevelt argued that it was a measure of benefit to the economy as a whole because all sectors of the economy were interrelated.

1938   Congress passes the Fair Labor Standards Act (FLSA), which established the nation's first federal minimum wage. Although coverage was very limited, it did establish a national minimum wage of $0.25 an hour to increase to $0.40 an hour by 1945. The legislation established an hours and wages division, whose administrator would be responsible for the appointment of an industry committee for each industry engaged in either commerce or goods production. The committees were to include representatives from employers, employees, and the general public, and were to make recommendations for the highest possible minimum wage in each industry that would not adversely affect employment. These committees were also supposed to be cognizant of each industry's respective economic and competitive conditions.

1949   In his State of the Union Address President Harry S. Truman calls for an increase in the minimum wage—the first since its last increase in 1945, which was the last in a schedule created in the initial FLSA of 1938. He argued that the minimum wage was central to his broader social agenda of attempting to bring the lowest paid workers up to a level that corresponded to the price and wage structure that had evolved immediately following World War II. As a result of these amendments to the FLSA, the minimum wage was raised to $0.75 an hour. These amendments also began a process of expanding coverage. All employees in retail sales were previously excluded from coverage. Now only those employees in retail establishments with more than 50 percent of their annual sales volume in the states in which they were located were excluded.

1961   Congress raises the minimum wage to $1.25 an hour and expands coverage to include an additional 7.6 million workers. These amendments were important because of the expanded definition of covered industries. Covered industries now included retail and service establishments with gross sales in excess of $1 million and who sold across state lines in excess of $250,000. The minimum wage now covered transportation workers in either urban or intraurban systems in which gross sales also exceeded $1 million. Gas station workers were also included if gross sales exceeded $250,000. Still, the law continued to exclude many workers who otherwise would be classified as "low-skilled" workers.

1966   Congress amends the FLSA again to cover an estimated 9.1 million workers. These amendments, along with the preceding amendments in 1961, are considered to be among the most important because of the expansion of coverage. These amendments raised the minimum wage to $1.60 an hour, where it would remain until amended again in 1974.

1981   President Ronald Reagan fires the PATCO air traffic controllers who went out on strike, which for federal employees was illegal. This action sent shock waves through the labor community because employers in the private sector came away with the message that if government can fire striking workers, they can too. This event is often seen as the beginning of an assault on organized labor. With this assault, membership in unions declined and a key constituency for increases in the minimum wage also declined. It was no coincidence that the greatest decline in the value of the minimum wage occurred at the same time that organized labor saw its greatest decline in membership. Reagan, who was no friend of organized labor, also opposed increases in the minimum wage, although he did support subminimums for teenagers. Many saw the Reagan years as an assault on labor generally. The next increase in the minimum wage would not occur until his successor George H. W. Bush was in office in 1989.

1981   The federal Minimum Wage Study Commission (MWSC) releases its report. The report concluded that a 10 percent increase in the minimum wage would lead to a 1–3 percent reduction in employment among teenagers. The report also concluded that the effects would be proportionately smaller for adults 20–24, and that on balance adults would be better off under a wage floor. Although the report did have something for everybody on all sides of the minimum wage debate, the report formed the basis for a new consensus that minimum wage increases specifically lowered employment for teenagers. For opponents of the minimum wage, this provided good ammunition. But it also fueled calls for a subminimum wage for teenagers. It may not be completely related to the report, but 1981 saw the inauguration of Ronald Reagan who opposed both unions and the minimum wage on the grounds that both were an assault to liberty, and the individual's liberty to negotiate their own working conditions, including pay, free from the fetters of government control. The year 1981, then, would mark the beginning of the longest stagnation of the minimum wage, which would also coincide with the greatest declines in union membership. The minimum wage, which had been raised to $3.35 an hour as the last phase of the 1977 amendments, would not be raised again until 1989.

1993   Congress significantly expands the earned income tax credit (EITC) as part of the Omnibus Budget and Reconciliation Act of 1993. Republicans and conservatives in Congress still opposed raising the minimum wage on the grounds that it would result in lower employment and hurt the poor. At a time when there were wide-ranging debates over reforming the nation's welfare system, the EITC was seen as a way to assist the working poor, reward work, and not lead to lower employment among the poor, who were also disproportionately unskilled workers. For single parents with two children earning a minimum wage of then $4.25 an hour, the maximum credit of $3370 when fully phased in by 1996 meant that these workers would effectively be getting a 40 percent boost in their income. The EITC functions like a negative income tax, which means that workers whose wages are too low to pay federal taxes get a check from the federal government. For conservatives who always argued the moral hazard of welfare assistance, the EITC was a measure that rewarded work, and would effectively offer an incentive to those who previously shunned work to enter the labor market, even if it was only the low-wage labor market. And for opponents of the minimum wage, this was viewed as a better way to assist the poor because it would not result in disemployment effects among the poor. At the same time, it was not clear that the EITC would not also be encouraging employers to pay low wages because they now understood that their workers' wages would be subsidized by government. Moreover, there was the additional question of what incentive would workers have to put their greatest effort in for their employers when 40 percent of their incomes was coming from the government instead of their employers.

1994   Baltimore enacts the nation's first living wage ordinance. Under this ordinance all companies that had contracts with the city to perform public services were required to pay a minimum hourly wage of $6.10 an hour at a time when the federal minimum wage still stood at $4.25 an hour. More than 130 municipalities have since passed similar ordinances, many of which also include provisions for benefits too. With this measure began what has come to be known as the living wage movement, which has been in response to two things. The first was the tendency of municipal governments to reduce costs by contracting out municipal services that were once performed by better paid unionized municipal workers to private contractors who weren't paying much more, if at all, than the minimum wage. And the second was that the federal minimum wage had failed to keep pace with inflation, and that it was insufficient to support a family. Although these ordinances were limited in their coverage, the living wage movement did call attention to the plight of low-wage workers. While it never materialized in the early years, the hope was that these citywide ordinances would lead to more encompassing citywide minimum wage laws. In more recent years with various municipalities enacting their own citywide minimum wages, the linkage appears to have been established.

1996   Congress finally amends the FLSA for the first time since 1989. The minimum wage was to be raised in two phases, from $4.25 to $5.15 an hour by 1997. This increase came amid considerable controversy. The Republican-controlled Congress was opposed for the same reasons they traditionally opposed it: it would lower employment and hurt small businesses. Congressional Democrats and President Bill Clinton favored it because they believed that those who work and play by the rules of the game should earn livable wages. The timing of the change was particularly important because it coincided with a major overhaul of the nation's welfare system. With the Personal Responsibility and Work Opportunity Reconciliation Act (PRWORA) of 1996, Congress ended welfare as an entitlement and made the receipt of temporary assistance contingent on participation in welfare to work programs. States would run their own programs, but assistance would now be time-limited, with financial inducements to move as many of their welfare caseloads into the labor market, as well as find ways to reduce out of wedlock births. There was certainly a sentiment among some that if former welfare recipients were going to be forced to transition into the labor market, then as a matter of fairness they needed to earn wages that would better enable them to stay there.

1996   The Australian Council of Trade Unions launches their living wage campaign as a claim before the Australian

Industrial Relations Commission. It was intended to mount a counteroffensive against the newly elected government that was committed to breaking union power and deregulating markets. It was about preventing the collapse of hourly wage rates in an economy plagued by chronic unemployment and underemployment.

1999 The British Parliament passes the National Minimum Wage (NMW), which effectively replaces the Trade Boards Act of 1909. This law created a uniform minimum wage covering the entire country. This act also created the Low Pay Commission (LPC), which was to act independently of Parliament and make periodic recommendations on the minimum wage. The purpose of the LPC was to remove the minimum wage in Britain from politics. By having an independent body make recommendations, Parliament would then be forced to publicly respond.

2007 Congress in its first 100 days of a newly elected Democratic Party majority in both chambers amends the FLSA to increase the minimum wage in three phases, from $5.10 an hour in 2007 to its current rate of $7.25 by 2009. This had been the first increase in the minimum wage since 1996, when a Republican-controlled Congress increased it only because the legislation also included a grab bag of goodies to business interests, especially small businesses.

2013 President Barack Obama calls for an increase in the federal minimum wage from $7.25 an hour, where it had been since 2009, to $9 an hour. He argued that in the world's wealthiest nation no one working full time should have to live in poverty. He argued that at a time when CEO pay was at its highest, it was definitely time to do something for the least advantaged members of society. But he also made it clear that it would be beneficial to businesses too. They would benefit from more customers with more money in their pockets to spend.

2013 On Labor Day fast-food workers take to the streets in a daylong strike for a $15 an hour minimum wage. This would be the first such strike among several periodic strikes for the $15 an hour minimum. Although it did not result in an increase in the minimum wage, it did call attention to the plight of low-wage workers, and could conceivably be the foundation for a nationwide social movement for a national minimum wage of at least $15.

2014   German chancellor Angela Merkel approves the country's first minimum wage of 8.50 Euros, which is the equivalent $11.75 an hour, to begin in 2015.

2014   President Obama proposes a minimum wage increase to $10.10 an hour in his State of the Union Address. This was in support of the Harkin–Miller bill to raise the minimum wage to $10.10. It is also against the backdrop of rising inequality.

2014   In February President Barack Obama issues Executive Order 13658 directing private contractors who are doing business with the federal government to pay their workers a minimum wage of $10.10 an hour. This minimum wage is limited in its coverage to only federal contractors, and does not apply to businesses across the board.

2014   Bill de Blasio is elected mayor of New York City on a progressive platform of addressing rising income inequality. Among his proposals was a citywide minimum wage to match other cities in the country that were already raising their wages. To some extent, his election did focus attention on these issues and the steps that local governments might take to address them.

2014   The Congressional Budget Office (CBO) issues a report on the minimum wage that states that an increase in the minimum wage to $10.10 an hour as proposed by President Obama could lead to 500,000 fewer jobs once fully implemented. Still, the report concludes that an increase in the minimum wage will be beneficial to the economy because more than 16 million workers will get raises and their increased purchasing power will fuel economic growth because greater purchasing power will lead to increased aggregate demand for goods and services.

2014 The Seattle, Washington, City Council passes a $15 an hour minimum wage and the mayor signed it. The law was expected to be phased in over seven years, beginning in April 2015. The seven-year phase-in applies to smaller businesses—those employing fewer than 500 workers. Larger employers—those employing over 500 workers—are expected to reach a minimum of $15 an hour in three years.

2014 The City of San Francisco is the second city in the United States to raise its minimum wage to $15 an hour.

2015 As of this writing at least 29 states and many localities have minimum wages that are higher than the federal minimum wage of $7.25 an hour. Of those states that have higher minimum wages, 16 have a mechanism for automatic adjustment of their wages so that they don't lose value due to a failure to increase the minimum wage. The increased number of states with higher minimum wages reflects the new reality that the federal minimum wage has failed to keep pace with inflation and its value has declined considerably. But it also speaks to states stepping into a void by the states that the federal government created by allowing the federal minimum wage to decline in value.

2015 The Los Angeles City Council votes to increase its minimum wage from $9 an hour to $15 an hour by 2020. The vote came amid workers across the country striking for a $15 an hour minimum, and in a city where almost 50 percent of the city's workforce earns less than $15 an hour.

2015 The City Council in Portland, Oregon, votes to raise its minimum wage to $15 an hour for city workers and contractors.

Glossary

Decile   This refers to each of 10 equal groups that the population can be divided into. If, for example, we are using this term to describe the wage distribution, it would be divided into 10 equal parts, with each part comprising 10 percent of the wage distribution. If we were then talking about the top decile of the distribution, we would be talking about the top 10 percent.

Deliberate Policy Hypothesis   This holds the rise in income inequality to be due to policy choices that were made. Rising income inequality is not due just to natural market forces, but to policy decisions that were deliberately made, or, in some cases, the failure to respond at all.

Disemployment Effect   When workers have lost their jobs directly as a result of an increase in the minimum wage.

"Effective Minimum Wage"   This refers to a larger segment of the labor market that does not earn the statutory minimum wage—the official minimum wage—but earn wages around that statutory minimum. It represents the larger low-wage labor market.

Efficiency Wage   When the efficiency of the firm increases due to an increase in wages. A minimum wage as an efficiency wage means that an increase in the minimum wage will result in greater efficiency because the higher wage leads workers to be more productive.

Employer of Last Resort (ELR)   This is the idea that government should create jobs programs and serve as the employer of last resort to those unable to find employment in the private marketplace. The wages paid in these programs would become the effective minimum wage.

Essentialist Arguments   These were arguments made by Progressive reformers in favor of minimum wages specifically for women. The minimum wage, they argued, was essential for the protection of their health and welfare because they were carrying the next generation.

Gini Coefficient   Also known as the Gini index or ratio, this is a measure of statistical dispersion intended to represent the income distribution of a nation's residents. It is commonly used as a measure of inequality. The Gini coefficient is a number between 0 and 1, with 0 corresponding to perfect equality and 1 corresponding with perfect inequality. Countries with coefficients further away from 0 are said to have greater income inequality than those countries whose coefficients are closer to 0.

Human Capital Theory   This theory holds that competitive markets guarantee that wages will be exactly equal to the workers' marginal productivity. In other words, wages are determined by the value that workers return to their employers. Employers, then, increase that value by investing in the human capital of their workers through training programs that will result in productivity. A minimum wage could also lead to employers making such investments in order to justify the higher wages.

Institutionalists   These are economists from the school of institutional economics that hold the standard model or competitive model to simply be a rationalization of a set of power relations. They categorically reject the notion that so-called market forces are natural. Rather, the power imbalance between labor and management requires the existence of labor market institutions that can effectively give them voice. These institutions have traditionally been unions and the minimum wage.

Liberty of Contract   This was a doctrine used by the Supreme Court to strike down efforts by states and then the federal government to pass maximum hours legislation and then minimum wages. The Court held that such legislation violated workers' liberty of contract—their ability to negotiate for themselves the terms of their employment.

Living Wage   During the early part of the twentieth century when Progressive reformers were pushing for minimum wages for women, a living wage spoke to a minimum threshold that they would need for subsistence. Since 1994, the concept refers to local ordinances requiring contractors providing municipal services to municipalities to pay a specified minimum wage.

Macroeconomic Model   This model holds that the economy benefits from a higher minimum wage in the long term because higher wages mean that workers have greater purchasing power, which in turn means that they can demand more goods and services in the aggregate.

Marginal Revenue Product   The amount of increase in output that results from, say, an increase in a unit of labor. If adding an additional worker results in a rise in total revenues, the firm's output will rise as a result. This is the criterion often used by firms to determine how many workers to hire. But it is also the criterion used to determine when to raise workers' wages.

Monopsony Model   When one firm or one industry possesses sufficient monopoly power that it can effectively establish wage rates. In a labor market where one principal industry, for example, fast foods, is the sole purchaser of low-wage and low-skilled workers' services, an increase in the minimum wage will not lead to lower employment. On the contrary, it might lead to higher employment because the higher wage effectively attracts workers.

OECD   This stands for the Organization for Economic Co-operation and Development. Countries that are members of the OECD are generally developed countries. The term has become shorthand for more developed industrial nations of the First World rather than developing nations of the Third World.

Pareto-Optimal/Optimality   A measure is said to be Pareto-optimal if in the process of making one group better off it does not make another group worse off. To be Pareto-optimal a public policy would have to be considered a win–win for everybody.

Rescheduling   This is an alternative to the standard model that holds an increase in minimum wages will lower employment. With rescheduling employment may rise following an increase in the minimum wage because employers may schedule their workers, albeit at higher wages, for fewer hours. The number of hours worked is determined by the hourly rate. Employment can increase because the number of hours per worker may actually decline while the number of workers working actually increases.

Scale Effect   One of the possible consequences of an increase in the minimum wage. Because an increase in the minimum wage raises costs leading to price increases, consumers then respond by purchasing less. Because demand has decreased, firms then produce fewer goods and services, which then results in lower employment. Employment is thus reduced through this scale effect.

Skills Mismatch Thesis   This holds rising income inequality to be due to a mismatch between the skills required by employers and those offered by workers. As the base of the economy has changed with new jobs either requiring workers with great skills or those requiring none at all, those who possess skills will command higher wages, while those who do not will be low-wage workers.

Standard Model   This model reflects the neoclassical synthesis in economics that in pure competitive markets, there is no such thing as unemployment because workers can always lower their wage demands until the point where employers will demand their labor services. A wage floor in the form of a minimum wage, then, prevents workers from selling their labor services at rates below that rate, with the result being that there will be lower employment.

Substitution Effect   When an employer in response to an increase in the minimum wage substitutes more technology for workers to improve efficiency. If the cost to the employer of higher wages exceeds the cost of technology, the firm may conclude that it is more cost-effective to make this substitution.

Supply-Side Effects of Minimum Wage   When an increase in the minimum wage effectively increases the supply of workers in the labor market because the higher wage serves to attract them into the market.

Universal Basic Income (UBI)   This is the idea that everybody should be entitled to a basic minimum income where the idea and level extend well beyond what we typically associate with minimum wages.

Wage Contour   A group of workers with similar characteristics working in similar industries and earning similar wages. For each group there is a group of rates surrounding a key rate, and these group rates are affected by changes in the key rate. Within an industry, the key rate is essentially defined as any rate serving as the reference point for that industry. By this theory, a minimum wage could serve as the key rate, or reference point, for the larger low-wage labor market.

Wage Floor   A floor beneath which wages may not fall below. In the form of a minimum wage, it prevents the cost of labor from dropping below that minimum.

"Washington Consensus"   This holds that skill-biased technical change is the source of inequality, stagnating wages for the average worker, and potentially long-term unemployment. This consensus also maintains that the economy could grow through a set of microeconomic policies of deregulation and privatization intended to achieve greater efficiency.

Webb Effect   The Webb effect is when greater efficiency results from higher wages because those higher wages led to workers increasing their productivity. Sidney Webb hypothesized that a legal minimum wage would lead to greater efficiency. This has come to be known as the Webb effect.

Index

About the Author

Oren M. Levin-Waldman is professor of public policy at the Graduate School for Public Affairs and Administration at Metropolitan College of New York. He is also a Research Scholar at the Binzagr Institute for Sustainable Prosperity. He is author of *Wage Policy, Income Distribution, and Democratic Theory* (Routledge); *The American Constitution* (Bridgepoint Education Co.); *The Political Economy of the Living Wage: A Study of Four Cities* (M.E. Sharpe); *The Case of the Minimum Wage: Competing Policy Models* (SUNY Press); *Reconceiving Liberalism: Dilemmas of Contemporary Liberal Public Policy* (University of Pittsburgh Press); and *Plant Closure, Regulation, and Liberalism: The Limits to Liberal Public Philosophy* (University Press of America). Among one of the researchers for Employment Policy Research Network (EPRN), his work has been published in *Policy Sciences, Review of Social Economy, Journal of Economic Issues, Challenge, Rhetoric & Public Affairs, Public Affairs Quarterly, Review of Policy Research, Regional Labor Review, Advances in Industrial and Labor Relations (AILR), Journal of Socio-Economics,* and the *Journal of Workplace Rights,* and he has also written several applied public policy studies. Currently, he is exploring the relationship between wage policies such as the minimum wage, wage contours, income inequality, and ultimately the impact that wage policy may have on civic participation. A member of the editorial board of the *International Encyclopedia of Public Policy,* which is connected with the Global Political Economy Research Unit, he has contributed several pieces. Professor Levin-Waldman has been an NEH

Summer Humanities Fellow at Princeton University. He is also on the editorial boards of *Perspectives on Work*, a publication of the Labor Employment Relations Association (LERA) and the *Regional Labor Review* published by the Center for Labor and Democracy at Hofstra University. In addition, he is a regular guest on "Westchester on the Level," a blog/talk radio show where he discusses economic policy for an hour every other week. He also writes regular columns in the *Yonkers Tribune* and LaborPress, and contributes frequently to the United Steelworkers' blog.